Food Culture in
China

Xinjiang
(A)

Nei Mongol
(A)

Hailongjiang

Jilin

Liaoning

BEIJING

Tianjin

Hebei

Ningxia
(A)

Shanxi

Shandong

Qinghai

Gansu

Shaanxi

Henan

Jiangsu

Xizang
(A)

Anhui

SHANGHAI

Sichuan

Hubei

Zhajiang

Guizhou

Hunan

Jiangxi

Fujian

Yunnan

Guangzi
(A)

Guangdong

TAIWAN

HONG KONG

Guangzhou

HAINAN

0   Miles   500

Food Culture in
China

JACQUELINE M. NEWMAN

Food Culture around the World
Ken Albala, Series Editor

GREENWOOD PRESS
Westport, Connecticut · London

Library of Congress Cataloging-in-Publication Data

Newman, Jacqueline M.
   Food culture in China / Jacqueline M. Newman.
      p. cm.—(Food culture around the world, ISSN 1545–2638)
   ISBN: 0–313–32581–2
   Includes bibliographical references and index.
     1. Cookery, Chinese. 2. Food habits—China. I. Title. II. Series
   TX724.5.C5N45   2004
   394.1′2′0951—dc22   2004012484

British Library Cataloguing in Publication Data is available.

Library of Congress Catalog Card Number: 2004012484
ISBN: 0–313–32581–2
ISSN: 1545–2638

First published in 2004

Greenwood Press, 88 Post Road West, Westport, CT 06881
An imprint of Greenwood Publishing Group, Inc.
www.greenwood.com

Printed in the United States of America

The paper used in this book complies with the
Permanent Paper Standard issued by the National
Information Standards Organization (Z39.48–1984).

10 9 8 7 6 5 4 3 2 1

Illustrations by J. Susan Cole Stone.

The publisher has done its best to make sure the instructions and/or recipes in this book
are correct. However, users should apply judgment and experience when preparing recipes,
especially parents and teachers working with young people. The publisher accepts no responsibility for the outcome of any recipe included in this volume.

*To Len for your many years of enriching my life, and for cooking
and consuming my other love;
and to Michael and Beverly for greater enrichment,
and for adding Polly, Leo, and more to the mix;
and to Justin, Ryan, Devin, Brett, Ben, and Emily who have added additional
pleasures, including devouring that other love.*

Contents

Series Foreword   ix

Introduction   xi

Timeline   xv

1. Historical Overview   1

2. Ingredients   29

3. Cooking   69

4. Regional and Provincial Foods   87

5. Meals   105

6. Eating Out   129

7. Special Occasions   153

8. Diet and Health   181

Glossary   203

Resource Guide   209

Selected Bibliography   215

Index   219

Series Foreword

The appearance of the Food Culture around the World series marks a definitive stage in the maturation of Food Studies as a discipline to reach a wider audience of students, general readers, and foodies alike. In comprehensive interdisciplinary reference volumes, each on the food culture of a country or region for which information is most in demand, a remarkable team of experts from around the world offers a deeper understanding and appreciation of the role of food in shaping human culture for a whole new generation. I am honored to have been associated with this project as series editor.

Each volume follows a series format, with a chronology of food-related dates and narrative chapters entitled Introduction, Historical Overview, Major Foods and Ingredients, Cooking, Typical Meals, Eating Out, Special Occasions, and Diet and Health. Each also includes a glossary, bibliography, resource guide, and illustrations.

Finding or growing food has of course been the major preoccupation of our species throughout history, but how various peoples around the world learn to exploit their natural resources, come to esteem or shun specific foods and develop unique cuisines reveals much more about what it is to be human. There is perhaps no better way to understand a culture, its values, preoccupations and fears, than by examining its attitudes toward food. Food provides the daily sustenance around which families and communities bond. It provides the material basis for rituals through which people celebrate the passage of life stages and their connection to divinity. Food preferences also serve to separate individuals and groups from each other, and as one of the most powerful factors in the construction of identity, we physically, emotionally and spiritually become what we eat.

By studying the foodways of people different from ourselves we also grow to understand and tolerate the rich diversity of practices around the world. What seems strange or frightening among other people becomes perfectly rational when set in context. It is my hope that readers will gain from these volumes not only an aesthetic appreciation for the glories of the many culinary traditions described, but also ultimately a more profound respect for the peoples who devised them. Whether it is eating New Year's dumplings in China, folding tamales with friends in Mexico, or going out to a famous Michelin-starred restaurant in France, understanding these food traditions helps us to understand the people themselves.

As globalization proceeds apace in the twenty-first century it is also more important than ever to preserve unique local and regional traditions. In many cases these books describe ways of eating that have already begun to disappear or have been seriously transformed by modernity. To know how and why these losses occur today also enables us to decide what traditions, whether from our own heritage or that of others, we wish to keep alive. These books are thus not only about the food and culture of peoples around the world, but also about ourselves and who we hope to be.

Ken Albala
University of the Pacific

Introduction

Food Culture in China illuminates the longest continuous food culture in the world, that of the Chinese. It describes foods eaten that have sustained this huge population, foods considered traditional, common, and good. The Chinese believe that eating appropriately is comparable to digging a well before becoming thirsty. Therefore, this book provides background and understanding about a culture that promotes health through eating what the Chinese consider good food and that believes that nothing is more important than eating.

In the 1300s, many Chinese lived to age 70 if they managed to avoid a communicable disease and could afford to acquire their food. What foods and food behaviors contributed to this longevity in an era when most people died near or before the age of 40? Chinese eating habits were considered one and fixed, but clearly the foods of this cuisine have changed and are changing in China and among the Chinese living abroad, so what were and what are their food habits?

With Chinese making up more than one-quarter of the world's population, each and every day more people are consuming the foods of this cuisine than those of any other cultural group. What food practices did their huge population maintain to survive? This book explores them and the fact that the Chinese gain pleasure from what they eat, speak a lot about their foods, adapt them as needed, and draw strength from them. This volume focuses on the Han, comprising almost 93 percent of the Chinese population.

Readers can gain appreciation of this food culture, one of the two most important cuisines in the world, the other being that of the French. In Chinese food, people have gained cultural health and happiness, and Westerners are now incorporating some of their foods and using some of their culinary techniques, and nutritional know-how. Many and perhaps most of them are variations large and small on what Chinese food really is. With supplies needed to prepare foods of this culture increasing outside of China, there is opportunity to cook what is believed to be real Chinese food and opportunity to understand what it is.

Therefore, this book develops an appreciation of Chinese cuisine. Its chapters discuss the food of China as both cuisine and culture. The historical information increases this knowledge and puts it in perspective. It provides background about the how, where, why, and when of Chinese foods, and details how food-related things came into being.

Ingredients are explored as major food groups, individual foods, and important Chinese food understandings, all major components of Chinese culinary thinking. Cooking in homes and restaurants speaks to what, where, why, and how this culture eats. So does detailing equipment, ordinary and special, needed to prepare their foods. These foundations of Chinese cuisine are the building blocks sitting under regional and provincial food information such as where different cooking styles and different dishes originated and where and how specialty foods play important roles in the food culture, north to south and east to west.

Like its people, Chinese food has roots and wings. The roots of the food culture began before the Xia Dynasty, circa the twenty-first century B.C.E. They have grown many fold. The world recognizes this cuisine as not monolithic; that is, many variations do exist. They are its wings and include but are not limited to the best-known Chinese provincial cuisines of Guangdong, Shandong, Sichuan, Jiangsu, Zhejiang, Fujian, Hunan, and Anhui.

Everywhere in China, people eat individual foods and food mixtures. This book explores Chinese foods and how they are prepared. It looks at particular equipment at home and in restaurants and how the Chinese eat their foods as meals and as snacks. It discusses special foods, including those used at banquets. It details Chinese table manners, current tastes, nationality and family differences, and types of away-from-home eating places; all of these are the food culture of the Chinese.

Eating out is the fastest growing trend in all countries; how the Chinese do this is another facet of their food culture. That is explored with reference to where and when they first ate out and what the forerunners of Chinese restaurants were. Other complexities of eating—such as the cultural protocols for the Chinese and those who join them at their tables, guest responsibilities, how to go and who goes to tea shops, and other food behaviors—are investigated, from those that are static to those that have changed.

Some cultures, the Chinese included, began using the sun and the moon to understand seasons in a given year and throughout many years. This book looks at their solar, lunar, and Georgian calendars and places important Chinese holidays in one or another of them. It delves into festival foods, those used for religious and other rituals, and those that mark family life-cycle celebrations. These parts of the food culture of the Chinese are also detailed, as are Chinese views about nutrition, diet, and health. Illustrating them and some Chinese medicinal and herbal perspectives helps explain some of the ways the Chinese treat their bodies with edible ingredients to keep them healthy and, if need be, to heal them. For centuries, Chinese people have been using specific foods to heal specific conditions.

Each chapter in *Food Culture in China* ends with a handful of recipes selected as illustrative of that chapter's topics. To make them is to taste content and intent. They are ancient, mid-period, or recent recipes, most made with easily available ingredients. They were chosen so when cooked together they constitute a meal for a family of four to six persons. This assumes the addition of a grain such as steamed rice or boiled noodles, should there be no staple food among the recipes in that chapter. To the Chinese, a meal must have a staple or grain food as its principle component.

Additional parts of *Food Culture in China* include a timeline of food-related dates, a glossary, and a resource guide and bibliography of mostly English-language references. A selection of English-language Chinese cookbooks is included to provide additional resources for ordinary, banquet, and regional recipes; so are lists of films, videos, CDs, and Web sites.

Savor them all when reading the pages of this book. They explore delicious aspects of Chinese cuisine. Eat Chinese food to gain personal tastes of understanding. Consult individuals and telephone directories for shopping sources that enable seeing Chinese ingredients and cooking them. Visit Chinese restaurants to taste those dishes their owners consider representative of their particular culinary corner of the world. Together, these experiences can expand knowledge of the cultural and culinary contributions that make up the food culture that is Chinese.

Note: Because the Chinese writing system uses characters or ideographs and not an alphabet, this book writes their spoken words in *pinyin*, the Chinese government's official spelling system that uses the Roman alphabet. With the exception of some names that still use older transliterations, such as Peking instead of the now accepted Beijing and Mao Tse-tung instead of Mao Zedong, only *pinyin* transliterations are used in this book.

Timeline

7000 to 5000 B.C.E.	Neolithic Period
	Agricultural communities were foundation of civilization.
	Cultivation of millet and rice and domestication of buffalo began.
5000 to 3200 B.C.E.	Yangzhou Culture
	Clay food vessels, including steamers, and baskets found in Ban Po village and other sites.
4000 B.C.E.	Dawenkou Culture
	Farmers along Yellow River associated with beginning of China's agriculture, that is, food crop experimentation. Dogs, pigs, sheep, etc., raised; but are rarely eaten.
2500 to 2000 B.C.E.	Longshan Culture
21st to 18th century B.C.E.	Xia Dynasty
	Period of Mythical Sages, includes father of agriculture and father of medicine.
18th to 12th century B.C.E.	Shang Dynasty
	Cast bronze vessels for food and offerings.

	Writings, some about food, found on oracle bones, bamboo, silk, etc. Assessing dates based on lunar eclipses written on the bones.
12th century to 221 B.C.E.	Zhou Dynasty (Spring and Autumn Period 722 to 481 B.C.E. and Warring States Period 403 to 221 B.C.E., respectively)
	Iron age begins circa 500 B.C.E.
	First hard evidence of chopsticks and crossbow for easier hunting.
	Confucius (551 to 479 B.C.E.), his *analects* influence food behaviors.
221 to 207 B.C.E.	Qin Dynasty
	Major unification of China 221 B.C.E.; Great Wall completed 220 B.C.E.
	Standardization of weights and measures.
202 B.C.E. to 220 C.E.	Han Dynasty (Western Han 206 to 25 C.E. and Eastern Han 25 to 220 C.E., respectively)
	Silk Road traffic supported; thereafter many more foods imported, some exported.
	Use of coins widespread, which expanded food purchasing.
	Main population adopted dynasty's name as theirs after major rebellion. Height of country's expansion under Emperor Wudi, who ruled for 50 years.
	Many foods codified under his rule.
	Foods incorporated from expanded regions of the area now Korea and Vietnam to Uzbekistan.
	Divine Husband's Classic of Materia Medica, authors unknown, written in Later Han.
220 to 265 C.E.	Three Kingdoms
265 to 420 C.E.	Jin Dynasty (Western Jin 256 to 316 C.E. and Eastern Jin 317 to 420 C.E., respectively)
220 to 581 C.E.	Six Dynasties
420 to 581 C.E.	Southern and Northern Dynasties
	Development of Zen sect, which proscribed eating behaviors.

Ben Cao commentaries about *Classic of Materia Medica.*

China reunified in 589 C.E., food culture was unifying as well.

581 to 618 C.E.

Sui Dynasty

Grand Canal constructed, allowing considerable north-south food movement; other canals repaired and connected.

Capital moved to Chang-An, now called Xian.

618 to 907 C.E.

Tang Dynasty

Many foreign religions in China; some influence food.

Commerce expanded and large increase of foreign trade.

Chinese goods and foods found in Baghdad and vice versa.

Increased contact with Japan and East Asia; much food exchanged.

907 to 960 C.E.

Five Dynasties and Ten Kingdoms Period
Foods maintained and little changed.

960 to 1279 C.E.

Song Dynasty (Northern Song 960 to 1127 and Southern Song 1127 to 1279, respectively)

Considerable codification of China's cuisine.

Madame Wu's Recipe Book written.

1276 to 1368 C.E.

Yuan Dynasty (also known as Mongol Dynasty)

Leadership under Temuchin and Jenghiz (Genghis) and Kubilai (Kubla) Qan (Khan) impacted foods with more lamb and other meats consumed. Foreign influences extensive, foreign contributions minimal.

Italian explorer Marco Polo in China 1275 to 1292; reports on country and food on his return. Chinese begin more traveling abroad, and bring more foods in.

1368 to 1644 C.E.

Ming Dynasty

Dynasty founded after expulsion of Mongols, whose foods were no longer in favor. Country expanded from Burma to Korea, and culture once again flourished.

Portuguese travelers arrive at Canton; they and other Europeans established settlements in Guangzhou and Macao. Christian missionaries among them converted thousands.

Essential of Materia Medica thoroughly revised in 1751.

Most famous overseas voyages took place when Admiral Zhenghe ordered five- to seven-mast huge ships to travel abroad; they reached Africa, exchanged Chinese items for similar things in ports; voyages hugged coastlines; returned with foods new to China.

1644 to 1911 C.E.
Qing Dynasty (also known as Manchu Dynasty)

Great cultural revival and more intercourse with the West. After Opium War in mid-1800s, much decadence, disease, and drugs destroyed people and places all over.

1912 to 1949 C.E.
Republic of China

Sun Yat Sen helped overthrow last emperor; country still had much political strife; began own form of communism.

Chang Kai-shek's Nationalist Party led moderates who were eventually overrun by Japanese. This impacted foods and reintroduced eating raw fish.

Nationalists fled to Taiwan in 1949.

1949 to present
People's Republic of China

During Cultural Revolution 1949 to 1976, Mao Zedong (1893–1976) denounced Western foods as he tried to feed China's millions of people, several millions of whom starved to death. He removed individual enterprises and designed agricultural cooperatives.

Western foods again allowed and popular.

American fast food (Kentucky Fried Chicken arrived in China in 1987, and McDonald's had 38 restaurants in Beijing in 1997) exceptionally popular.

1

Historical Overview

China is a large agricultural country in the middle of the eastern edge of Asia. Its people make up more than a quarter of the world's population. They call their country *Zhongguo*, which translates to Middle Kingdom, and use this name because they see their land and country as below the heavens but above the earth. They believe it evolved along the Yellow River and began many thousands of years ago.

Excavations of hundreds of Paleolithic and Neolithic settlements along the Yellow River, which is known to the Chinese as the *Huanghe*, provide images and knowledge of their culinary beginnings. Other sites elsewhere in the country do likewise. Many are from at least seven thousand years ago during what is known as the *Yangzhou* Period, circa 5000 B.C.E. In those days, people went hunting and fishing, and they gathered their food. Craftspeople working pottery, jade, and bronze made food-related items for the people and for the rulers.

Later the people became farmers and herders, and the farmers grew several kinds of millet and other grains. Today the Chinese refer to these grains as their staple foods. In their national language, they call them *fan*. Nongrain foods that are used to flavor the *fan* include vegetables and meats and are called *cai* foods.

During these earliest years, the Chinese people separated into two agricultural groups, some living in the drier north, others in the warmer and wetter south. The northerners primarily grew millet along with other grains. The southerners harvested mostly rice as well as other grains. Both gathered fruits and vegetables, planted some of them, and continued to fish and hunt. To protect what they grew and collected when they settled down, they built walls around their villages.

About six thousand years ago (circa 4100 B.C.E.), in the time of the *Dawenkou* culture, the Chinese people raised dogs, sheep, and pigs, and later chickens and goats. Only occasionally did they eat meat from these animals. Wheat and barley came into their food culture some five hundred years later, probably from the west. Other foods entered later still, but from the Near East, and some came from the Indus River valley, as did cattle. These foods illustrate acceptance of new-to-them food items, making wheat, barley, and later beef the first imported foods to become part of the Chinese food culture.

LAND

In early days, the size of China was about a quarter of what it is today, and it was not just in one location. Since the dawn of agriculture, villages in what became China have grown. A typical village started at a Neolithic site known as Banpo Village. It was near the city once called *Chang-An* that is now pronounced "shi-an" and spelled *Xian*. There are other places where Chinese culture began, some long known, others newly discovered. All of them came together in later prehistoric times. They eventually became what is now the third largest country in the world, a country that leads the world in producing several crops, including rice, potatoes, and tea.

The people in what was called Qin lived mostly in the temperate climate zone, and as they expanded southward, tropical areas became part of their country. During these Qin times (221 to 207 B.C.E.), China was one-third its current size. The southern expansion included what are now three of China's provinces: Guangdong, Guangzi, and Yunnan. These three provinces are where most of China's fruits and vegetables now grow, perhaps because there are up to three growing seasons a year. In addition to southern expansion, the country grew as it expanded north and west. It reached its greatest size during the Qing Dynasty (1644 to 1911 C.E.). Late in the 1940s, it became known as the People's Republic of China (PRC) and today is not quite as large as it was in the Qing, when all of Mongolia was included.

Archeological finds and written materials from the Han through Yuan Dynasties (202 B.C.E.–220 C.E. and 1276–1368 C.E., respectively), show Chinese food strongly influenced by foods of southern and western Asia.

Even with this incorporation and expansion of old and new foods, the Chinese still ate mostly grains or *fan*, used fresh and pickled vegetables as the standard accompanying *cai* dishes, and reserved meat dishes for the elite and for special occasions such as festivals and ancestor sacrifice. Snacks, known and popular since early times, included fruits, nuts and seeds, and dried and pickled foods. The unearthed tomb of King Wudi's consort found her stomach full of dozens upon dozens of melon seeds.

With vast terrain in eastern and central parts of Asia, the People's Republic of China now encompasses about 3.7 million square miles, or 9.6 million square kilometers, and is the world's third largest country. To put things in perspective, this country occupies a quarter of all terrain in Asia and one-fifteenth of all land in the world. China is just a bit larger than the United States. It extends almost 3,400 miles (5,500 kilometers) north to south and about 3,100 miles (5,200 kilometers) east to west. It has coastlines on the Yellow Sea, the East China Sea, the Taiwan Straits, and the South China Sea. Depending on how measured, this country has more than ten thousand miles of coastline edging its land and circling the thousands of coastal islands.

China shares land borders with more than a dozen countries including Vietnam, Laos, Myanmar, India, Bhutan, Nepal, Pakistan, Afghanistan, Tajikistan, Kyrgyzstan, Kazakhstan, Russia, Mongolia, and North Korea. Within its huge landmass is the Yangzi, China's longest river, which flows west to east for more than 3,800 miles (6,380 kilometers) and empties into the East China Sea. The Yellow River or *Huanghe* is north of the Yangzi and about five hundred miles shorter, or 3,278 miles in length (5,464 kilometers). Below both of them is the Pearl River or *Jujiang*, which is about 1,318 miles long (2,197 kilometers), one-third the length of the Yellow River.

The United States and China are close to the same physical size, and seasonal differences do match from one to the other in similar latitudes. However, most of China's fertile land is in the east, not in the midwest of the country as it is in the United States. China has three different physical components or areas. The first is the fertile eastern region with elevations under 1,500 feet. The second is in the southwest where the Tibetan Plateau averages 13,000 feet above sea level. The third is northwest with broad desert basins ringed by mountains. Similar to the United States, China's eastern side is edged with water; but its western side does not. It shares borders with many of the already mentioned countries. Another difference is that China's main rivers flow west to east, while the main river in the United States flows north to south.

China has many lakes that dot the country and are sources of considerable marine life. Its land, only about 11 percent arable, is home to many indigenous and imported plants and animals. With so little land to grow things, it is a wonder that this second most populous country in the world can feed its more than 1.2 billion people. It does so because to the Chinese, nothing is more important than eating. That mindset, plus their understanding of their own food history, helps the Chinese know where and how food is procured, prepared, and presented. They understand who eats what and why, and they deem everything that moves as edible, palatable, and socially appropriate.

AGRICULTURE

Most of China's hundreds of ancient settlements and villages, from the Yellow River to the Pearl River, began during Paleolithic times. Prehistoric and Paleolithic findings, and those of the Neolithic period until the sixteenth century B.C.E., show that the Chinese people not only gathered, fished, and hunted for edibles, but also learned to plant several grains. After fire was discovered, their food knowledge expanded with this ability to cook and with animal domestication.

Since the Yangzhou culture, circa 5000 to 3200 B.C.E. and probably before, the Chinese diet was heavily grain-based. In northern areas, they flavored their grain, mostly millet, with the various beans they planted or foraged. Later they flavored wheat and barley, and even rice, in a similar fashion. South of the Yangzi River, where rice was the staple grain, flavoring foods included foraged and planted items such as roots, beans, and greens.

All grains, when cooked, become more digestible. If crushed somewhat and mixed with hot water, they make an instant gruel-like food that is somewhat digestible. It was not until Han Dynasty times (202 B.C.E.–220 C.E.) that any of the grains were ground into flour, made into various shapes, and cooked into or with foods. This cooking made them totally digestible. With the advent of flour the Chinese made dumplings and noodles, and both became popular.

Early Chinese folk continued to hunt and seek out aquatic food, while water buffalo, particularly in the south, helped with the arduous task of plowing. They still do. Farming in southern and northern regions is still mostly a manual task. Penned animals assured a supply of meat, most only slaughtered for special events and holidays. Artifacts and later writings show an additional use for the grains that were planted; they were made into and consumed as fermented beverages.

The Chinese probably boiled water for drinking. Besides eating some foods as they found them, they dried, salted, pickled, and boiled those they grew and harvested. They put some food directly on the fire, others on it but in containers, and they spit meat on thin pieces of wood and/or bamboo and put that on the fire. Probably a little roasting and braising was done and a little frying of foods. Stir-frying, which in restaurants today is the main Chinese cookery technique, did not evolve or become important until about the Ming Dynasty (1368–1644 c.e.).

In this large area that became China, land and climate differences impacted what could grow and therefore what was available to eat. The Chinese people, not a totally homogenous group, ate differently as dictated by where they lived; by how they procured, prepared, and presented their foods; by ancestral influences; and later by differences in their economics. Beliefs such as Confucianism, Daoism, Buddhism, Islam, and others impacted what they ate as well, as did what animals they raised and foods they planted. Even with these differences, land use everywhere in their country showed many similarities, perhaps because of an oft-repeated Chinese saying that proposes eating five cereals for support, five fruits for assistance, five animals to nourish, and five vegetables to sustain.

As to specific foods, seeds radiocarbon dated circa 5000 b.c.e. show that mallow, botanically known as *Malva sylvestris,* was a popular vegetable then; it is not cultivated now. Soon after that early period, popular plant foods grown included cabbages and other vegetables. Most popular were melons, cucumbers, gourds, mustard greens, various members of the onion family, and taro. These same foods are eaten today, but how they are consumed differs. Early on, the Chinese ate foods with their fingers and later used spoons. They did not begin to use chopsticks until about the Shang Dynasty (circa 1600 to 1045 b.c.e.). Beverage consumption included soups, boiled water, and fermented beverages; it still does. The fermented drinks were also used for offerings.

PEOPLE

Where did the Chinese people come from? Thousands of years ago some, but not all, were indigenous to the area. Others at that time and thereafter came from central Asia, some probably as Arabian traders, others as monks from India, still others from farther afield and for other reasons. Those not originally there came by one of many land routes that traversed Asia, some by roads that later became known as the Silk Road. Others climbed over mountains, and some arrived by sea. These ways of arriving are still points of entry, as are cities with airports for those who now come by plane.

In early times, the people who lived in this region called themselves Hua or Huazia. They eventually changed their name to Han, naming themselves after the Han Dynasty. The country they lived in became known as Zhongguo, or the Middle Kingdom. The name China was from a group of rulers known as the Qin, sometimes spelled *Chin*.

Today, close to 93 percent of the more than 1.2 billion people in China consider themselves Han. The government calls the others their minority nationalities or ethnic minority peoples. Purportedly, there are 55 major non-Han ethnic groups, sometimes called the country's other nationalities. Many of these populations see themselves as more finely divided than the 55 minority groups designated by the government. Together, they and the Han speak more than four hundred languages and dialects different from the official language of China, called *Putonghua*. The Han and the minority populations, more often than not, live in different regions of the country and practice different religions. Where they live and their religious beliefs impact foods that they eat.

Most non-Han populations live in the country's north and northwest. Some are scattered in border regions in the southeast and southwest of the country, and a few live in most provinces and in the three major cities, but these numbers are small. They are concentrated in about two-thirds of China's landmass and primarily speak their own languages. About half have their own written languages, and many practice the Islamic religion, which forbids the use of China's main meat, pork.

Minority populations make up about 7 percent of the total Chinese population, and they are growing. The largest is the Zhuang people, whose population is between 15 and 16 million, and the smallest group is the Lhoba, whose population barely exceeds two thousand. The five largest ethnic minority populations are the Zhung, Hui, Miao, Uygur, and Yi peoples. Of the others, 18 groups have populations of more than 1 million each, and the 10 with asterisks after their names have populations of more than 5 million each. The 18 groups are the Bai, Bouyei, Dai, Dong, Hani, Hui, Kazak, Korean, Li, Manchu, Miao, Mongolian, Tibetan, Tujia, Uygur, Yao, Yi, and Zhuang. Six minority populations have fewer than ten thousand people each. They are the Drung, Hezhen, Lhoba, Moinba, Orequen, and Tatars. The other minorities with fewer than 1 million persons are the Achang, Blang, Bonan, Daur, Deang, Dongxiang, Ewenki, Gaoshan, Gelo, Jing, Jingpo, Jino, Kirgiz, Lahu, Lisu, Moanan, Mulam, Naxi, Nu, Pumi, Qiang, Russian, Salar, She, Shui, Tajik, Tu, Uzbek, Va, Xibei, and Yugur.

Some of these populations see themselves as one group, while others do not—nor do they like the groupings assigned by the government about 50 years ago. For example, one group given the appellation of Yao in 1949 believe themselves to be more than 20 distinct groups whose names include Pan, Shanzi, Ao, and Baiku, among others. The Miao, called *Hmong* in the United States, also believe themselves to be several groups, each known by the color of its dress or headdress, including the Black Miao and Blue Miao, and so on. And there are others. Names and numbers aside, as some of these people mix and intermarry their ethnicity continues to impact Chinese food as never before.

LANGUAGE

The official language of China is most often called Mandarin in English. In Chinese it is called *Putonghua*, and it is spoken by about 70 percent of the population. Everyone living in the 22 provinces, five autonomous regions, and the three municipalities of Beijing, Shanghai, and Tianjin is taught to speak this national language in school.

Chinese writing is a pictorial language whose pictographs are also known as characters or ideographs. When written, the characters are called calligraphy in English and *shufa* in Chinese. Like Chinese food and culture, China's written language is ancient and has a continuous history. The pronunciation of some of its words has changed over time, as have some meanings. For example, the city called *Xian* used to be called *Chang-An*, and the transliteration for non-Chinese readers of dynasty names, such as *Zhou*, have also changed. Zhou is *pinyin* romanization of an early Chinese dynasty that was spelled *Chou, Tcheow,* or *Ch'ou* in older transliteration systems, as are *fan* and *cai*, words that replace *fan* and *tsai*. The older transliteration systems included Wade-Giles and Yale. Another transliteration change into *pinyin* is the dynasty now spelled *Xia*. It was written *Hsia* in an earlier system. But not every Chinese transliteration has changed; some remain the same. The Shang Dynasty is an example, as it is spelled *Shang* in virtually every system.

While there were many ways to transliterate the Chinese spoken word, there is only one written Chinese language. Dialects are regional ways to pronounce Chinese written words, and there are five major dialects spoken by very large population groups. They are Cantonese, Fujianese, Shanghainese, Toishanese, and Hunanese. Most are in the south and the east and used by groups that prefer to speak their own dialects rather than the national language.

Han people in one part of China should understand each other because they all study the national language, but not all do. If they are literate, they can all read one another's written words, but that is not so when they speak. Therefore, it is not uncommon to see a Chinese person trace characters on his or her hand when what was said has not been understood. This is not an option for the non-Han minority peoples, whose languages are not related to Chinese and who do not use Chinese ideographs. Most ethnic minorities use their own languages, and they are encouraged to learn them. If they live in autonomous minority regions, in school they learn their own and the national language.

Chinese is the world's only major tongue that still uses a pictographic nonalphabetic and nonphonetic language. Unlike food, which can be recognizable, the sounds their pictorial words make when spoken cannot be understood by anyone who has not learned them. So to solve that problem, in 1958 the Chinese government developed what they believe is a uniform way to best sound out or pronounce words in their language. The full name of this system is *Hanyu pinyin*, most often shortened to *pinyin*. Since 1976 it has been used for virtually all transcriptions done in China and elsewhere. All major newspapers in the United States and other countries use it.

However, not every word is transliterated using *pinyin*. For example, the spelling of some names, places, and people remain in an older system. An example is the name of the capital city of *Peking*, more popular than the *pinyin* word *Beijing*. It is not uncommon for both *Peking* and *Beijing*, to be used interchangeably in and outside of China. While the Chinese culture stresses continuity, this return to a common transliteration illustrates a change back.

While all Chinese people learn the national Chinese language in school, minority children living in mostly minority areas learn that and one of the 53 different minority languages. These tongues can be categorized into the nine language groupings of Altaic, Japan-Korean, Tibeto-Burmese, Austro-Asiatic, Dai, Miao-Yao, Austronesian, Indo-European, and Chinese. There are 21 minority languages that use their own writing systems, and some have no written language except for some prayers and songs.

ETHNIC CUSTOMS

Most Chinese ethnic groups have beliefs that are neither Confucian nor Buddhist nor Dao, the main ones of the Han population. The largest religious belief is among the Muslims, who practice their Islamic faith.

There are many Muslims among the Bonan, Dongxiang, Hui, Kazik, Kir-giz, Ozbek, Salar, Tajik, and Uygur peoples. In alphabetical order, the other main religious practices in China include animism, Christianity, Daoism, Hinayana, Lamaism, polytheism, shamanism, and totemism.

Minority populations can have their religious and nonreligious prac-tices. Some have their own marriage and death customs, their own festi-vals, and their own festival foods. Some minority practices are similar to those of the Han, and others are not related at all. For example, there are more than a hundred special festivals specific to one or several different population groups. Many groups have their own dress, usually worn only at festivals and at their own life-cycle practices such as weddings and fu-nerals. Some groups, including Kazak and Mongolian peoples, were no-madic herdsman; some still are. Others are hunters and fishers, such as the Hezhes who now may be city, suburban, and rural dwellers working in small businesses, in factories, and on local farms.

The Han Chinese use food to mark ethnicity and calendrical, family, and social events, as do most minority groups. The foods many minorities eat on a daily basis may not resemble the food Han people eat. Some of these foods are dictated by religion, such as those of the Islamic faith, and others by custom and culture. As in many other countries, when these people move and settle away from family, friends, and cultural cognates or marry people from different regions, ethnic groups, and religious groups, food habits can change quickly; and in China many of them have.

A few examples highlight some differences between what minorities and the Han eat. For example, among the Bai people, rice is the staple grain, but instead of being steamed plain the rice is prepared pilao/pilaf style and with other ingredients. Dai people adore roasted and not steamed fish, and their staple grain, which is rice, is cooked in bamboo tubes. Dong people like oil tea and drink lots of it. Koreans consume *kim-chee*, their beloved pickled vegetables, at every meal. Miao people love sour soups and sour-tasting main dishes and enjoy one or more at every meal. Mongolian and Kazak people consume tea with milk, drink mare's milk, adore braised mutton, and eat very few vegetables. Tibetans love a roasted barley called *tsampa*, eat very few vegetables, and like their tea mixed with milk, dried cheese, salt, and sometimes butter. The Naxi eat loquat meat, and they and Hui and She minorities put whole fruits such as longans into their tea, peel and all. They like to drink that tea with white rock sugar. Uygurs and others consume baked flat bread called *nang* instead of or in addition to rice, and they like their meat skewered and roasted, preferably over an open fire.

EARLY FOOD HISTORY

The start of Chinese civilization is shrouded in myth, yet documented in Chinese literature. Some say this country called Qin began in the so-called Legendary Period, a time also known to the Chinese as the Period of Mythical Sages. That was before 2000 B.C.E. and before the earliest Chinese dynasties or succession of sovereigns of a particular family, called *Sandai*.

The first dynasties, known in English by their Chinese names, are called Xia, Shang, and Zhou. The Xia Dynasty dates from about the twenty-first to the sixteenth centuries B.C.E. The Shang Dynasty follows, continuing until about 1045 B.C.E. The Zhou Dynasty follows the Shang and ends about 221 B.C.E. Chinese people refer to everything that happened in China by associating it with or near a specific dynasty.

A few of the early dynasties and times before them are not totally fixed in fact or history. One way to learn more about them and the foods consumed during them is to look at early Chinese legends or myths. One important myth tells about a dozen Celestial Sovereigns, an almost additional dozen Terrestrial Sovereigns, and nine Human Sovereigns. Each of these mythical people is said to have reigned for eighteen thousand years. The Chinese interpret this to mean that their culture began thousands and thousands of years ago. Another Chinese myth tells of Suiren, a sovereign who knew and taught how to make fire. Another speaks of a ruler who knew how to fish using nets. Yet another speaks about how to domesticate and raise animals.

One mythical ruler, who may have existed, is Shennong. He knew and taught his people about agriculture. Both he and another ruler known as Huangdi may be mythical, though current research leans toward their being real. No one is 100 percent sure. Real or imaginary, Huangdi is known as the Yellow Emperor. He and Shennong are considered the fathers of Chinese medicine.

Passed orally from one generation to the next, the myths and artifacts tell about early Chinese times, as do very early Chinese books. Two important early volumes are the *Shijing* or *Classic of Poetry*, and the *Shujing* or *Classic of History*. They extend what is known about Xia times, even though they were written after that dynasty ended about the eighteenth century B.C.E. They may have been written as late as the Han Dynasty. Ancient stories and artifacts tell that early rulers celebrated important agrarian rituals; one honored the planting season by turning soil with a jade hoe, and another marked the start of winter by making sacrifices to heaven.

Myths, books, and early writings on oracle bones, bamboo strips, pieces of silk, bronze artifacts, and other materials also tell how and what the Chinese ate. They show that China was not a primitive culture, that its agriculture was feudal, and that Chinese farmers were tenants or were given land on condition of service or payment, irrespective of what that land might produce. They also indicate the importance of food to the early Chinese people.

Like the country and the people, Chinese cuisine has a long history. Food use, cooking methods, serving principles, and table manners originated many thousands of years ago. The Chinese people understood that food was basic and critical. Food was often unavailable due to floods, drought, and other physical calamities, and they honored it when it was and still honor it when it is there for them. In early days and today, the Chinese use food to survive, to communicate, to maintain social groups, and to express individual and group identity. Through food, they find connections to past, place, and people.

The Chinese know that their country's food is famous. They know about special banquets that serve very fancy food known worldwide as haute cuisine. They know that their basic foodstuffs can be made into thousands of different dishes. Even with this knowledge, they prefer to eat a lot of plain grain, their staple food. The amount of staple grains or *fan* a Chinese person consumes is about 90 percent of their diet.[1]

Now, as in ancient times, only a small number eat meat daily, and those who do eat only a small amount, perhaps just a few small pieces. Everyone uses vegetable foods to accompany and flavor their *fan* or staple grain foods. They eat lots of vegetables, and they eat them and other *cai* foods because they love how they flavor their *fan*.

The food that the very earliest Chinese people ate began with or before Peking Man and his earlier brethren. Peking Man, or *Sinanthropus Pekinensis*, found in Anyang in China in the 1930s, was unearthed at a Paleolithic site at Zhoukoudian, some 30 miles from Beijing. Found with him were food-related artifacts, associated food waste, and hearthlike places to cook food. Now called *Homo erectus pekinensis*, this humanoid and the food things he was buried with tell a great deal about ancient Chinese food and food sources. They also tell about how early Chinese people consumed food.

Almost all early artifacts, including those found in China, are determined by radiocarbon dating. The ones found in Anyang at a site called *Hemudu*, and others found elsewhere, confirm that the Chinese culture was large, in more places than originally thought, and quite sophisticated.

Found with Peking Man were toothed sickles, footed millstones, rollers, containers to cook in and to eat food, and millet seeds. All dated from about 5500 B.C.E. Many other items were unearthed elsewhere in the Yellow River valley; still others were uncovered north, south, and west of there; and some were found in caves.

Many early items come from later times; others were dated as from a lot earlier. For example, rice grains from about 6000 B.C.E. were found in the Hunan Province at a site called *Pengtoushan*. Other grains and artifacts were located in the Zhejiang Province, in the Jiangsu Province, and near the city of Shanghai. Most recently, still others have been found at several sites near Sichuan, another of China's 22 provinces. Together, these artifacts confirm rice as the principal staple in south and central parts of China and millet as the staple in northern locations. They show rare use of wheat and barley until later, hemp use later still, and sorghum (*kaoling*) as not used until some time after that.

These finding confirm that early Chinese people cooked their staple foods and made them into a gruel we now call *zhuk* or *congee*. They confirm that the people added things to this watery cereal or to plain water to make soup or stewlike foods, and sometimes enhanced them with vegetables, fish, meat, and/or poultry. Overall, these archeological findings tell where, how, and with what Chinese gastronomy began. They show bone and bamboo tools being used to hunt and plow, and early cooking materials mostly made of clay. Findings include three different early vessels made and used for boiling and three important others used for steaming. They were called *ding, li, hu* and *xien, zeng,* and *fu*, respectively.

CHANGE IN FOOD CONSUMPTION

Chinese food culture has always been evolving. The first reason is that food resources came from ever-expanding areas and foods and their availability did influence what people ate. Chinese cuisine accepted the introduction of foreign foods, such as wheat and barley. The building of 11 canals, probably begun in the Warring States (403–221 B.C.E.), helped move foods from one area to another. One expedition Emperor Wudi sent to Turkestan in 139 B.C.E. brought back pomegranate, sesame, coriander, clover, alfalfa, grapes, horses, and more. Many of these were adopted and adapted into Chinese cuisine.[2] Later, in the Sui Dynasty (581–618 C.E.), more foods moved east and west. When the Chinese fixed older canals and built the Grand Canal, completing and connecting almost all of them in the Song Dynasty (960–1279 C.E.), these major engineering feats made possible the shipment of more foods with grain payments to the Imperial Palace via the massive waterway that was 40 paces wide.

A second reason this cuisine changed was its early and continued appreciation of food and health. The Chinese have always believed that food and medicine are one, both providers of nutrition and health. They pay particular attention to the right foods and see them as not only ensuring good health but also prolonging life. Their appetite for good food seems part of their nature, perhaps traced to much starvation and marginal living. They use philosophic opposing forces to maintain balance, harmony, and good health, dividing almost all foods and health conditions into two forces, *yin* and *yang*. These forces permeate every aspect of their culture, and Chinese physicians treat illness as an imbalance between these forces. They recommend *yin* foods to treat *yang* health conditions and *yang* foods to treat those that are *yin*.

A third item promoting change is their interest in and desire for food. The Chinese have always made demands that required expanding food sources. This was done by China's early rulers, later imperial courts, and ordinary people. Demands were made by emperors to feed the people. They were made in the name of scholarly gourmandism and to help businesspeople and officials. These desires and demands resulted in more and different foods, additional restaurants, more elite eating, and more fancy haute cuisine-type foods.

The fourth reason for change is China's long, continuous food culture. Chinese food history has thousands of years of openness to new ingredients and changing cooking methods coupled with reliance on past practices. For the Chinese people, eating permeates, dominates, and perhaps best explains life. Their most varied cuisine has not only used foods in new and more varied ways than others, but it has also done so for the longest time, and its people delight in so doing.

Food and cooking played important roles in early Chinese culture. The most important for its rulers was *shih*, or providing food for the people. In early dynasties, *shih* had several meanings including to feed, to eat, and to drink. *Shih* also meant excellent grains. That last meaning shows the importance of staple foods in the Chinese diet, an ancient importance that still exists today. Grains were so important to ancient rulers that many bronze vessels were made to store them and the alcoholic beverages made from them. They were so important that rulers were buried with them.

Alcoholic beverages in early days were more important than today, and they were different. Then they were brewed from molds, not fermented from sugars as is popular in the West. Concurrent with drinking alcoholic beverages, the leaves of the wild tea tree, indigenous to southwest China, were brewed and consumed, often for medicinal purposes. Plain boiled water and infusions from different plants and animals were also used medicinally and for quenching thirst. Most Chinese were and still are wary of uncooked food and drink. They learned that cooking tenderizes foods otherwise difficult to consume and digest, and that cooked foods and beverages can be healthier than raw, uncooked ones. It was common then and is still common today to boil all water before drinking it hot or at room temperature.

Consuming large amounts of tea came later, about 316 B.C.E., in what is now the Sichuan Province. There, planting and keeping tea plants, botanically known as *Camelia sinensis*, made this crop very manageable, particularly when kept at bush height. Tea moved to other parts of southern China, and later in the Tang Dynasty Lu Yu (birth date unknown, died in 804 C.E.) encouraged the correct use of tea. His book *Chajing* or the *Classic of Tea* became very popular and helped make tea an important Chinese social beverage.[3]

In ancient times, tea and brewed drinks were stored in pots and large vessels, many called *ding*. Most early containers were made of hardened clay; later ones were made of bronze. Recently discovered oldies were radiocarbon dated as more than seven thousand years old. Early Chinese rulers, including those in the Zhou Dynasty, thought the huge cauldrons so important that they used them as their main symbol of power. Officials of all aspects of food preparation did too. During the Xia Dynasty, foods and beverages were cooked and stored in clay containers and later prepared and stored in bronze vessels. This practice continued into the Shang and Zhou Dynasties.

HISTORICAL OVERVIEW

After the Sandai or three first dynasties of Xia, Shang, and Zhou, the imperial dynasties of China begin in the Qin (221 B.C.E.) and continued until the end of Manchu rule in the Qing Dynasty in 1911 C.E. During the Qin, various feudal states of China were unified under one emperor. That was about the same time some parts of the Great Wall of China were built to protect against marauding northern tribes. During the short Qin Dynasty, cooking techniques and sharp tools used to prepare food expanded rapidly. Food was cut into smaller pieces to reduce cooking time. Not all foods were cooked, though most were, and the few eaten raw were often thin-sliced and pickled for ease of chewing.

During the next four hundred or so years of the Han Dynasty, which followed the Qin in 202 B.C.E., grains and vegetables and meat broths and stews remained popular, their use and variety expanded. Other cooking techniques became important, some even more important—such as frying, roasting, brazing, steaming, and drying foods in the sun. It was during the Han Dynasty that grains were milled into flour and noodles were made by mixing flour with water to form a paste. In ancient days, noodles were called *bing*; now the word *mein* is more commonly used. Those made of wheat flour were first introduced in the north, where wheat was more common. Using flour to make dumplings followed, and the use of flour for steamed buns and baked cakes became popular in every part of China sometime before the Tang Dynasty (618–907 C.E.).

The range and variety of prepared foods and cuts of meats began to increase, indicating a developing sophistication and more discriminating tastes. Archeologists found some of the foods and equipment used to prepare them painted on murals and reliefs in Han tombs. Others were illustrated in later times, and even more were written about or pictured still later. These murals and writings show equipment such as pots with flat bases sitting on waist-high rectangular fire-benches and others placed over the fire on their own three legs or feet. Still other flat or rounded-bottom cooking vessels were set on trivets.

Books that discuss Han times, but were written after them, mention foreign fruits including pomegranates, grapes, walnuts, sesame seeds, and black pepper. They mention new vegetables including eggplant, spinach, coriander, green onions, cucumbers, and carrots. These foods became more popular as time went on, as did local foods including the *lizhi*, *longyan*, and *cumquat*—whose spellings may be more familiar as *lychee*, *longan*, and *kumquat*. In ancient Chinese books and poems, it was easy to identify foreign foods. They used the ideograph or character *hu* in front of the word. In those times, *hu* meant barbarian or from a western region, and the word *hu* was dropped when use of a food became commonplace.

From the Han through the Tang Dynasties, which ended in 907 C.E., knowledge about foods and cooking made many advances. Dairy products were popular and breads and cakes more so. Bakers sold their wares on the streets, as did others. There were many more restaurants, some served by blue-eyed, white-skinned waitresses who were probably the offspring of the many Arabian merchants who visited or lived in China at that time.

In the Tang Dynasty, cereals and other staple foods began to be accompanied by more *cai* dishes, some new and others from ancient or more recent texts. One such was the *Qimin Yaoshu* of the Northern Wei period (386–534 C.E.). Referred to as the QMYS and in English as the *Essential Techniques for the Peasantry*. This book by Jia Sixie is the oldest Chinese food volume preserved in its entirety. It discusses agriculture, aquiculture, preserving, brewing, and dairying, and its close to 300 recipes include many for vinegars and relishes. The QMYS lists more than 160 ancient written sources the author used to write this book. Many were volumes recorded as early as the second century B.C.E. One was written by Fan Shengzhi, whose extant materials were said to detail agriculture in the first century C.E.

The QMYS discusses peeling, cutting, and soaking foods in ash, water, or brine and other methods of preservation. This fantastic fundamental resource of early Chinese food history discusses teahouses and restaurants and foods and beverages, and it has recipes. It also discusses color, shape, taste, and aroma in prepared foods.

The writings in the QMYS closely follow rules set down by Confucius (551–479 B.C.E.), an early sage who wrote about proper conduct, filial piety, food behaviors, and other topics in a book attributed to him called *The Analects*. In the QMYS are recognizable Confucian suggestions that meat quantities never exceed those of staple foods, and that there are three important culinary essentials: cutting, flavoring, and precise control of cooking temperatures or heat.

The QMYS has one chapter each for Sichuan peppercorns and for ginger; discusses apples, pears, plums, apricots, persimmons, chestnuts, hazelnuts, and edible fungi; and reports on breeding and butchering pigs, ducks, chickens, horses, donkeys, mules, sheep, and goats. It also has many herbal cures, 24 vinegar variations, 40 different wines and beers, and how to make a black bean mash. That mash may have been the first known soybean-related condiment. The recipes in the QMYS are typical northern cuisine, as are one for scrambled eggs with chives and another for a sweet and sour deep-fried fish.

Other books written during these same times also speak of earlier days and people. Some mention Emperor Tang, the founder of the Shang Dynasty, who appointed a prime minister widely credited as the cook who formalized theories of Chinese cuisine. He is given additional credit for categorizing foods according to their origin, be they vegetable, land animal, or marine life. He also grouped foods based on three of the five elements, namely, fire, water, and wood. To him, *penttiao*, or cooking foods, meant what the syllables mean individually. *Pent*, in ancient times meant to cook, and *tiao* to season. His ideas may have originated from the oracle bones or from bamboo and wooden strips with food information on them, even some from Confucius. The bamboo records, called *ce* or *dian*, were about food circa the third or fourth century B.C.E., and the oracle bones were more divination about future food-related wishes.

Other books about this minister or the ideas he promulgated include the *Annals of Linzi County* about early Chinese people. The *Zhouli*, or *Rites of Zhou*, saw dietetics mentioned as first among the branches of medicine. These and other writings about this trusted minister say that he knew about the five basic tastes and could tell where water came from just by its taste. The *Zhouli* also discusses more than 2,000 people who handled food for the emperor and his entourage. These include more than 300 people who tended to solid food, 836 who worked with beverages including fermented ones, 94 who were icehouse personnel, and so forth. The larger number attending beverages shows Chinese emphasis on drinking in those days.

In other earlier writings, such as in the *Shijeng* and the *Chuci*, ancient poetry anthologies, 44 food plants were mentioned. Most were similar or exact matches of foods and seeds found in early Han tombs (202 B.C.E.–220 C.E.). These same foods were in use in Tang Dynasty times (618–907 C.E.) and are almost identical to those used today. The content of all these books shows how important food and medicine were to early Chinese people. They are still important.

By the Tang Dynasty (618–907 C.E.), culinary arts rose to new heights. As early as the seventh century, many foreigners lived in China, two hundred thousand alone in Guangzhou, the southern city that used to be called Canton. Their presence increased the use of foreign foods and flavors, and Chinese foods began to include more sugar and spices. They became a common part of Chinese food then and still are today. Prosperity at this time gave rise to yet more restaurants. Bean curd popularity increased, particularly among Buddhists and other vegetarians. Though known earlier, this coagulated soy product did not become very popular until Tang times.

Equipment for cooking changed at this time, and the wok (*guo* or *kuo*) appeared in homes during the Tang Dynasty. In some it replaced the pot and the steamer; in others it was used in tandem with them. The wok was known in Han times, but it was mostly used to toast grains, an additional technique to make them more digestible. Long peppers (not the capsicum variety), ginger, and betel leaf also became popular during this dynasty and were cooked in the wok. Additional special foods and dishes from central Asia and Persia came into the cuisine, including slices of raw fish and boiled lamb, baked and roasted mutton, sesame buns, and steamed bread.

Dim sum (*dianxin*) became very popular during the Tang Dynasty. Its origins were Cantonese, and *dianxin* was the northern way to say it. In Guangdong Province and in Guangzhou it is also called *yum cha*. This morning or noon snack-type eating of many small dishes translates in Cantonese as "dot the heart." It is popular in the south, where many people went to and still go to restaurants early in the day to enjoy these labor-intensive small bites. Chefs in the north now make them and use more items with ground wheat and ground rice than do their counterparts in the south.

Various grains, different from one region to the next, are used to make dumplings and other small items for dim sum. Some are steamed, fried in shallow oil, deep-fried, braised, or baked. In the Tang Dynasty, there were many recipes for dim sum and for other foods. According to the *General Annuls of Shandong*, Prime Minister Duan Wenchang compiled 50 volumes of *dianxin* recipes just from those eaten in his Shandong Province. His popular books became known as the *Food Menus by Revered Zhu Ping*.

The Song Dynasty (960–1279 C.E.), which followed the Tang, was a time of sophisticated recipes and cooking equipment detail. Use of woks and long handled flat-bottomed pans called *pau* increased. So did use of vegetable pots and bamboo baskets for steaming. Other items used to prepare foods then included large spoons, ladles, long chopsticks, and bowls; all of them used more and more than before. Many came in sizes and shapes familiar today.

During Song Dynasty times, peasants continued to consider rice, salt, soybean sauce, vinegar, tea, and firewood as necessities of life. The increased use of the wok made cutting even more important. Ingredient shape and heat transmission gained importance, as did different flavors and other necessities to make foods cook and taste better.

In the Song, an important technological advancement occurred in printing. That allowed for widespread distribution of recipe books, food monographs, and written records about markets. A cookbook called *Zhunggui Lu*, by a Madame Wu, was written sometime during this dynasty (960–1279 C.E.). It is considered one of the earliest Chinese cookbooks of this era, and it is an important one because common people could buy a copy. The plethora of written recipes and details about the culinary and the extensive practice of preparing good food made some call this period a golden age. Others limited that expression to mean that the Song was the golden age of Chinese *sushi*, as the Chinese ate thin slices of raw fish somewhat akin to the way *sashimi* is eaten today. However, they did not eat raw fish on rice, as *sushi* is currently served.

This practice of eating some foods raw was known, though not extensively practiced. Animal foods, mostly marine, and vegetables were consumed raw. Restaurants pickled and served raw vegetables and raw fish, as well as other kinds of cooked fish, meat, vegetables, and fruit. Pork, lamb, and goat were the most common meats eaten. A few vendors did sell rabbit, pheasant, venison, donkey, wild cats, and even horsemeat, camel's hump, owl, and magpie, but most people ate rice, wheat, beans, and millet. Some flavored their grains with but a few small pieces of the items just mentioned, and they ate the necessities previously mentioned. Markets sold cooked food, most purchased and taken home to eat. Most popular were congees and dumplings, main meal dishes, soups, and teas. Others sold raw foods, and some sold equipment including braziers, spoons, chopsticks, bowls and cups, and steamer baskets. During this period, the first the use of tables, then stools, came into fashion, and the rich were the first to get up off the floor and use them.

Though China was making coins then, items generally were acquired by bartering. That was true in shops, inns, and the marketplace, including night markets that existed for those who could not shop during the day. Day and night, vendors specialized in a single product or in related ones, many belonging to guilds specializing in different kinds of foods, such as butchers, grain merchants, and others.

In the Jin and Yuan Dynasties that followed (1115–1234 C.E. and 1276–1368 C.E., respectively), coinage became more commonplace, bartering decreased, and markets became centralized, with more seasonal foods available. However, not everyone shopped at these markets. Porters were known to bring foods to the homes of the affluent, and itinerant merchants plied streets and alleys, selling their wares at the front or back doors of those who wanted and could afford them.

Distilled liquor became commonplace, readily available, and sold in specialized shops. Firepot use gained popularity, emulating the Mongol rulers. In 1271 the Mongol ruler Kublai Khan, who had named his empire Yuan, saw his Mongolian dishes in common use. Perhaps this was because *Yinshan Chengyao* or the *Essentials of Dietetics* was a guidebook for imperial dishes and things hygienic. This copiously illustrated book, which became known as the YSCY, downplayed fish and vegetables and emphasized lamb and other Mongolian meats. It flavored foods with condiments of Middle Eastern origins, such as the spice asafetida in meats and mastic and a licorice-flavored, originally Middle Eastern resin made from *Pistacia lentis-*

cus in breads. The YSCY added new foods and new ways with foods. It had hundreds of recipes, including one for well-seasoned stuffed sheep intestines. This book included many new texture foods and flavorings. Even sherbet was added to Chinese cuisine.

The YSCY had 236 recipes, most included for their therapeutic value. Among them, nearly a hundred are considered rare and precious dishes. It discusses foods forbidden to pregnant women and precautions to take when drinking alcoholic beverages. It has recipes for infusions, syrups, and meat broths. While the Chinese did borrow many foods including mutton from their Mongol conquerors, mutton was popular only in the north. It was hardly ever used in the south and was even disdained there.

Early cooking began in boiling water, but the popularity of grilling and firepot cookery came into use from the Mongol people, as did information touted in the *Essentials of Dietetics*. About the same time, spoon use for eating rice and cooked dishes began to decline, though spoons did play important roles in serving foods. In their place, chopstick use began to increase, particularly for personal food consumption.

A famous painter known as Nizan (1301–1374 C.E.) wrote many books, one titled *Cloud Forest Hall Collection of Rules for Drinking and Eating*. It may be China's first book with recipes actually designed for ordinary households. In it were many for vegetables and seafoods and some for making soy sauce, brewing rice for alcoholic beverages, cooking noodles and wonton, and boiling and steaming crabs. This collection advised how to open and prepare clams; cook chicken, mushrooms, and wheat gluten; and make basic alcoholic and nonalcoholic beverages. Nizan may have published the first recipe to quick-cook meat. His book is probably the first to make what is now called *surimi*, imitation seafood made of fish. Included in it is a recipe for making imitation scallops using river fish. While most of Nizan's recipes are simple and for ordinary foods, a few are complicated, such as those on how to stuff a lotus and how to use a goldfish stomach. Fancy or holiday foods in his book include how to barbecue pork and goose and ways to make a jellyfish stew.

Later, in the Ming and Qing Dynasties (1368–1644 C.E. and 1644–1911 C.E., respectively), local flavors and cooking techniques reached maturity. Regional differences were no longer thought the consequence of geography or climate because regional foods were used everywhere. Food use, particularly during the Qing, was not too different from today. The ways Ming and Qing differed from earlier dynasties were the increased number of cookbooks and medicinal tomes and the fact that even more food hawkers came to the home or at least to the courtyard gate, some using a monkey ringing a bell to call attention to their presence.

Along with culinary salespeople came tailors, barbers, shoe repair folk, and other merchants, all touting and selling wares in local neighborhoods. Soon thereafter, some of these vendors stopped going house to house and set up shop on street corners or in small market areas. Some of the first to do so sold tea or noodles served in bowls. Their wares soon included new food imports such as sweet and white potatoes. Sweet potatoes, which came from the Philippines, were roasted and sold at street corners more than were white potatoes, which had come from Peru. Both were incorporated into many southern Chinese foods. Also roasted were two other imports, corn kept on the cob and peanuts. These four foods, recent additions to the Chinese culinary, quickly became popular. Popular too, but not new, were *tangjen* peddlers selling fancy lollipop-type figures made by melting sugar. When they first became known is unsure.

At this time, special foods took on considerable importance, as did the chefs who made them. Some chefs were available for rent for special occasions; others cooked for the less affluent. There were more recipe and meal choices, and Yuan Mei, a famous poet (1716–1798 c.e.), spoke and wrote about both. He saw the need to use the very best ingredients and condiments and believed that chef and marketer must understand the natural properties of foods to use them properly. For example, he wrote that pork needs to be thin-skinned and fragrant. His 300-recipe book, *Suiyuan Shidan*, which translates to *Sui Garden Recipes*, became a bible for dishes and for practical yet artistic menus.

Crops from around the world continued to come into China, and most were readily accepted. The pumpkin, mango, capsicum pepper, tomato, guava, and turkey, and foods from elsewhere in Asia such as bird's nests and shark's fins, became known. Today, the use of the last two items remains small but they are nonetheless important parts of the Chinese culinary. By the late 1400s, China exported more foods than before. Pack animals had transported them, tea included, to the West until the 1300s. While early amounts may seem small, thousands of animals had trekked what became known as the Silk Road and other routes each year. Hundreds of boats then replaced people and animals; they could and did carry even more Chinese food ingredients far from home.

In 1644 the Manchu, who were a nomadic people, invaded China. They established the last dynasty, named Qing, which in Chinese means pure. Their first three rulers were well versed in Chinese literature and continued the custom, practiced since the third century, of compiling the official history of the previous dynasty. These histories included what each ruler and his entourage ate and when. They and the many Jesuit missionaries who came from Europe in the 1500s had considerable impact on the court. During these times, the Chinese people continued to drink large amounts of alcoholic beverages, and some of them carved and carried their own drinking containers. A very special one, made out of a rhinoceros horn, symbolized health and happiness; and there were many others.

During late Ming and in Qing times, meals were served on a more regular basis, namely twice a day. It was common to eat at six or seven o'clock in the morning and at about half-past one in the afternoon. Snacks or light refreshments were served at six in the evening, not in the morning as dim sum is today, and they were also served at other times. Imperial tables used more rare and expensive land and sea delicacies. Cooking was Han style mixed with Manchurian—that is, mixed northern and southern styles—and every food was valued for its aroma, color, form, flavor, and texture. In Qing times, many dishes were given auspicious names such as dragon boat fish, evergreen consommé, dragons swimming among gold coins, yellow croaker in snowy chest, and lantern bean curd.

Europeans began to arrive in large numbers during the Qing dynasty. The first were the Portuguese. They came by sea, and many returned home with huge amounts of tea, peaches, coriander, and other foods. In the 1400s Jesuit priests came to Macao and then to Beijing. They and the other Europeans slowly established enclaves in Shanghai, where the British joined them and developed a presence in Hong Kong. Only one new cooking item came into prominence in the late 1800s, the Mongolian firepot with its funnel-shaped charcoal brazier. Later, in the late 1900s, another one did, the electric rice pot.

MODERN CHINESE FOOD

The Chinese respect all food, be it *fan* or *cai*, and care for and about it. They speak about it at meals, offer it to guests day and night, and do not waste a morsel of it. *Fan*, their word for rice and other grains, also means meal. It is used in the common greeting of *chifan* to say hello, even though it literally means "Have you eaten?"

Chinese food, the world's longest uninterrupted food culture, garners great respect the world over. More people say that it is the best-tasting food in the world because it has the three needed requirements: geographic variety and use of all manner of food, a long-established elite, and very well-developed culinary practices. Many say that more people in the world eat and enjoy Chinese food on any given day than any other cuisine.

After a revolution and the disbanding of the Qing Dynasty in 1911 C.E., food maintained its critical importance. Different influences impacted meals, particularly those served in restaurants. Perhaps the most important was when the huge court staff of the Qing was disbanded and many kitchen officials and court chefs opened their own restaurants. One, the Fangshan Restaurant in Beijing, still serves Qing Dynasty dishes.

Other large food changes happened when China ceded Taiwan to Japan in 1895. This island remained under Japanese rule for 50 years, and when the Japanese departed they left many influences on Chinese cuisine. One, eating raw fish, had started earlier and was popular in the Song Dynasty. It had fallen into disuse but returned to fashion during and after the Japanese occupation.

There was a period of government-dominated disinterest in food. This was during the years Mao Zedong ruled China after 1949 to the mid-1970s. Mao saw to it that important chefs were sent to the countryside to dig potatoes. His government decreed the exact moment when everyone everywhere in the country should pick a crop, be it ripe or overripe, ready or not. Foreign foods were officially considered inappropriate during these times; their use dropped precipitously.

After Mao and since 1999, when Hong Kong was returned to Chinese control after the 99-year British mandate, the popularity of Western foods escalated. Some were new, others rejoined Chinese cuisine after having been deemed unacceptable by Chairman Mao. Today, Western foods are very accepted and considered "in" by some. Although they are only a small part of the food culture, their use is growing, particularly among the young; and often by young and old between meals and at meals eaten away from home.[4]

During the first half of the 1900s, some nontraditional foods did come into use, including monosodium glutamate, popularly known as MSG. This new seasoning, really a modern technique for an old one that was now made by bacterial fermentation, came from Japan. It was adopted by many chefs and households, particularly those in the south. They had previously used kelp or fermented wheat for the same savory taste sensation.[5]

In the mid- to late twentieth century interest in nutrition increased. Nutrient analysis was added to some cookbooks[6] as the general diet continued its emphasis on grain foods and foods to flavor them. Mongol and

Woman buying food in modern shop, Guangzhou. Photo © TRIP/T. O'Brien.

Manchurian food use continued to decline in the south since the increases made during Yuan and Ming Dynasties. Pride in Han food was renewed during Ming and Mao times. Some continues today but is mixed with foreign foods and food ideas. The greatest impact is the incorporation of non-Chinese ingredients prepared with Chinese taste, and some eating of westernized fast foods, particularly among the young and by others when away from home.

In the last few decades, snack food use increased, as did the use of sweets. This can be found throughout the diet, in dishes and candies between meals and after them, and in products available for sale in larger markets. Western-style fast food plays a larger role in children's diets, and soda is consumed by young and older people. Attention to meals and use of fresh foods are diminishing; frozen and prepared food use is increasing. The Chinese diet continues to change as it always has, reacting to internal and external impacts. What began with the importation and incorporation of wheat and barley continues, but with greater rapidity. Travel and TV are modern canals transporting ideas about foods; they enhance incorporation of new foods with new ways to prepare and eat them.

Where the Chinese cuisine of tomorrow will come from and what it will be are anyone's guess. One can assume that some people, particularly the affluent, will always enjoy old-style banquets, rare exotica, and lots of

Western foods. The number who knew Chinese haute cuisine was small and may remain so, but should it grow it might grow exponentially due to today's information-age technology, availability of expensive foods or faux ones to replace them, more prepared foods, decreasing numbers of well-trained professional chefs, and greater intermingling of minority populations with the Han.

ANCIENT RECIPES

The dynasty most commonly associated with each recipe is incorporated into its title. As written, the recipes are not exact originals because most early recipes did not have amounts, times, and/or temperatures included, while these do. They have been adapted, but only slightly, and rewritten in the style of modern recipes, their ingredients given in American measures. They were selected to be cooked together as an entire meal, but they do not need to be. To be a complete Chinese meal, rice or noodles or another staple grain needs to be added to these dishes, if not already included. Consult the Resource Guide for other sources of ancient recipes to make a meal representative of a single dynasty.

Southern Song Dynasty Shrimp Appetizer

- 1 pound whole fresh shrimp
- 1/2 cup plus 1 teaspoon coarse salt
- 1 tablespoon fresh ground black pepper
- 1/2 cup or more Chinese rice wine
  1. Wipe shrimp dry and remove all swimmerets (appendages under the abdomen can be peeled, but the Chinese prefer not to).
  2. Put the shrimp into a glass bowl with the half cup of salt and mix well. Then cover and refrigerate for six hours. Remove, drain well, and put them into a dry glass bowl.
  3. Mix the ground pepper and the remaining salt with the shrimp. Put them into a dry one-quart canning jar.
  4. Cover with rice wine, close the jar, and refrigerate for three to five days, stirring them once each day. Then drain and serve. Quartered hundred-year eggs and pickled ginger are fine accompaniments.

Yuan Dynasty Carp Soup

- 1/2 pound fresh carp, scales and bones removed, each half cut into two pieces
- 1/8 teaspoon ground coriander

- 1/8 teaspoon fresh ground black pepper
- 1/2 teaspoon coarse salt
- 1/8 teaspoon ground Sichuan pepper
- 8 cups chicken broth
- 1 small onion, cut into one-inch pieces
- 1/2 cup Chinese rice wine
- 1 teaspoon minced ginger shoots or chives
- 1 tablespoon Chinese red vinegar or rice vinegar

1. Dry fish with paper towel, then mix ground coriander, black pepper, salt, and Sichuan pepper, and rub all sides of the fish with this mixture. Set this aside for 15 minutes to absorb some flavor.
2. Put the rest of the ingredients into a pot, bring to just under a boil, and simmer for three to five minutes.
3. Add seasoned fish and simmer for five minutes, then serve.

Tang Dynasty Empress Chicken

- 1 whole broiler/fryer chicken
- 2 tablespoons dark soy sauce
- 1/2 teaspoon salt
- 1/4 teaspoon freshly ground pepper
- 2 cups vegetable oil
- 3 scallions, trimmed, then cut into one-inch pieces
- 1/2 onion, cut into one-inch pieces
- 2 tablespoons minced fresh ginger
- 3 cups chicken broth
- 3 cups Chinese rice wine

1. Clean the chicken and remove any materials adhering to the underside of the breast or rib areas. Blanch it in boiling water, remove and wipe it dry with a paper towel. Brush the chicken with the soy sauce and refrigerate, covered or in a plastic bag, for at least four hours. Remove and rub inside and outside of the bird with a mixture of salt and pepper, and set aside for half an hour until it comes to room temperature.
2. Heat the oil and fry the chicken for 10 minutes, turning it often. Drain well on paper towels.
3. Put the chicken into a large casserole, add scallions, onion pieces, and ginger root as well as the chicken broth and the wine. Cover the casserole and put it into a 375 degree oven for one hour.

4. Remove the chicken from the oven and let it rest for 10 minutes. Strain the liquid and boil it until reduced to about half a cup.

5. Cut the chicken into small pieces, place in a warmed serving bowl, pour reduced sauce over it, and serve.

Northern Song Dynasty Dungpo Pork

- 1 piece fresh pork belly, about two pounds, cut into two-inch squares
- 1 teaspoon salt
- 2 tablespoons soy sauce
- 4 tablespoons Chinese rice wine
- 1 tablespoon sugar
- 3 scallions, trimmed, then cut into one-inch pieces
- 2 tablespoons minced fresh ginger

1. Rub the salt into the sides and bottom of the pork pieces, not into the top or skin side, and put the pork into a plastic bag, tie it and set into a bowl, and refrigerate for four or more hours. Remove and drain the meat, and wipe it dry with a paper towel.

2. Put the pork into rapidly boiling water and boil for 10 minutes, remove and drain, then put the pork into a very large casserole, skin side down. Repeat this process two more times. The pork should be in a single layer.

3. Mix the rest of the ingredients, bring them to just under the boiling point, and pour this over the pork. Cover the casserole and put it into a 350 degree oven for two hours, then remove the meat and put it into a heat-proof bowl, skin side up and still in a single layer. Cover and set this into a steamer over rapidly boiling water. Steam for two hours, checking the water every 15 minutes to make sure there is enough water in the bottom of the steamer and that it remains boiling. Remove the meat, keeping the skin side up, to a preheated serving platter.

4. Put the all the liquid remaining in the casserole into a pot and bring to a boil, then reduce it to about a quarter of a cup. Pour this over the pork, and serve.

Ming Dynasty Stir-Fried Chinese Cabbage

- 1 pound non-heading cabbage such as Chinese celery cabbage
- 1/2 teaspoon vegetable oil
- 1 garlic clove, peeled and sliced
- 4 slices fresh ginger, sliced into thin strips
- 1/2 teaspoon salt
- 1 teaspoon sesame oil

1. Cut cabbage into one-inch wide pieces.
2. Heat oil and fry garlic and ginger about half a minute until aromatic, but not burned.
3. Add cabbage pieces and stir-fry for one minute, then add salt and 1 tablespoon water, cover and steam for one minute. Remove cover and cook one or two more minutes, stirring all the time.
4. Add sesame oil, stir, and serve.

NOTES

1. J. M. Newman and R. Linke, "Chinese Immigrant Food Habits: A Study of the Nature and Direction of Change," *Royal Society of Health Journal* 102 (6): 268–71 (1982); J. Jing, ed., *Feeding China's Little Emperors* (Stanford, Calif.: Stanford University Press, 2000).

2. J. M. Newman, "Savoring Diversity of the Silk Road," *Flavor and Fortune* 10 (2): 5, 24–26, 32 (2003).

3. Lu Yu, *The Classic of Tea*, trans. F. R. Carpenter (Boston: Little, Brown, 1974).

4. David Y. H. Wu and Sidney C. H. Cheung, eds., *The Globalization of Chinese Food* (Honolulu: University of Hawaii Press, 2002).

5. I. K. Goldberg, "Super Science: Monosodium Glutamate and Chinese Restaurant Syndrome," *Flabor and Fortune* 1 (1): 10–12 (1994).

6. Christine Y. C. Liu, *Nutrition and Diet with Chinese Cooking*, 5th ed. (Ann Arbor, Mich.: Author, 1983).

2

Ingredients

This chapter explores ingredients, including soy sauce, bean curd, and other items important to the Chinese cuisine. It looks at them as food groups in order of their importance, staring with the staple foods the Chinese eat, which are mostly grain foods. These make up anywhere from 60 to 90 percent of the calories a person in China consumes each day, depending upon economic and other circumstances. Affluent people consume fewer calories from staple foods and are increasing their animal food intake, but even so the staples are the mainstay of their diet.

Flavors and mixtures that season and accompany staple or grain foods are discussed next. While some attention is paid to ingredients from the past, major emphasis is about ingredients in the Chinese diet today. Not every ingredient is included because, in general, the Chinese eat every plant and every animal and do not have any taboos about food. They do have concerns, though, about when to eat them.

FOODS CONSIDERED CHINESE

What makes a food Chinese? Does soy sauce really make a food Chinese? What about bean curd? Surely the way a food looks, smells, and tastes depends upon ingredients used and how the food is prepared. But do Chinese dishes and their cuisine have to include soy sauce or bean curd? The answer is not now, and certainly not long ago. For those who lived a thousand or more years ago, there is no guarantee they even knew these two foods.

It is thought that soy sauce, as it is known today, did not exist in the early years of the Chinese empire. If it did, sauces used then were different from ones known and used today. With respect to bean curd, it is not clear how people coagulated soy milk, which is what bean curd is, or when it was prepared for the first time. If these foods, thought quintessentially Chinese today, did not exist in China's early years, that raises interesting questions as to what makes food recognizable as belonging to the Chinese food culture.

Soy sauce and bean curd are not unusual Chinese foods today, but they once were. Unusual ingredients did and do exist in the Chinese cuisine and have for quite some time. Does a food need to be unusual to look and taste Chinese? Unusual foods now include birds' nests and sharks' fins; they and others are discussed in chapters 7 and 8, but these foods are more important for special occasions and medicinal use. Not every Chinese person has eaten them, so how can they be typical Chinese foods?

The origin of soy sauce is not part of early Chinese literature. When it first appeared is unclear, as is how it was made. The word for soy sauce now is different from what it was in ancient times. Furthermore, most modern soy sauces are fermented liquids. Detailed information about this type of fermentation did not exist much more than a thousand years ago. When soy sauce was first written about, there were no details as to how it was made. Therefore, early soy sauce types can not be compared to those made today, and there is no assurance that they were the same sauces. To complicate matters further, almost all sauces from thousands of years ago had names other than those in use today. Thus, there is no assurance as to which, if any, was soy or which was another Chinese sauce. What is known is that the Chinese word for soy sauce first found its way into print during the Song Dynasty, a period of time starting in 960 C.E. Was this sauce known before someone wrote about it? If so, how long before that? That will never be known for sure, nor will we determine how long before Song times soy sauce may have been known.

What about bean curd? When was it made for the first time? When was the first time this Chinese food was consumed? One legend has it that Prince Liu An, who lived from 179 to 122 B.C.E. during the Western Han Dynasty, invented the way to make this white coagulated soy milk food. Chinese people lived thousands of years before this prince did. Does that indicate that early Chinese people who did not eat bean curd were eating Chinese food? Again the question is what makes Chinese food recognizable. Some say that Chinese dishes are a mixture of ingredients. Are roast duck and many other one-item Chinese dishes Chinese?

ANCIENT CHINESE TASTE CONCEPTS

Chinese foods have been written about for more than two thousand years. The earliest writing is attributed to a chef-minister appointed by an emperor in the Shang Dynasty. This legendary man, I Yin, was considered the master chef of that dynasty. Circa 1600 B.C.E., he never mentioned soy sauce or bean curd. He did speak about ginger and cassia (a spice whose taste is quite similar to cinnamon), and he mentioned mushrooms, fish paste, and salt. More importantly, he discussed harmonious blending of foods and spoke of sweet, sour, bitter, pungent, and salty flavors. He was the first to mention balancing and transforming foods when cooking them. His thoughts represent what is important to Chinese food today.

I Yin's early statements match those of a famous and more modern Chinese author, Lin Yutang, who said in 1937 that the whole culinary art of China depended upon the art of mixture.[1] From I Yin to Lin Yutang and on to today, ingredients mixed in a particular way make foods Chinese. How foods are mixed and used can determine whether the foods are Chinese, as can which ones make up a meal and how dishes and meals are eaten.

In discussing food for the emperor in a book of the same name, author John D. Keyes in 1963 wrote of five imperial seasonings: salty, sweet, sour, peppery, and spicy.[2] But he wrote that Cantonese chefs consider six taste sensations when preparing a dish: sour, sweet, bitter, salty, peppery, and natural. The natural taste he refers to means the unadulterated taste of the raw food itself. Some word definitions change over time; one such is the taste of natural.

There are many similarities among ancient and modern taste sensations and their definitions. Which foods were and are the best examples of each of these tastes? The sweet I Yin refers to as *kan* came from adding malt sugar or honey to foods. Today, the Chinese still use the word *kan*, and they still make many foods sweet, but more often they do so with sugar. Honey was popular in ancient times, while sugar as we know it was not.

Sour, also attributed to I Yin and those who followed, was called *suan*. An example of a *suan* food in both ancient and modern times is the *mei* fruit. This food some consider a plum is really closer to an apricot, and it was and still is a popular Chinese fruit. Today, vinegar is a more common sour taste than is the *mei* fruit.

The salty taste was called *hsien;* now it is more commonly called *shiyan* or just *yan*. While the ancient Chinese had salt, it was not easy to get. But when it was available, they made pickled vegetables, sauces, and other long-lasting foods. They prepared or preserved foods with salt or with items naturally high in this taste, such as seaweed. Soy sauce, which is salty, was not known before the Han Dynasty (202 B.C.E.–220 C.E.), and its use in the thousand years that follow the Han is uncertain. Salt and soy sauce are used today for this taste sensation, and salt is used to make soy sauce and almost every other fermented sauce. Salt and fermented sauces are often found in many but not in every Chinese dish.

Another ancient Chinese flavoring term was *bitter*. It used to be and still is called *ku,* and it was and still is important among Chinese culinary tastes. Many hundreds of years ago, smartweed (*Polygonum hydropiper*) was a popular bitter-tasting food. But this vegetable is unknown today. A more modern food with a similar taste sensation is bitter melon. Other bitter foods used then and now include strong wines, beer, and quite a few herbal decoctions.

Another early Chinese taste was pungent, and I Yin called this taste *hsin*. Today it is known as *ciji*. Examples of pungent foods then and now are garlic, onions, ginger, and cassia. Sichuan pepper is also a good example, but when it came into use is not clear. It may not have been known in I Yin's time, and culinary historians agree that, if it was, it probably was not popular. While pungent is not considered a primary taste in most Western cultures but rather thought of as a combination of piquant, acrid, peppery, and/or spicy, the Chinese have always considered it a primary taste.

The last taste attributed to I Yin was savory, and he called it *jiang*. These days, the Chinese word for savory is *xian*. This taste was and is found in meats, fish, thick bean pastes, and mushrooms, among other foods. The Chinese recognized this basic taste sensation in ancient times. Japanese coined the term *umami* for it, and that word is now universally used as savory, and considered a primary taste.

Besides these five early basic tastes, the Chinese did and still do flavor foods with another taste sensation, namely that of animal fat. While this taste has no special name, it is believed important, and the word used is either *fei* or *feipang*. Not every one of these tastes was popular at all times. Some were seasonal and not popular year-round. Ancient writings such as in the *Zhou Li* and the *Chi Li* speak of using a little sour in spring, not having too much bitter in summer, avoiding an excess of pungent in autumn, and not having much salty food in winter.

MODERN TASTE EQUIVALENTS

The Chinese speak about specific ingredients for each of the aforementioned tastes (Table 2.1). These are not universally agreed upon because region, heritage, and other factors impact who believes which foods represent the taste under discussion. Cane and/or beet sugars are the most common sweets in use today, along with ripe fruits and other sweetmeats. Sour includes not only vinegar, but also lemon and related tastes. Bitter includes the aforementioned bitter melon and other foods with similar tastes, including medicinals, wine, beer, and other alcoholic beverages. Pungent foods include anise, fennel, cloves, and black, white, and Sichuan pepper. Salt still means using salt along with soy and other sauces.

The Chinese consider all sauces, not just fermented ones, salty, and they call them all *jiangs*. To them, savory includes various fish pastes, oyster and other fish sauces, meats, mushrooms, monosodium glutamate (MSG), and pickled foods. Technically speaking, savory includes all foods with glutamates, including those just named and others such as the tomato.

Table 2.1
Five Chinese Tastes and Some Representative Foods

		Tastes		
Sweet	*Sour*	*Salty*	*Pungent*	*Bitter*
beef	carrot	abalone	adzuki bean	apricot
Chinese date	celery	bean leaves	almond	asparagus
foxtail millet	cherry	beans	bean sprouts	beer
frog	chicken liver	black mushroom	dried fish	bitter melon
lotus root	eel	black seaweed	garlic	cherry
melon	jellyfish	carp	ginger	loach
onion	plum	chestnut	horse lung	millet
orange	pork liver	clam	kumquat	mutton
oyster	red seaweeds	cloud ear fungus	long cabbage	pickled scallion
peanuts	red turnip	dried persimmon	mud snail	river shrimp
potato	scallion	eggplant	peach	sea cucumber
shark's fins	tomato	gingko	river crab	sheep heart
shrimp	walnut	matrimony vine	taro	spinach
spleen	watermelon	pig kidney		stone parsley
watermelon	wheat	prawn	yellow seaweed	strong wine
white radish	wild birds	sea urchin		white seaweed

Notes: Foods can have more than one taste, depending upon how prepared and other factors. Regional and minority differences are not represented.

Fermented foods, though not a taste category or a basic taste, are important when cooking Chinese food. Many of them have glutamates as part of their composition, and glutamates enhance other flavors including bitter and pungent. Fermented foods were used in China's culinary, and some of the earliest were fermented meat pastes, followed by the fish pastes. Later, beans including the soybean were fermented and made into pastes and sauces. Bean curd, after its invention, was fermented too. Called *fuyu*, this coagulated and then fermented soy food can be referred to as stinky tofu or Chinese cheese. However, bean curd is made from a vegetable, not a dairy product, and while its aroma is strong, this acquired taste is loved by most Chinese.

Fermented vegetables and fruits are ancient and modern, many called pickles. Those fermented from fruits and vegetable liquids are more apt to

Making tofu. Photo © TRIP/F. Good.

be called wines. To the Chinese, the word for wine is *jiu* and it is used for all alcoholic beverages. They do not distinguish between wines and liquors or amounts of alcohol in any one of them. Peoples in Western societies discuss differences in alcoholic content of these beverages, and their names often regulated by law based upon their alcoholic content. In China, all alcoholic beverages except for beer are called *jiu*, and beer is called *pijiu*.

CHINESE FOOD CATEGORIES

In the Chinese diet, the most important foods were and still are the staple or starch foods, which they call *fan*. Examples include rice and rice products, wheat and wheat products, and foods of other grains and seeds, including millet and sorghum. The Chinese serve one or more of these staple foods at every eating occasion called a meal. They do not consider times when minimal or no staple foods are present to be meals. This is an important distinction. Snacks can and do have small or medium amounts of *fan*, while meals always have the majority of their calories coming from *fan*.

Sauces and other fermented foods and spices flavor staple foods, as do vegetable foods, animal foods, fruits, fats, and others. Foods that flavor staple or *fan* foods are called *cai* foods. No meal is complete without both *fan* and *cai* foods. When both are not consumed and when *fan* is less than *cai*, the Chinese consider that eating occasion a snack. All meals and snacks are not the same everywhere in China. There are regional differences in type, volume, and content of *fan* and of *cai* foods, and there are localized differences. Regional differences are discussed in chapter 4.

Because staple foods are so important, these are discussed before foods that flavor them. The Chinese think that vegetables are second in importance when flavoring *fan* or staple foods; vegetables follow what Westerners consider seasoning items that come after *fan* foods. Animal foods follow them, including fish, poultry, and meats from four-legged animals. Then come fruits, and last among ingredient groups are alcoholic and nonalcoholic beverages.

STAPLE FOODS

There are many staple foods used in China. The two most important are rice and wheat. To illustrate the extent of staple food usage, about 35 percent of all calories consumed in China come from rice; wheat accounts for about 15 percent and is increasing. Other staples make up about another

10 to 15 percent of all calories. Rice intake remains constant throughout the country, though people are actually eating less of it because the population is growing, and rapidly. General food availability is increasing and broadening, and except for rice, individual intake of each staple food is less and less year by year. Affluence changes eating behaviors. In China, as elsewhere, more animal foods are consumed each year, replacing calories from carbohydrates.

Rice

Rice is a basic and important food to those Chinese whose heritage is from the south, particularly those from or with family from south of the Yangzi River. This river is often considered the rice-wheat divide of China, with rice consumed in lesser quantities north of it. The Cantonese word *chifan* literally translates as "eat rice." It is used to mean eating, a meal, and food. The word for rice itself is *dao* or *mi*. Throughout China, rice is used as a grain and as a flour, and when the latter, it is made into noodles, rice paper, several kinds of alcoholic beverages, rice vinegars, and other things.

This ancient grain has been cultivated as long as Chinese civilization itself. Rice grains were found at several Neolithic sites. While China's four-thousand-plus-year-old civilization is often fixed around the Yellow River, rice and other items from the Shang Dynasty are emerging north and south of both rivers, most recently in the villages of Sanxingdui and elsewhere. Like the origins of this culture that has not just one location, there is not just one variety of rice. Rather, there are many, their differences considerable, especially to the Chinese. They can be based upon length of the grain, its thickness, its color, and its taste.

Careful examination of the many types of rice show varieties that do not look or taste alike. There are differences in starchiness, aroma, and exterior and interior color, and differences in variety, processing, and polishing. The process of removing the exterior husk is called milling. There are differences in preparation of this staple food before its sale. For example, if cooked just a little it is called converted rice, and if cooked longer before drying with or without other processes, it is called instant rice. These two preparations are new to China.

Most Chinese do not like rice that is commercially precooked. They prefer raw white rice, and they like it rinsed many times to remove excess starch before they cook it. They also prefer their rice milled and very white. As to the cooked product most, but not all, Chinese like it dry and fluffy, the grains not sticking to each other. For this, many believe that long grain rice can work best. There are others who prefer a milled medium grain white rice, particularly those who live in eastern areas of China and in Taiwan. They like their rice shinier, a little stickier, and a bit nuttier in texture.

Another type of milled white rice is glutinous rice. This is a usually short grain rice. It is the thickest and starchiest of rice varieties. While a few Chinese do eat this type of rice all the time, most use it for special dishes, particularly as a stuffing or as a wrap around something. Glutinous rice goes by the names of sticky rice and sweet rice; it is stickier than other rice types, and some say it does taste nuttier. It is available, as is all rice, ground to be used as a flour, as a rice vinegar, and as an assortment of alcoholic rice beverages.

Less milled rice is called brown rice. Not all brown varieties cook in the same amount of time because some have different amounts of the hull or bran removed. All brown rice takes longer to cook than polished white rice. Many aromatic rice varieties, white or brown, are called jasmine rice. Rice can be cooked plain and cooked to have yellow or tan-colored rice crusts, also called rice cakes. These are most often made from fully cooked long or medium grain rice varieties that are dried and then fried until very crisp. Rice crusts can be used in dishes called sizzling rice. No matter the variety, rice as flour can be made into rice noodles and other rice products.

There are black and red rice varieties. The color is mostly due to the color of the seed coat or husk. Black rice is usually higher in gluten than white rice, takes longer to cook, is stickier, and is a little nutty. Red rice is reddish-brown in color, and its cooking times are also longer than for white rice. Some red rice is colored or infused with a red dye; others are colored using a red mold; and still others are naturally brownish-red. Most red rice is used to make fermented red rice products such as red rice wines, red wine lees (the residue left when making rice wine), and red bean curd. These are popular products, particularly in the province of Fujian. The grains of red rice are usually not as long as black rice grains. Because red and black rice get most of their color from the husk, both are milled very little if at all. Chinese rice vinegar also comes in colors—black, red, or clear. These vinegars can be milder, less acidic, and somewhat sweeter than their Western counterparts; and black rice vinegar is a good though different substitution for Italy's balsamic vinegar.

Wheat

Wheat, though used as a grain, is rarely used plain. However, there are very few Chinese recipes for wheat berries, as the whole grain is called.

Most often, wheat is ground and made into noodles or steamed bread. While noodles can be made from rice and other flours, most are made from wheat or mixtures of flours such as wheat and rice flour. Examples of noodles not made from rice or wheat include cellophane noodles made from mung bean flour, and those made from sorghum, millet, buckwheat, potato, soybean, manioc, yam, lotus root, water chestnut, and other flours.

The noodles made using mung bean flour are also known as transparent noodles, though they are really translucent when cooked. Noodles can have flavors added, such as shrimp noodles made adding powdered dried shrimp to wheat flour or spinach noodles made by mixing dried ground spinach with flour. Some packaged noodles are called vermicelli, an Italian word often used for long and thin noodles. There are hundreds of other noodle varieties based upon raw ingredients and shape of the finished product. All are loved in one region or another of China and are more popular than rice in the north. The same is true for steamed breads and other staple foods. One difference is that southern Chinese prefer their noodles made with eggs, while northern Chinese prefer theirs whiter, eggless, and made with wheat starch.

Noodles, north and south, are symbolic of long life. They come in many shapes, long or short, thin or thick, round, oval, or flat. When thick, they can be boiled, baked, fried, or steamed. When thin, they do not bake well, but can be made in most other ways. The flattest kinds are called sheets, wrappers, skins, Chinese pancakes, Peking doilies, mushu pancakes, or spring roll wrappers. They can be shaped by rolling, pulling, cutting, or pressing the dough. Appreciated most when fresh, they are also popular partially or completely dried.

Noodle products were in use at least as early as 500 B.C.E. but did not become popular until the Chinese mastered the art of grinding large amounts of flour. In early days, many were hand-stretched by pulling a batch of dough thin, then twisting, stretching, pulling and stretching, and then pulling, stretching, and twisting again, and so on. They still are prepared in that fashion and were and are called lamien. They are popular particularly in Fujianese restaurants, where noodle makers are a featured attraction in their eatery windows. While noodles can be made with any type of flour, those of wheat, which naturally has gluten, stretch best.

All types of noodles are appreciated, and some are more popular than others. Wheat noodles are the most sought after in most regions of China. Noodles may first have been used outside of China when traders along what is now called the Silk Road brought or bought them there. While

Making wheat noodles, Wuhan. Photo © TRIP/F. Good.

most food historians believe they developed separately in Italy and in China, the earliest records for making them are found in China.

Millet

Millet is probably China's oldest staple grain. Known as early as 5000 B.C.E., different types are thought to be the first grains used in China. While there are many varieties, consensus is that foxtail millet and common millet, both called *shu*, were early and important foods. They were found and used in northern China, and perhaps used quite early in the south as well. Still known as *shu*, both types of millet are found in glutinous and nonglutinous varieties. No matter the type, millet is used less frequently today than either rice or wheat.

Barley and Sorghum

Barley may have been domesticated almost as early as millet. Both were mentioned on oracle bone inscriptions. They were plentiful foods and were and are called *damai*. Barley was radiocarbon dated from at least Shang Dynasty times (sixteenth century B.C.E.), and recently some barley and millet found in China dated even earlier than the Shang. It is unclear where each one of these staple foods originally came from.

Sorghum is a grain also called *kaoling*. That name is close to its Chinese name of *gaoliang*. It probably did not get to China until later than the previously mentioned grains. Today, its primary use is in making alcoholic beverages, particularly *maotai*, a popular, well-known, and very high-alcohol-content liquor. Grains including barley and sorghum are readily available and inexpensive, and less-affluent Chinese eat a lot of them. Some say they prefer one over the other or like both of them more than wheat or rice.

Maize and Other Staples

Maize, also known as corn, is technically not a grain. It probably has a short history as a staple food in China, but a few scholars believe that at least one variety came to China early and from Africa. Others say it did not arrive in China until after Columbus discovered America. All agree that at least by the 1600s it was a common staple food. Other nongrain staples such as sweet potatoes, white potatoes, and peanuts are also used in large amounts. They probably came about the same time corn did. Each of them and other lesser-known staple foods are used as grown, and are also used after drying and grinding into flour and made into many starch products including noodles and dumplings.

Buckwheat, rye, and oats are among other grains known. Their use is minimal except in the far north of China. The same is true of other seeds and grains including Job's tears, which is a tall grass and a minor staple food. Flours ground from a variety of dried beans and pulses are in use, but they have minor roles in the Chinese diet except for mung beans, already mentioned, which are used in cellophane noodles.

SAUCES AND SPICES

In general, sauces and spices flavor staple foods, vegetables, and animal foods; spices more than sauces are used in herbal medicinal extracts. Soy sauce is probably the most common Chinese flavoring ingredient today, and it is certainly the best known. Use of it and all sauces and flavoring liquids varies depending upon region. The sauces discussed next are but a small fraction of China's sauce larder.

Soy Sauce

Soy sauce or *jiangyou*, as it is now called in Chinese, is a thin liquid made by fermenting soybeans with a few other ingredients. It probably originated as a means of preserving foods, not as a flavoring agent, and probably because of its high salt content. A possible early source of this sauce may have been the liquid remaining after straining a thick paste. No one is certain because many early words for sauces or pastes are no longer in use, such as *hai* for the thinner ones and *haithan* for thicker ones. Thick sauces were used at the end of the Zhou Dynasty (221 B.C.E.), but they are not believed to be similar to a single one in use today. Thick or thin, most early Chinese sauces were made by fermenting meats. Later, other animal products were used, including fish and shellfish.

The current Chinese term for soy sauce came into the printed language in an early Song Dynasty tome sometimes translated as *Madam Wu's Recipe Book*. It also was found in Lin Hung's *Basic Provisions for Rustic Living* volume written during the Southern Song Dynasty.[3] Both were written during the Song Dynasty. The first of these volumes describes soy sauce use when cooking meat, crab, and vegetables; the second uses soy sauce to flavor vegetables and seafood. Before that, *Essential Techniques for the Peasantry* or *Qimin Yaoshu* (QMYS) did report sauce used in the sixth century C.E., but how similar this was to soy sauce is not known. Specifics about its culinary usage are unknown because it was used as a salve for hemorrhoids.[4]

There may be other soy sauce precursors. But none have been positively identified with soybeans and with culinary intake. In addition, early and unusual usage calls the sauce *yu* and not *jiang*, its current word. That is odd because *yu* meant oil in those days, and soy sauce is a water-based liquid made without oil, nor is oil incorporated after it is made.

For the past thousand or so years, soy sauce has been made from roasted ground soybeans and wheat, fermented with a starter or mold. There have never been standards for its color, saltiness, or added ingredients. The best ones take months or years of fermentation; imitations and those made from hydrolyzed vegetable protein can be made in hours or days. Most people cannot taste differences but react to the amount of salt and other added ingredients. Chinese in the United States, at least, mostly use the soy sauce their parents did or the first one they ever purchased. In a recent study, American-born and Chinese-born respondents claimed use of a particular brand because their parents did. Not one of them had ever tried a different brand, nor had they or their families ever made any fermented sauces, soy included.[5]

Soy Sauce Varieties

Dark soy sauce is one of the two main types of soy sauce. It is brewed longer, made with less salt than many other soy sauce products, and has molasses or another caramelized sugar added. When a bottle of dark soy is shaken, it clings to the glass and takes some seconds or minutes before the glass clears. This is a good way to identify it should the label not say dark or black soy sauce. This type of soy sauce is also marketed as double black soy sauce. Dark soy sauces redden or darken foods made using them.

Thin soy sauce is saltier and not as viscous as dark soy. It does not cling to the glass container when shaken, and it only slightly tints foods made with it. This type of soy sauce used to be referred to as light soy sauce. Now, both *light* and *lite* have legal definitions in many countries as to content, so that term is rarely used. In the United States, *light* means that a food item has at least 25 percent fewer calories or is reduced in its sodium content by the same amount. Some light or lite soy sauces are reduced in one or the other of these, up to 40 percent. Premium or aged soy sauce definitions are more general than legal and usually mean that the fermentation process was not accelerated chemically and there is no added hydrolyzed protein. Superior soy sauce also has no definition; it can be a brand name or hype about the product. Labels on soy sauce must state whether hydrolyzed protein, molasses, caramel coloring, or other ingredients are in that particular product.

Other types of soy sauce include thick soy sauce, which has more molasses and/or another sugar added and sometimes some starch, such as cornstarch. Mushroom soy, particularly popular in Shanghai, Fujian, and other regions of south China, is usually a thin soy sauce made with the addition of straw mushrooms or their extract. Rarely is the black forest mushroom, commonly known by its Japanese name of shiitake, used in mushroom soy, and rare is the container indicating which type of mushroom was used to make it. Shrimp-flavored soy sauce is popular in China's eastern regions. It is made using brined shrimp in the processing. There are other seafood-flavored sauces such as abalone sauce and scallop sauce. Most are thick; not all have soy sauce in them; and most are related to or made like oyster-flavored sauce, discussed below.

Other Bean Sauces

No matter the kind, bean sauces are almost always thicker than soy sauce and are often used or made with it. They are very popular in eastern regions of China and in the Sichuan province. Most are made from yellow or black soybeans, are highly salted, and are fermented. They were probably the most ancient thick nonanimal pastes made in China. As with soy sauce, most are made with wheat flour. Sweet ones have lots of sugar with other flavorings added before or during manufacturing. Fermented black beans, though technically not a sauce, are thought of as and called black bean sauce. All are heavily salted and mixed with spices and ginger, and the beans look raisinlike. Newer varieties are made into sauce by rinsing and mashing the beans lightly. Some manufacturers add vinegar, salt, sugar, many seasonings, and even soy sauce; and some brands have garlic and chili peppers as well.

Sweet bean sauce is akin to thick soy sauce with fewer seasonings than black bean sauce. Brown bean sauce is usually made from whole or fermented yellow soybeans with salt, sugar, and other flavorings added. Hoisin sauce is a sweetened, thick, reddish-brown bean sauce made with vinegar, garlic, sesame seeds, soy sauce, and some chilies and spices added during or after the fermentation process. Barbecue sauce, also thick, can be called *sacha* sauce. It is made from fermented soybeans and can have vinegar, tomato paste, chili, garlic, sugar, and various spices added. It has a sweet/spicy taste, and many varieties include or are fermented with baby shrimp, known as krill or brill.

Oyster Sauce

Oyster sauce is a thick, brown condiment popular in the south of China. It is made from oyster extract and other items used in soy sauce manufacture, and can have cornstarch, monosodium glutamate, and/or another form of preservative. Of all Chinese sauces, this one usually has the lowest sodium content; individual product labels need reading to verify this. Early forms of this sauce and varieties sold in Asian countries use pieces of oyster in their manufacture. In the United States, only liquid extract from cooked oysters is allowed, so they are labeled oyster-flavored sauce. Related sauces can be made with scallops, abalone, and other shellfish, with or without soy sauce or hydrolyzed vegetable protein. There are vegetarian oyster sauces, most made with mushroom extract.

Shrimp Sauce

Shrimp sauce is not a variant of oyster sauce. Most popular varieties use heavily brined shrimp with a preservative, and some are not even sauce but rather dried cooked pink shrimp. The strong aroma associated with shrimp dissipates when cooked, and resultant dishes have a mild shrimp flavor. Other seafood sauces are thin and smell strong; most are also mild tasting, and they get milder the longer they cook. Some shrimp sauce is used as a dipping sauce. These sauces are particularly common in regions near Vietnam and/or are used by Chinese who have lived in other Southeast Asian countries.

Chili Bean Sauces

Many chili bean sauces are called pastes. They are related to the bean pastes, but many do not have a single bean in them; that is why they are listed separately. In general, these sauces are thick and made with fresh and/or dried hot and/or sweet chili peppers and vinegar. Sometimes they have oil and garlic added, and a few brands add crushed tomatoes. Chili oil is different. It is not a true bean sauce, usually has no beans, and is an oil with chili peppers in it or the peppers strained and removed after the oil is infused with their taste. Most often, the oil used is fresh or toasted sesame oil.

Rice Wines

China's most famous rice wine, made for more than two thousand years, is *shaoxing*, and they say the best is made in the Zhejiang province. Rice wines are usually made from glutinous rice, millet, a special yeast, and local mineral and spring waters, and are somewhat akin to an amber-colored sherry. However, they have higher alcoholic content, namely 18 percent. It is common for rice wines to be aged buried in earthenware containers for 10 or more years. Parents make or buy then bury a bottle at the birth of a daughter. They unearth it to drink at her wedding.

Wines lose taste and aroma when heated. Chinese cooks add theirs in two batches, some with the sauce ingredients, the rest just before serving; this preserves taste and aroma. Rice wines are used in braised dishes, in stir-fry cooking, and in clay-pot and Yunnan pot cookery. The latter is particularly popular in the Fujian province and looks as if an upside-down funnel is in its center with a hole at its top; this allows steam to enter when cooking. Some rice wines, particularly those from Fujian, can be thicker; they are made from the dregs or leftovers of red rice wine. These dregs are called wine lees, and they have pieces of rice in them.

Plum Sauce

This newer sauce, called duck sauce in the United States because it is frequently served with duck, is usually made with sugar, plums, vinegar, salt, ginger, and chili peppers. This jamlike condiment, sometimes called *dukjiang* in China, is more piquant than sweet, as well as somewhat tart. It is used as a dipping sauce, and newer recipes use it cooked into a dish.

Sesame Oil and Sesame Paste

Both sesame oil and sesame paste are made by grinding toasted white sesame seeds with the oil pressed from that residue mixed with the seed paste. Amber in color, sesame oil is known as *mayou* or *xiangyou* and has a strong, pleasant aroma. Less expensive brands can be blends with other oils such as soy. Labels that do not say 100 percent sesame oil can be such blends. The Chinese like to sprinkle a few drops of sesame oil on cooked vegetables just before serving; it provides a wonderful aroma and fine taste.

Sesame paste, usually called *zhimajiang,* is by some considered a sauce or *jiang.* Similar to the consistency of peanut butter, it is a common cooking ingredient in southwestern China. Sesame paste is viscous and best blended with hot tea or warm water before using to soften it. This allows easier mixing into other items such as marinades and cooking liquids.

SPICES AND OTHER SEASONINGS

Individually and as mixtures, spices and seasonings impart flavor to Chinese dishes. The most ancient were cassia, cloves, and fennel. Cassia, is related to cinnamon and known as *guipi.* It is mentioned in the *Elegies of Chu* written in the fourth century B.C.E. It is used as quills cut from the tree's bark or ground and mixed with other spices. Cloves, called *dingxiang,* were in use by or before the third century B.C.E., as was fennel, called *huijiang.* Both were and are used whole or ground. These three spices have been common in cooking, and fennel and cloves were used to sweeten the breath. Actually, chewing cloves was a requirement before speaking with the emperor. Somewhat later, anise, basil, black and white

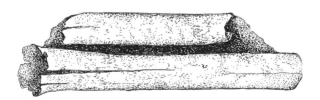

Quill of cinnamon (cut from bark).

pepper, cardamom, mace, mustard, nutmeg, star anise, tamarind, and turmeric came into use. Listed below, the spices and herbs are not in order of importance or use; such differences can be regional. Instead, they are in alphabetical order.

Anise

This popular licoricelike flavor comes not from anise seed but rather from star anise, a spice unique to the Chinese cuisine. Botanically known as *Llicium verum,* this star is eight-pointed and is the dried flower of an evergreen sometimes called clove flower. It is related to neither cloves nor anise, and it is commonly used in marinades and red cooked dishes. The seed is discarded before the dish is consumed. Star anise is also used ground and is the major component in a flavoring called five-flavor powder. This spice mixture usually has five ingredients, a number the Chinese consider lucky, but it can have more than five ingredients. Thought to have some curative properties, it is sometimes made into a healing tea. Chinese star anise is not toxic, but Japanese star anise does have some toxicity and should not be fed, especially as tea, to infants and children and those with health problems.

Five-flavor powder can include some or all of the following: cinnamon, cloves, fennel, ginger, licorice root, Sichuan peppercorns, tangerine peel, and of course star anise. Star anise alone or in a mixture is popular in braising, barbecuing, and roasting meats, and sometimes in vegetable dishes.

Star anise.

Apricot and Other Fruit Seeds

The apricot seed, *Prunus armeniaca,* is inside the hard stone or pit of the apricot. It is used to season dishes, is popular in traditional Chinese medicines, is bitter, and can be toxic if too many are eaten. Even when having just a few, they should be cooked 20 minutes or more.

Olive kernels, another seed called *ganiankeng,* are native to and from a special Chinese olive. Like the apricot seed, they are found inside the pit or stone, in this case inside the Chinese olive pit. The stone of this particular seed looks very different from other olives because it comes to a point at either end. Some use this pit as a toothpick. Not bitter tasting, the seeds of the Chinese olive can be purchased around the world. They are processed by heating, then rolling and flattening the internal seed. Apricot seeds are not rolled, and many that are sold have not been heated. That is why users need to cook them for at least 20 minutes. The rolling process extracts natural oils not always considered healthy, as does cooking these and other fruit pits. Pine nuts are a common Western cookery substitute for olive seeds.

Coriander

The herb *Coriandrum sativum* flavors Chinese food when used fresh; so do the dried seeds. A member of the carrot, dill, parsley family, it is commonly known by two other English names: cilantro and Chinese parsley. It was used in ancient China by or before 200 B.C.E. Its most popular uses are fresh and in leaf form when cooked in a dish and to decorate one.

Ginger

Known in Chinese as *zijiang* and botanically as *Zingiber officinale,* many call this plant ginger root. Grown underground, but not a root, this popular seasoning is a rhizome with many segments or knobs. It was used in China thousands of years ago and is popular today. Exactly when it became a seasoning item is not known, though Confucius (551 to 479 B.C.E.) and others mention it. Many Chinese use it both fresh and dried as a medicinal; in cooking it is mostly used fresh. Immature ginger, known as young ginger, is used, but it has pinkish tips and a stronger taste. It is popular in the south of China. Chinese do not use dried ginger interchangeably with fresh ginger, nor do they use fresh young ginger instead of older ginger. Young ginger is common in some beef dishes and best mixed with coarse salt for 15 minutes, then well rinsed before using. Preserved ginger

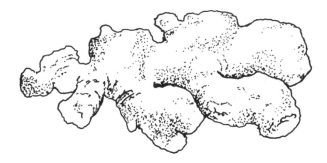

Fresh ginger root.

is sometimes called stem ginger, and it is found in a supersaturated sugar solution. Prepared this way, it is commonly found in sweet dishes. Fresh and slightly dried and preserved gingers are a recent snack; both are sold coated with coarse sugar.

Monosodium Glutamate

Monosodium glutamate, or *weijing,* commonly known as MSG, is what the Chinese call a flavor enhancer. It brings out taste and provides its own savory meaty taste sensation. Thought to be ancient, though few Chinese records so indicate, MSG was first manufactured by the Japanese at the end of the 1800s. It became very popular after a new fermentation process to make it was discovered in 1909. Since then, virtually all MSG is made by this bacterial fermentation process. With no major indications of the Chinese using MSG before the 1900s, it first began to appear in Chinese and Western cookbooks after that. Foods naturally high in glutamates, as are MSG, mushrooms, kelp, and tomatoes, all enhance the savory taste sensation. Prior to 1909, Chinese used kelp and other seaweed to get the same effects.

Mustard

Mustard seeds are used whole and ground. Most ground varieties are from yellow mustard seeds. The ground seed is mixed with water, oil, or both and can serve as dipping sauce. Taiwanese restaurants commonly serve this mustard mixture on a small saucer next to chili paste; some even make these two items look like the *yin/yang* symbol. They use either or both to dip their deep-fried and steamed foods in. Mustard, as powder or paste, can be incorporated into dishes for piquancy. Black and white mustard seeds are rarely ground for Chinese dishes, but sometimes they are used whole.

Rock and Other Sugars

When referred to as slab sugar, rock sugar is compressed brown sugar layers. It is processed differently than Western supermarket-type brown sugars. Pieces of slab sugar or lumps of clear or amber sugars are used in cooking. Those not in slabs can be found as large crystals. They are commonly called rock sugar and can range from clear to light brown. Slab or rock, they are eaten as candy and used in beverages, braised dishes, and medicinals, and as glaze to make roast meats shiny. The Chinese in the eastern part of the country, particularly in Shanghai, adore sweet dishes made with one of these sugars. Maltose, as a thick black liquid sugar, also sweetens many Chinese dishes. It is commonly made from sprouted barley seeds and used in stir-fried and baked dishes and in snack foods.

Sichuan Pepper

Sichuan peppers are actually berries and are sometimes called *fagara*, Chinese pepper, anise pepper, wild pepper, Sichuan peppercorns, or prickly ash. They are also called flowering pepper because the berries look like open flowers. No matter the name, these dried fruits are not a true pepper or true prickly ash, nor are they related to white or black pepper. They are piquant reddish-brown berries unique to China and popular throughout its western regions, particularly in the Sichuan province. Botanically known as *Xanthoxylum simulans*, they come from a shrub or bush often seen as a hedge around homes and hotels. These berries were used in ancient China, though when for the first time remains a mystery. They are best when toasted, and good when ground and mixed with equal amounts of salt. This mixture is used to dip meats and fried foods.

Tangerine Peel and More

The dried peel of the tangerine is from a special variety of the mandarin family. This citrus peel is loved in soups, braised dishes, sauces, and sweets. It is common throughout China, but used most often in southern regions, left whole or minced.

Sacks of spices and other dried foods at Chengdu market, Sichuan Province.
Photo © Art Directors/TRIP/Tibor Bognar.

Other popular seasonings include basil leaf, white and black sesame
seeds, cloves, powdered curry mixes, fenugreek, nutmeg, black cardamom,
coriander seed, cumin, chili peppers, and various herbs such as licorice
root, red, black, and brown dates, the nuts and seeds already mentioned,
and chestnuts, cashews, peanuts, pine nuts, and walnuts.

VEGETABLES

In general, vegetables are the second most important food group after
fan or staple grain foods. They are adored by the Chinese, who eat many
different kinds at almost every meal. Popular are garlic, scallions, and ginger, all leafy greens, and all manner of peas and beans. Many vegetables
are eaten at a meal; fewer and lesser amounts are consumed as snacks. The
Chinese probably consume more different kinds of vegetables and eat a
greater volume of them than people of most other cultures. They like
them lightly seasoned with sesame oil, vinegar, rice wine, simple and
complex stocks, flavored oils, and/or herbs and spices. They also flavor
them with a chili pepper or two and sometimes top them with peanuts or

other nuts. Common and popular vegetables vary by season and region. Those listed below are associated with Chinese cuisine and listed in alphabetical order, not in order of use or preference.

Asian Eggplants

These include the long, thin purple variety some refer to as Japanese eggplant. They are 7 to 10 inches long and popular throughout Asia. Eggplants are in the *Solanum* botanical family, and the Chinese call them all *aigua* or *quizi*. Most popular are the thin purple ones. The Chinese do eat slightly fatter, white-skinned varieties, small, round green ones, and others in a myriad of shapes, sizes, and varieties. They are not familiar with fat, black-skinned varieties. They have used eggplants for thousands of years, at least since 700 B.C.E., and prefer theirs almost seedless, young, sweet, and with low water content.

Bamboo Shoots

An ancient Chinese vegetable, there are several dozen varieties of bamboo shoots, a perennial member of the *Dendrocalamus* family. The Chinese call them *tianzhu* or *zhusun*. Besides their culinary popularity in dishes, the Chinese like them plain and pickled and use their leaves as food wrappers. All parts of the bamboo plant are used medicinally, be they leaves, stalks, or roots, and they are used fresh and dried.

Beans and Peas

Already discussed with reference to their use in sauces, beans are eaten many other ways. Sugar snaps and other peas are eaten after minimal cooking; the Chinese like them bright green and crisp, their stringy edges removed for easier and tastier consumption. Peas are members of the *Pisum sativum* family and eaten as flat snow peas and fatter sugar snaps, both consumed shell and all. The former are ancient; the latter a newer vegetable. The flat peas called snow pea pods or *xuedou* are believed to have been part of the Chinese culinary for hundreds if not thousands of years. The Chinese call both of them either *helan* or *hedau*. In English, the fat ones, called melting mouth peas, are about a hundred or so years old. Other beans and peas are used in long-cooked dishes.

Long beans, also called yard-long beans and sometimes asparagus beans, are members of the *Vigna unguiculata* leguminous family. They grow to about 18 inches in length, are thin, and as a string-bean-like green vegetable they are starchier than ordinary string beans, can have a pale or dark green exterior, and are called *doujiao*. Appreciated somewhat crisp, the Chinese either oil-blanch them for a minute or two or boil them. Then they are stir-fried or long-cooked, all techniques to enhance their flavor and texture.

Soybeans are used not only to make soy and other sauces, but are also eaten fresh after boiling, or reconstituted from the dried bean, then long-cooked. They are never eaten raw. They can be prepared many different ways, even made into a milk. To do that, dried soybeans are soaked, then ground, and their liquid is then pressed out. The Chinese drink this soy milk. They also coagulate it, then press out excess liquid, and call it *doufu* or bean curd. Different amounts of water can be pressed out, with the bean curd then called soft, firm, or pressed bean curd. The Chinese also cook firm bean curd with soy and other seasonings; this makes brown bean curd that is sometimes called spiced bean curd.

This food item, called *doufu* in Chinese and *tofu* in Japanese, though those English spellings are not always so differentiated, has been known since sometime during the Han Dynasty. Some say King Liuan, who ruled circa 160 B.C.E., invented it. There are many ways to use this protein-rich food, whether fresh, dried, fried, smoked, or fermented.

Bean Sprouts and Other Shoots

Young sprouted plants are popular Chinese vegetables, particularly those grown from the mung and the soybean. Mung beans are members of the *Phaseolus* botanical family and called *yacai* by the Chinese. Soybeans are members of the *Glycine max* family and called *dadou*, which means big bean. Used for more than four thousand years, they and other sprouts are started in the dark and grown until their white bodies are about two inches long. As such, those from the mung bean are known as *douya*, and those from the soybean with their larger heads are referred to as *dadouya*. Sprouts are preferred with no green leaves protruding, which is why they are grown in the dark. While every part of a spout is edible, heads and tails of each individual sprout are removed in many fancier dishes and always in very fancy restaurants. That way, they look and taste better, and their crispiness is accentuated.

Pea shoots and sweet potato shoots are prized for their leaves and so are not grown in the dark. As green vegetables, their leaf tips are expensive and considered special foods. Pea shoots, *Psium satvium*, called *doumiao*, are more common and more popular. Sweet potatoes are detailed below, their shoots less prized. Other young leaves are used, but these are most popular and most common.

Bok Choy and Other Cabbages

Bok choy in *pinyin* is called *bakcai;* it is commonly called by its Cantonese name of *paicai.* A loose-leaved, eight- or nine-inch, white-stalked vegetable, it has dark green leaves and is in the *Brassica* family. This leafy vegetable and others in the *Chinensis* family have been used by the Chinese for thousands of years. There are many varieties, all preferred small and in their younger, less-developed versions, and all also eaten when mature and full-grown. There are other species such as the Shanghai, with shorter, light green stems and lighter colored leaves, and literally hundreds of others. Some are related, some not; some are spinachlike, others different; some have big leaves, others big stems; and some grow on land, others in shallow pools of water.

Many cabbages are used, including napa, Chinese celery cabbage, and others; many are in the *Brassica* family. They have many names in Chinese and English, including Peking or Chinese cabbage, *Tientsin, suichoy,* and *huangyabai,* among others. Also used are varieties in the *Pekinensis* group that have longer leaves with stalks raging from white to dark green. Some cabbages are smooth, others curly; some are headed and round and the size of a basketball, others flat-leafed and known as *taigucai.* They can be sweet or bitter, with *gaicai* or mustard greens among the most bitter.

The texture of most cooked cabbages is preferred with crispness preserved, mustard greens being the exception. Early written records tell us that many kinds were part of the Chinese culinary at least since the fifth century B.C.E. Seeds and other artifacts more recently removed from ancient tombs show that some were used hundreds of years earlier.

Chili Peppers

Chili peppers are recent additions to Chinese cooking as they became popular only five to six hundred years ago. Today, they are used extensively in everything from sauces to complete dishes. Most dishes loaded with them are associated with foods of the Sichuan and Hunan provinces. Many different red and green spicy and sweet pepper varieties are used; each can have a different piquancy. Before their introduction to China, items other than chili peppers gave spiciness to the foods, most notably Sichuan pepper and white pepper, as well as some ingredients no longer used.

Chinese Chives

Several varieties of this flowering vegetable are used, others not. Most Chinese chives are about 8 to 10 inches long and thin, and resemble blades of grass. Some have a rounded head at their top. All are members of the *Allium* family, and most are called *jiucaihua*. Those with heads, open or closed, can be called flowering chives. Some are yellow and more related to leeks, others white, but only because they are grown in the dark.

Chinese Flowering and Nonflowering Broccoli-Type Vegetables

This is a group of green vegetables that do not head as does American broccoli. Their flowers can be yellow or white, their stalks and leaves white to dark green. Some varieties are in the *Brassica parachinensis* family and related to the cabbages; others are not. As a group, some have been known for hundreds of years, others for thousands, and many are called *caixin*. Those in *Brassica oleracea* are known as *jielan*, and those with yellow flowers or *Brassica rapa chinensis* are known as *youcai*. These latter ones have a few open flowers and thick stalks that should be peeled before cooking. Most broccoli-type vegetables are preferred somewhat crisp.

The nonflowering dark green vegetables in this group include the mustard cabbages mentioned above, which are in the *Brassica juncea* group. There are many varieties, most quite ancient; some have thinner leaves and most are used before they flower. Red or green ones belong to the *Amaranthus* family and are known by that name; the Chinese call them *xiancai*. Garland chrysanthemum is another popular green vegetable; it is in the *Chrysanthemum* family and called *tunho* by the Chinese. There are *Impomoea* vegetables including water spinach, which the Chinese call *ongcai*. Some call this item hollow-stem vegetable because its stems are exactly that, hollow. Another popular vegetable is stem lettuce, a member of the *Lactuca satvia* family, called *wosum* by the Chinese. Also popular are various types of watercress in the *Rorippa nasturtium* family, and a popular and ancient green known as Chinese celery. This latter item, a member of the *Apium graveolens* family and called *qincai*, is thinner, with darker stems than celery found in the Western world. It has a more intense flavor and aroma and is included in dishes to enhance appetite. Not all leafy vegetables used in ancient times are still in use. For example, the licorice-tasting fuzzy leaves of the *Perilla* family are rarely used by the Chinese today, they but are a part of Japanese cookery.

Cilantro

Cilantro is sometimes called Chinese parsley and is better known as coriander. This member of the *Coriandrum* family has been mistaken for flatleafed Italian parsley. However, its wide, flat leaves are a different shape. Ancient and used as vegetable or garnish, this herb has a strong distinctive taste and aroma. Called *yuansai*, its leaves and sometimes the stems are used in cookery; the seeds and roots rarely are, but are used for their medicinal value.

Daikon, Jicama, and Other Root Vegetables

In English, some root vegetables are referred to by their Japanese or Hispanic names; daikon and jicama are respective examples. Daikon looks like an oversized carrot; different varieties come in different colors. The most popular one is long and white; others are white and light green or all light green. Most are in the *Raphanus* family and known to the Chinese as *luobo* or *quingluo*. There are other unrelated vegetables, including all manner of turnips, that are sweet or have a peppery aftertaste. When older, many get bitter. Other than baby ones, all are peeled before use. Jicama, a short, fat turnip variety, is a member of the botanical *Pachyrhizis* family and called *shage* by the Chinese. Vegetables in this group are used cooked and/or marinated when raw, then pickled and made a little sweet. All of them are considered crisply refreshing.

Taro, an ancient root vegetable, is a member of the *Colocasia* family. It comes in many sizes and varieties, is popularly known as *yuzi*, and is always peeled. It must be cooked before eating, whether tiny or melon-sized. There are hundreds of different varieties, all somewhat starchy, some with dark threadlike fibers throughout their white or yellowish interiors. Some are wet taro and grown in swampy land; others are dry taro because they and most other root vegetables grow in dry soil.

Lotus root, a member of the *Nelumbo* botanical family, is known as *lianou*. This ancient Chinese food, though grouped here, is really a tuber, not a root. All parts of lotus plants—that is, seeds, leaves, flowers, and stems—are eaten. Sweet potatoes, also a tuber but not an ancient Chinese food, have been part of the Chinese culinary for some five or six hundred years. Members of the *Ipomoea* family and called *ganshu*, sweet potatoes are popular in and around Fujian Province, where they are used fresh and dried, and ground into flour; elsewhere they are disdained and called poor man's food. These and many other roots and tubers are used dried and ground into flour and adored for their young shoots eaten as green vegetables.

Ginger

Ginger, already mentioned in the spices and seasonings section, is a rhizome used young, old, and preferably fresh. Particularly loved by those from Guangzhou and other southern regions, some people peel it before use. Young ginger, rarely peeled, is stronger and often mixed with coarse salt, then rinsed before using. This removes some of its bitter and astringent taste. Ginger is also an important medicinal and is made into a popular tea.

Mushrooms

Technically all mushrooms are fungi. Some are commonly known by their Japanese names, as are the shiitake and enoki. The Chinese call the former forest mushrooms or simply black mushrooms. Foraged fresh and dried, they have been used for millennia. This most popular Chinese mushroom is now cultivated, grown commercially on freshly cut oak logs. The enoki is a yellowish-white mushroom that grows fatter, shorter, and in many more colors when foraged than the skinny cream-colored cultivated varieties found in supermarkets. Oyster mushrooms can be cultivated or foraged, and if foraged can be white, tan, or in shades of pink, blue, or yellow.

All of these and most mushrooms are used fresh or dried. The only fungi rarely used fresh are those known as cloud ear or wood ear. Most popular black or white, the latter found more in sweet dishes, these *moer* types are prized for their crisp texture. Dried mushrooms, gathered or cultivated, are best reconstituted in warm water. The Chinese most often prefer them reconstituted from dry because they have a more intense flavor than do fresh mushrooms.

Silk and Other Squash and Related Gourds

Silk squash is a spongy zucchini-type vegetable 10 to 20 inches long, most often ridged, and sometimes incorrectly called Chinese okra. Botanically in the *Luffa* family, there are several varieties, most called *sigua*, and most needing their skin and, if there are any, ridges removed. When seen cut and in a cooked dish, this food has a light green exterior and white interior. Bottle gourd is related but in the *Lagenaria* family. A Cantonese treat known as *hulu*, bottle gourd is preferred long-cooked, whole or mashed. Chayote, called *hezhang*, is another related vegetable, but in the *Sechium* family; in the West it is also known as mirliton or christophene. More gourd than squash, the Chinese use it like a squash, cut up and stir-fried, seed and all. There are many other squash and gourd-type vegetables, most preferred young. They are cooked in a myriad of ways, quickly or for long periods of time.

Water Chestnuts, Other Bulbs, and True Nuts

All of these are popular fresh or dried, and as flour. The water chestnut, called *mati* and a member of the *Eleocharis* family, is popular canned but preferred fresh. It must be peeled and can be stir-fried or prepared in a variety of other ways. The horned water chestnut, correctly known as water caltrop, is botanically *Trapa bicornis* and is called *lingjiao* by the Chinese. It grows in water, leaves protruding, is very ancient, and must be cooked. It is quite starchy, with a hard black shell-like exterior that is difficult to remove.

Lily bulbs are white and found in or at ground level near beautiful flowers of the same name. Called *baihe*, the rounded bulb is eaten fresh or reconstituted from dried, and it is used as a medicine. These bulbs are not tiger lily or *jinzhen*, which have other English names including golden needles, yellow flower, and lily stems. Rather, the lily bulb is an unopened flower of the *Hemerocallis* or daylily family. Dried ones take a long time when soaked, to be reconstituted, and are often long-cooked, while the tiger lily, a bud in the *Lillium lancifolium* family, is ready to cook after soaking it 10 or 15 minutes. Tiger lily buds are most frequently partnered in dishes with cloud or wood ear fungi. Another bulb, arrowroot, is called *cigu* and is of the *Sagittaria* family. It is round with a thin, brown skin that is always removed. Somewhat sweet and starchy, this bulb is very popular as a flour used for thickening purposes. When fresh is used in stir-fry and longer-cooked dishes.

Peanuts, now part of the Chinese culinary, have been in use about five hundred years, maybe a bit longer. They and other nuts and seeds are popular in some regions and for some purposes, as are apricot seeds and olive kernels already mentioned. They and walnuts, almonds, and other nuts are used as seasonings, as foods, and when ground as flours. They are also used for their medicinal value.

Winter, Fuzzy, and Other Melon-Named Foods

Technically fruits, many melons are used as vegetables in China. The winter melon, botanically *Benincasa hispida*, is grown until about the size of a basketball and called *donggua*. It can have a dusty white exterior, a dark green skin, and a white interior. Rarely eaten raw or pickled, it is most often cut and cooked in a dish after seeds and skin are removed. It can be used whole as a container to steam foods in, and if it is, the white fleshy interior is eaten with the contents. It is sold whole or in slices when fresh and, if found heavily sugared, as candy during Lunar New Year and at weddings. It is available year-round because, when whole, it stores well.

The fuzzy melon or *jiegua* is in the same botanical family as winter melon. It is about the same size as a zucchini and has a hairy exterior. There are other popular melons; one mentioned earlier is the bitter melon or *kugua*. Botanically known as *Momordica charantia*, it tastes quininelike, akin to tonic water and, as the English name suggests, is indeed bitter. Its bumpy exterior is pale green. Removing seeds before cooking or blanching it for a minute or two reduces this bitter taste.

ANIMAL FOODS

In China, meat is consumed in smaller quantities than are creatures from the sea. Animal flesh from roving creatures has less prestige than foods from animals that live in water. All animal protein is eaten in smaller quantities than either vegetables or staple foods. However, Chinese are consuming more and more animal foods as their affluence increases. Most meats and foods of the sea are consumed fresh, but they can be dried. As such, meats are made jerky-style, and shredded fish or whole pieces from rivers or the sea are dried or fermented. There are no taboos, so all meats can be consumed; those that are unusual are discussed in chapter 7 because they are more popular at banquets and on festival occasions than as everyday foods.

Seafood

The Chinese adore shrimp, fin fish, mollusks, crabs, and virtually every other manner of seafood. They also consume lesser known items such as the sea cucumber, called *beche du mer* in French, and they eat turtle and eel, and fish maw, which is the air bladder of some fish. It is found dried, fried, and hanging from ceiling hooks in many Chinese markets. They love fish tails, adore the cheeks of fish, and eat every part of virtually every sea animal.

In general, Chinese prefer white-fleshed fin fish but do eat all manner of freshwater and saltwater varieties and all types of oysters and clams. They prefer them alive until just before cooking and love shrimp made drunken style, which is alive until poached in wine just minutes before eating. They eat every manner of crustacean, some pickled, and adore all tiny eggs or sperm, which Westerners call roe. Some fish and crustaceans are farmed; they can be seen swimming in large tanks in restaurants, assuring freshness until the cooking moment. The Chinese cook and eat frogs as tadpoles and when fully grown. During the Song Dynasty, raw fish slices were popular; they are regaining popularity since the thousand-year hiatus between Song times and now, and the Chinese eat clams, particularly the neck of the huge geoduck, sliced and raw. Raw fish consumption might have resumed when Taiwan was ruled for 50 years by the Japanese, or it may be the result of increased trade, travel, TV, and other exposures.

Meat and Poultry

The Chinese eat all animals, though some are no longer legal because they are considered endangered, such as camel and bear. Pork is the most commonly consumed meat, so common that the same word is used to mean both meat and pork. Muslims do not eat pork for religious reasons; they eat mutton and goat meat. Other Chinese prefer these least of all, even though mutton was touted as one of four meats in the eight delicacies of Zhou Dynasty cuisine. When speaking about meat from a pig, a joke is told that the Chinese eat every part of that animal except the oink. They also eat every part of other four-legged and two-legged animals, be it skin, meat, fat, or entrails, and they eat parts cooked from fresh, dried, and ones preserved in salt or oil.

Animal foods can be braised, poached, boiled, stir-fried, baked in clay or salt, potted, simmered, or cooked in a mother sauce, which is a soy sauce mixture used and reused from one similar meat to another. The Chinese cook some animal foods Song Dynasty-style or dried and very finely shredded, looking like hairs on person's head. They salt their meats, and seafoods too, and make them into pastes, but these days less frequently than in ancient times. Some meats are still pickled sometimes, and rarely, if ever, do the Chinese eat any meat raw.

Except for vegetarians, all Chinese eat chicken and duck, the most commonly consumed two-legged animals. There is less use of goose, pigeon, and other small birds, mostly due to economics and availability. Sausages are made from most meats, primarily pork meat and pork liver, secondarily from duck meat and duck liver. Nothing is wasted. Even animal blood, primarily pork, is used after coagulation. They steam, slice, and eat blood as is or cut up and incorporated into a soup or cooked dish. Chicken, duck, other poultry, all meats can be boiled or roasted, pressed, cooked and dried—some just heavily salted and set aside for later consumption. Pressed poultry preserved in salt is called Nanjing style.

In ancient China, farmers kept six animals as livestock. They were considered important along with the five classical grains. They were written about, and bones and seeds have been found in burial plots. The animals are the horse, ox or cow, sheep, pig, dog, and chicken. All are raised, but not all are consumed. Some are eaten frequently, others primarily for seasonal strength or health reasons, such as dog. Ancient literature indicates that horse was never considered a food item, but records show that some was eaten, albeit rarely. It should again be pointed out that there has never been any taboo against eating horse or any other animal.

Some animals are not eaten with legal cause, a concern about their extinction. As to dog, it was popular during the Han Dynasty but disappeared thereafter. By the Tang Dynasty it became repugnant and was hardly a table food. Today, it is consumed in winter in some areas of south China, but most Chinese still consider it repugnant and do not eat it.

Besides popular meat and sea creatures, the Chinese eat some less familiar items such as the seahorse. However, these are mostly used for medicinal purposes. Tiny birds, once popular as single-bite foods, are no longer abundant; some are virtually extinct, so their use diminished, as has other unusual animal consumption that is legal but in short supply. Those that are consumed, most for special occasions, include birds' nests, sea cucumbers, and others, and they are discussed in chapter 6, their main use being at banquets and other festive and festival occasions. In ancient and dynastic China they were not used as everyday foods.

Eggs

The Chinese eat animals that lay eggs and the eggs that they lay. Popular are chicken, quail, pigeon, and duck eggs fresh and in several preserved forms. Preserved eggs are usually duck eggs that were put up in salt, brine, or a mixture of ash, clay, and/or limestone. The ones buried in ash and similar things are called thousand-year eggs, but that is a misnomer. More accurately, these eggs are buried or covered and put in large crocks in one of many mixtures for about 90 to 100 days.

Salted or brined eggs, when peeled, have cloudy whites; the color of their yolks intensifies to deep orange. They look softly coagulated, taste very salty, and are popular in recipes and moon cakes. Ash, clay, limestone hundred-day eggs are transformed, too, and after peeling their whites are translucent black, their yolks gray-green. When first opened, they have a strong hydrogen sulfide aroma that dissipates quickly. The brined eggs are popular in cooking; the buried black albumen ones are most often eaten as is, cut in halves and served with pickled ginger. They are most popular in the south of China.

FRUITS

The Chinese eat a large variety of fruits plain and prepared in many ways. When fresh, they like them large and lovely, and often share one among many people, cutting it into slices or wedges. They also use fruits in long-cooked or minimally cooked dishes. Fruits can be symbolic, with some used as temple offerings, others as ornaments. When fresh, the Chinese prefer most of them at their peak of ripeness, but do intentionally eat some less than ripe; a peach is one example—they like green ones and ripe ones. Listed below are less familiar fruits, in alphabetical order. It is interesting to note that individual fruits, like many foods, have gone in and out of popularity. One such is the apple. Apples were popular when the Silk Road was well-traveled, then until recently there was minimal usage. Now they are again popular, and China now grows many varieties to meet this renewed interest.

Citrus Fruits

This group of fruits originated in Asia, many believe in China. They include the orange, mandarin, tangerine, lemon, pomelo, and others. All were in high regard in ancient times, and many were presented to the court as tribute foods. Citrus fruits common in the West are not discussed.

One citrus fruit unique to China and India is a variation of the common citron. Known as Buddha's hand or finger citron, the Chinese call it *fuhou*. It was a popular potted plant, used as a gift and in Chinese traditional medicine. Often depicted in art, it is believed to bestow good fortune on households that keep it. The skin was and still is preserved in sugar or syrup and eaten on New Year's and other special occasions. It can be cooked in a few holiday-type dishes, valued for its thick skin; there is almost no pulp in this fruit.[6]

Cumquats are citrus and called *qintou*. In English they can be called golden mandarin. Small, oval, and orange, they are about the size of a very large date, grow on low trees, and unlike other citrus fruits are eaten skin and all. Their skin is quite sweet, their interior unusually tart.

Litchis and Tree Fruit Relatives

The litchi and related tree fruits originated in China, known at least since Han Dynasty times. Litchi, also spelled *lichee* and *lichii* in English, is spelled *lizhi* in *pinyin*. It is an especially prized fruit; its trees are planted in areas called gardens, and they bear fruit for a hundred or so years. Ladies of many a royal court wrote of their fondness for this sweet fruit and its cousins, the longan and the loquat (*lonyanguo* and *pipa*, respectively). All are subtropical single-stone fruits with white flesh, and all are used fresh and dried. These fruits have traditional Chinese medicinal properties, as do their bark and leaves.

Peaches

Domesticated in China and popularized there, peaches may also have origins somewhat west of China; perhaps they traveled to China on early trade routes. Since coming, they have become an important symbol and an important food. The peach or *tao* is symbolic of long life, and a common Chinese god carries the peach of longevity in his hand. Aside from the fruit's delicious taste, peach wood—which is not consumed—is revered and considered a protection against evil.

Persimmon

The pollen of persimmon have been found in Neolithic sites in north China. This is a fruit considered indigenous to China. Persimmons can be pointed at the top or flat-topped and are popular in traditional Chinese medicine. Wild persimmons are sometimes known as date-plums, no doubt because they are the size of a date. Called *shi* in Chinese, persimmons can be anywhere from this date-plum size to as big as an apple, depending upon the variety. They are eaten fresh and dried, and many are cooked from the dry state.

BEVERAGES

The Chinese have consumed alcoholic beverages for thousands of years. They also drink both hot and cold water that has first been boiled, a lot of tea, and most recently soda, canned juices, bubble teas, and slushy-type drinks.

Cold Beverages

Cool or iced drinks were familiar to China's early ruling classes and intelligentsia. Iced liquor and clear, cool wines were written about in early Chinese poetry. Recently, cold soda has become popular; its use is increasing. Carbonated beverages or soda hardly existed prior to Chairman Mao (1893–1976); he banned those associated with the West.

Beer use, particularly in Qingdao where Germans taught the Chinese how to make this beverage, has been popular since the late 1800s when a German-style brewery was built there. By the early 1900s there was some bottling of health waters from mountain streams near the brewery. After that, beer and health waters became popular; they were bottled in many regions. Cold tea never was popular, but some at room temperature is sold on the streets in hot weather. Tea, as a hot beverage, was first reported in 59 B.C.E. Its leaves were a tribute item sent to the emperor's court. It became very popular after Lu Yu told about and touted its benefits.

Soup

All types of soup were and are the beverage of choice at mealtimes. In some regions of China, such as Fujian, and at banquets in many regions, several soups are consumed at a single meal. Most often, thick soups are consumed early in a meal and thinner ones nearer the end. A Chinese expression says that "soup fills the cracks," meaning the spaces left empty at a meal. The expression "rice fills the cracks" can be used for fried rice served at the end of a banquet.

Tea

In China, tea is consumed without sugar and most often without anything added to it. Southern Chinese prefer theirs green, but also drink oolong and black tea. The western Chinese prefer theirs in bricks and oxidized until black. There are hundreds, if not thousands, of different teas to select from, but every one is made from leaves of the plant *Camel-*

lia sinensis. Differences, as is also the case with wine, depend upon where leaves were grown and how they were handled after picking. All tea leaves are dried; most are somewhat or considerably oxidized, which is a process often incorrectly called fermentation. Those dried for the shortest time are considered white or green; those dried somewhat longer are termed oolong. Tea leaves dried longer still are called black tea by Westerners; the Chinese call this red tea because the infusion made from them is reddish. There really are finer gradations than just these three. Chinese refer to teas as white, yellow, light green, green, red, and floral. The latter group has things such as jasmine or litchi flowers added, and there can be other additives.

Chinese believe that tea is beneficial. Even so, except for the Cantonese, most do not drink it at regular meals. They do drink a lot of it with snacks. Overall, they believe that tea reduces fatigue and creates a sense of well-being. They drink lots of it, and when entering a home a guest is always quickly presented with some. Many treatises have been written about this beverage and how to grow and brew it. Perhaps the most famous is *The Classic of Tea* by Lu Yu, written in the 800s.

Water

In ancient China and today, most water is boiled before being consumed for sanitary reasons. Little water is consumed plain, other than a few bottled health waters. More commonly, the liquid people drink is the liquid left after making noodles, cooked vegetables, and other foods. These waters and soups are their liquids of choice. They drink them at and between meals; and they use them when making sauces for their cooked dishes.

Wines

Wines are ancient beverages. In China, they were and are made from grains, fruits, vegetables, and more. Popular as medicinals and for social drinking, alcoholic beverage use has continued for thousands of years. Through several historical periods, the Chinese consumed excessive amounts, and they developed many games to play while so doing. They wrote about being inebriated and having drunken brawls; their poetry honored this condition. Confucius (551–479 B.C.E.) and others thought inebriation dreadful. Since raucous times during his generation and thereafter, society has spurned this behavior. For the past few hundred years, writings refer to drunkenness as something to be shunned. Therefore, there is much less drunkenness at the banquet table than in earlier times.

RECIPES USING MAJOR INGREDIENTS

Grains such as rice and noodles made from rice and other grains are the basic starches at meals. The most popular meat at ordinary meals is pork, a food rarely served at a banquet. Meals can begin with spareribs or another taste-tempting appetizer, and during a meal a best-loved vegetable such as Chinese broccoli, or *gailan*, or any other steamed or stir-fried green is served. In the south of China, greens are loved and typically made with *fuyu*, fermented bean cakes. In the United States, the most-ordered restaurant dish is beef and broccoli. In China, one of the most beloved is soy sauce chicken. For vegetarians and other health-conscious people, there are many dishes made without meat. Yangzhou fried rice is made without soy sauce and with or without meat; it can go with any these foods. After a meal, a popular fruit such as the mandarin orange or kumquat might be served. Any or all of the following popular dishes use common ingredients. A guest, treated as one of the family, would be served several of them.

Sweet and Sour Spareribs
- 2 pounds spareribs, cut (by the butcher) into one-inch strips
- 3 tablespoons dark soy sauce
- 3 tablespoons sugar
- 3 tablespoons orange juice
- 3 cloves garlic, minced
- 3 tablespoons Chinese rice vinegar
- 3 tablespoons catsup or 2 tablespoons tomato paste mixed with 1 tablespoon water
- 3 tablespoons Chinese rice wine or dry sherry
- 1 to 3 tablespoons corn syrup
- 3 tablespoons cornstarch mixed with 1 cup cold water

1. Cut sparerib strips into two or three sections.
2. Mix soy sauce, sugar, orange juice, and garlic, and marinate the ribs in this mixture. Cover and put them in the refrigerator for 12 hours or overnight.
3. Heat oven to 400 degrees Fahrenheit. Put ribs on racks in a deep oven-proof baking pan. Cook then for 50 minutes, turning every 10 minutes. Remove from the oven and cut into individual ribs.
4. Bring vinegar, tomato product, rice wine, and corn syrup to the boil. Add cornstarch mixture and stir until thickened, then pour over the ribs and serve.

Greens with Fuyu

- 1 pound spinach, *gailan*, or any other green leafy vegetable
- 1 tablespoon *fuyu* (fermented bean cake), mashed
- 1 tablespoon thin soy sauce
- 1 tablespoon corn or peanut oil
- 1 to 2 cloves garlic, minced

1. Wash vegetable and cut off any tough or broken stems, Drain well, or use a salad spinner to remove excess water.
2. Mix mashed fermented bean cake with soy sauce and set aside.
3. Heat oil, add the garlic, and stir-fry for 10 to 20 seconds, then add the greens and stir-fry for two minutes. Add two tablespoons water and continue to stir-fry until all the greens are soft and wilted.
4. Add bean cake mixture, stir well, and cook another minute, then serve.

Stir-Fried Beef and Chinese Broccoli

- 1/2 pound flank steak
- 1 tablespoon salted black beans, rinsed and lightly mashed
- 1 clove garlic, minced
- 2 thin slices peeled fresh ginger, minced
- 1 teaspoon corn or peanut oil
- 1 teaspoon cornstarch
- 1 teaspoon thin soy sauce
- 1 teaspoon Chinese rice wine or dry sherry
- 1/2 teaspoon sugar
- 1 pound Chinese or Western broccoli, stems removed and cut into two- or three-inch pieces or bunches; blanched for 1 minute, chilled in ice water, and drained well
- 2 tablespoons corn or peanut oil
- 1 tablespoon cornstarch mixed with 2 tablespoons dark soy sauce

1. Cut flank steak into thin strips about one-quarter inch by one-quarter inch by three inches in length.
2. Mix black beans, garlic, and ginger, and set aside.
3. Mix the teaspoon of oil, cornstarch, thin soy sauce, rice wine, and sugar, and stir in the flank steak strips. Mix well, then set this aside for up to half an hour.

4. Heat two tablespoons oil and add the black bean mixture. Stir-fry for no more than half a minute, then add meat mixture and continue to stir-fry for one more minute, then add the broccoli. Stir-fry another minute or two until the meat has lost most but not all of its pink interior color.

5. Add cornstarch mixture and stir-fry until it thickens and all is mixed well. Be careful to do this in no more than one minute, then serve.

Cantonese Soya Chicken

- 1 whole chicken, three to four pounds
- 2 cups thin soy sauce
- 1 slab Chinese brown sugar or 1/4 cup brown sugar
- 1/2 cup Chinese rice wine or dry sherry
- 1 tablespoon sesame oil

1. Clean and dry chicken with paper towels.
2. Put soy sauce, brown sugar, and rice wine into a six-quart pot. Add 1/2 cup cold water and bring to the boil.
3. Add the chicken, return liquid to the boil, add the sesame oil, and cover the pot. Reduce the heat immediately, then simmer for 15 to 20 minutes, depending upon the size of the chicken. Turn it every 5 minutes during this time. Then turn off the heat and allow the chicken to remain in the pot an additional 20 minutes without removing the pot's cover.
4. Remove the chicken from the pot, and reserve the sauce. *Cool the chicken for half an hour, then cut it into bite-sized pieces and serve.

*This liquid in the pot is called a mother sauce. It can be reused if refrigerated in a jar with a tight lid. It keeps best when covered with melted solid shortening, at least half an inch, that will solidify and seal out air. It should be stored in the refrigerator and can be reused many times. It is best when refreshed with half each of the soy sauce, brown sugar, rice wine, and sesame oil after every other use. When reusing it, remove the solid shortening and set it aside. Then remelt it to reseal the remaining sauce before refrigeration the next time.

Yangzhou Fried Rice, Vegetarian Style

- 6 medium-size dried Chinese black mushrooms, soaked in warm water for half an hour
- 1/2 cup fresh or frozen peas
- 1/2 cup bamboo shoots, diced the size of the peas
- 1/4 cup carrots, diced the size of the peas
- 1/2 cup fried gluten or bean curd squares,[†] diced the size of the peas
- 1/2 cup firm tofu, diced the size of the peas

- 2 teaspoons corn or another bland vegetable oil
- 2 eggs, beaten
- 4 cups precooked rice, must be at room temperature or cooler
- salt and pepper to taste

1. Remove mushroom stems, and dice mushrooms about the size of peas.
2. Mix the mushrooms with the peas, bamboo shoots, carrots, gluten squares, and tofu. Set aside.
3. Heat half the oil. In a wok or large fry pan, fry the eggs as a single pancake until just set, turn over and fry another half minute, remove from the pan, cut into thin two-inch strips, and set aside.
4. Heat the other half of the oil and stir-fry the vegetables three minutes, and set aside.
5. Return eggs to the pan, add the rice, and stir gently for one minute, then add the vegetables and stir-fry two or three minutes until heated through. Add the salt and pepper, and serve.

†Fried gluten and/or fried bean curd squares can be purchased in the refrigerator sections of large Chinese markets, or they can be made at home by cutting one-inch squares of fresh gluten or fresh bean curd, pressing out the excess water, and deep frying them—a few at a time—until golden.

NOTES

1. Lin Yutang, *Importance of Living* (New York: Reynal and Hitchcock, 1937).
2. John D. Keys, *Food for the Emperor* (San Francisco: Ward Ritchie Press, 1963).
3. H. T. Huang, as cited in *Science and Civilization in China*, vol. 6 (Cambridge, UK: Cambridge University Press, 2000).
4. Ibid.
5. J. M. Newman, "Soy Sauce Favorites: A Tasting," *Flavor and Fortune* 8 (1): 29 (2001).
6. Frederick J. Simoons, *Food in China: A Cultural and Historical Inquiry* (Boca Raton Fla.: CRC Press, 1991); J. M. Newman, "Buddha's Hand Citron," *Flavor and Fortune* 5 (4): 5–6 (1998).

3

Cooking

This chapter discusses cooking techniques, who cooks, how and with what, differences by region and people, and cooking terminology. The Chinese have many different terms and different techniques for cooking foods; the ones discussed here are but a few. They like to be very specific and differentiate among cooking techniques when they speak about food and how it is prepared. A topic often discussed is the many different cooking techniques and the subtle differences between them.

Some methods used by the Chinese are common in many cultures, such as boiling, deep-frying, and pickling. However, they are not always done the same ways. For example, while some consider boiling a single cooking technique, the Chinese speak about and use many different ways of boiling foods. One is plain cooking in water that continues to boil; another is quick-boiling then removing the pan from the heat source; and still another is putting food in boiling water but reducing the temperature gradually. There are also deep-boiling, plunging food in boiling water then rinsing, and others.

Boiling is not the only cooking method where subtle differences are discussed, practiced, and given different names, and where each is considered different and important. Steaming also has a variety of different techniques and names. Two examples are indirect steaming, with no contact with steam as the source of heat, and direct steaming, where the steam encompasses the food. Still other culinary methods have important differences. Some Chinese cookbooks discuss 20, 30, 40, 50, and even more variations of heating and cooking food, each with its own Chinese word and its own detailed description. Some chefs and even home cooks take pride in knowing and using more than a hundred different cooking techniques.

One particular technique, first used by the Chinese and later adopted by others, is called stir-frying. This method may be several thousand years old and probably took root in Han Dynasty times (202 B.C.E.–220 C.E.). However, it was different then and far from the most important cooking technique in ancient China, where it was used primarily to toast grains. It did not become commonplace until several hundred years ago. In part, today's uses may have been initiated and necessitated by limited fuel supplies. Stir-frying spread to the rest of Asia, then to the rest of the world. It will always be associated with Chinese food but was not the first, nor is it now the most important, technique used by the Chinese.

A look at some important techniques, but not in order of importance as this can vary by region, helps to understand them and the attention to detail that is Chinese cooking. While volumes have been written about all the techniques the Chinese use, there is no one way to categorize them. Therefore, they are generalized and discussed in broad categories, with only some differences within each one explained. Equivalents closest to the Chinese cooking method are given, and a Chinese word transliterated into *pinyin* is provided.

BOILING

Called *zhu*, boiling was and is a very important way to cook Chinese food, perhaps the very first such cooking method using fire. As mentioned, it is not thought of as a single cooking technique, but rather as many. When done in lots of liquid at a rolling boil, the Chinese call it *cuan*. However, if the food or foods are dropped into the boiling liquid and quickly removed, this plunging or blanching is called *shua*. When food stays in the boiling liquid for more than just a quick in and out, the Chinese word is *tang*. When the liquid is brought to the boil, the food put in, and the temperature immediately reduced so that the food is cooked at a lower temperature, as in simmering, the Chinese call it *dun*.

Another technique of cooking in hot liquid is to put food in broth. When that liquid starts to boil, the heat is reduced, and the food is long-cooked, a braising called *lu*. If the broth is seasoned with soy sauce, the technique is called *chiang*, and in English known as red-cooking. This term is further differentiated if the food is cooked with or without wine and the soy sauce added to broth, stock, or plain water. Without soy sauce, the word is *bai*, which means white, and the word *lu* may be added. *Lu* cookery is done with or without seasonings such as star anise or a stick of cassia (the cinnamon Chinese use). If the cooking is done in a liquid and in a special pot called a firepot, with or without soy sauce, the name changes to *shuan*. Sometimes, when food is steeped and the water never boiled, the cooking technique is called *tsui*.

STEAMING

Another popular Chinese cooking method is to steam foods. Steaming may have been the second cooking technique ancient Chinese people used. To steam, food is often put in bamboo containers called baskets. The baskets with a bamboo cover on top sit over simmering or rapidly boiling water; this technique is called *zheng*. However, if the food is not in direct contact with the steam (as in the top part of a double boiler), this is a different technique called *dun*.

There are many others cooking techniques involving putting food into or above a boiling or simmering liquid, and there are different Chinese names for each of them. Because the Chinese care about each and every

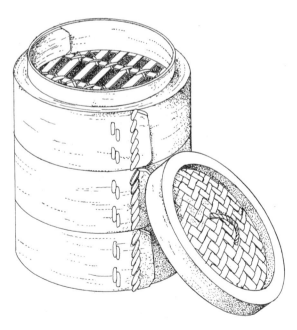

Bamboo steamer baskets.

subtle difference, these require specific words to help differentiate differences that Westerners generalize about and call moist-heat cooking.

DEEP-FRYING

Plunging foods into hot oil—deep-frying them—was not commonly done in ancient China. Other than in restaurants, it is still not common today. But when it is done, the Chinese differentiate major ways. One is generally called *qinzha*, but sometimes specified as *kanzha*. The former term means fried in lots of oil after the food item has marinated in a liquid; the latter means frying foods that were first coated in batter. Should the foods have first been marinated and then fried, some would use the word *yen*. When a food is fried until it is very crisp, they call it *suzha*. Should the food be wrapped in a piece of paper, dough, or a leaf, the word changes to *zhibaozha*. When a food has its own skin, such as a piece of chicken or duck, or a food is wrapped in a poultry skin, then the word most used is *cuizha*.

ROASTING AND SMOKING

The Chinese generally call roasting *kao*, and they mean cooking in a closed oven. Westerners may be more familiar with the term *bake*, which Chinese generally limit to nonmeat items. Roasting can be called *anlukao* when done with the food hanging on a hook in the oven. Southern Chinese restaurants often have many long hooks holding chickens and ducks cooked this way visible in their front window. When food is roasted over an open fire, the Chinese word is *minglukao*; to Americans this is barbecuing.

Smoking is a cooking technique related to roasting; the Chinese call it *xun*. To them, it requires foods set over continuously produced smoke from wood, tea leaves, or the like. To roast, bake, or smoke a food that is coated in rock salt and then put it into an oven is called *yenji* or *chu*. To roast a food that is first coated with clay is *nikao*. Roasting, baking, and smoking are cooking techniques using dry heat; they can involve many other subtleties and types of dry heat cooking. One difference is whether this cooking is done in a closed space or an open environment. Another, like smoking, can use different types of fuels as the heating source. All of these have special names associated with them.

PAN OR WOK COOKING

This technique can be done in any kind of pan. For the last several hundred years, the Chinese have been doing it in woks. The word *wok* is Cantonese; it is *guo* in China's north and sometimes *kao* elsewhere in the country. Woks usually have rounded bottoms; they are China's main cooking pots today because they are very versatile. They can be used to deep-fry and boil, to steam if one places a cover on top, and to pan-fry or stir-fry without a cover. Traditionally, the Chinese put the wok into a charcoal fire pit. In modern kitchens, if used on an electric stove, a wok needs to sit on a ring to assure that it does not tip over.

Most Chinese foods are pre-prepared before cooking. One technique is dry marinating or coating the foods in flours and/or spices. If that is done, the Chinese word is *pan*. Dry sautéing or cooking in a wok or pot without oil is *hui*. The current and most famous technique of cooking in a wok is stir-frying; this is called *chao*.

To stir-fry, the Chinese heat the wok before putting food in it. In standard stir-frying, after the wok is hot but before it smokes, oil or another liquid is added before adding another food. This technique traditionally requires food to be cut into bite-size pieces, diced, cut into strips, or sliced. Then, after the wok is heated and seasonings—such as garlic, ginger, scallions, or shallots—are added, with or without oil, everything is tossed continually as it fries; hence the name stir-fry. The seasonings are tossed until fragrant, about 20 or 30 seconds, then the main ingredients added, starting with the one that needs the longest time to cook. Sometimes the meat is added first and removed when half cooked, then vegetables are added one by one, by longest to shortest time needed to cook. After all vegetables are partly cooked, the meat is returned to the pan, and when everything is three-quarters cooked, additional seasoning items such as soy and other sauces, vinegar, salt, and sugar are added and tossed as they stir-fry. A thickening agent such as cornstarch, water chestnut flour, or arrowroot is mixed with water and added about one minute before a dish is finished. If cornstarch is used, the dish is stir-fried until the sauce thickens and clears; other thickeners are cooked until the sauce reaches the desired consistency.

When foods are raw and not coated, the general Chinese term for stir-frying is *senchao*. When the meats or vegetables are coated with starch, this different technique is called *liu*. *Pao* or quick-frying is similar to *chao*, but the main food or foods take less time to stir-fry, and some are coated with egg white. There are other related techniques such as to fricassee or *shao* a food. To the Chinese, that means to first stir-fry the food, then add water or stock and simmer until done. Another related cooking technique is *jian* or pan-frying. In this technique, foods are fried in a small amount of oil until crisp (many are marinated before frying), then finished off or cooked in one of several additional manners.

PREPARING COLD FOODS

Most Chinese food is served cooked and hot, or warm. All of the afore-mentioned cooking techniques can be used alone or together to prepare foods to serve at any temperatures, cold included. Most times they are served hot and from the pan, but sometimes foods are served at or below room temperature. Serving cold food is not new to China. Years ago, cool or chilled foods were eaten a lot more than they are today.

There are several ancient recipes for cold food, and the Chinese do have a Cold Food Festival (see chapter 7). To serve foods cold or chilled, they had icehouses. Ice was also used to ship, store, and make some foods cold. Most chilled food was cooked first. One method was and is to heat foods and then let them set; this method of jelling is called *tung*. Other foods could be precooked, allowed to cool, and served at room tempera-ture. Still others, albeit only a few of them, were and are served chilled.

HOME AND RESTAURANT MEAL PREPARATION

In ancient times the Chinese ate two meals a day, while for the last thousand-plus years they have eaten three a day. This difference can be partially explained by the way meals are defined, which is detailed in chapter 5. Most but not all cooking for these meals was done by women. They stayed at or near home to raise the children and prepare meals for the entire family. Some did work in the fields near home, and many took children and foods to the fields, where they made some of these meals, then ate them there. Sometimes they brought cooked foods; other times someone made a small fire to warm the foods they brought; and sometimes they cooked the meal there. At the end of the day they went home and cooked the evening meal or snack. In some regions of China and in more recent times, the evening meal was the main meal.

More recently, most women work outside the home, and cooking is shared by some or all of the adults, male or female, and some of the older children. Most recently, many Chinese rarely cook at home. Lots of them eat the main meal at their workplace canteens or cafeteria-type facilities. The meals can be a perk, if free, or the food may be considered part of the salary. In other workplaces, employees pay for what they eat. Those who cook at the workplace can be men or women.

In cities, eating out—buying food from street vendors at corner stands and eating in restaurants—is becoming more common. Some is done on the way to or from work. It was less common for people or families to eat out at night, except on special occasions, but that is changing. In Chinese and many other Asian cities and towns, there are many street vendors selling food, but few places to sit and eat. So people line up, buy something, and eat it on their way to or from work.

Lunch and dinner meals were not commonly eaten out, mostly because of the expense. In China, at least, most salaries could not support that luxury. This has been true for hundreds upon hundreds of years. However, on holidays and for special life-cycle events, eating out was and is a special treat often indulged in and done extravagantly. When Chinese go out to eat, many generations do so together. On weekends and holidays, when income allows, many go out for *dientsin, dim sum, yumcha,* or whatever they call it. This snack-cum-meal is becoming more popular, and is detailed below.

For those who cook at home, shopping often is a daily activity. Until recently, very few homes in China had refrigeration. While more do now, the Chinese still prefer fresh food, neither chilled nor frozen. They adore their fruits and vegetables at the peak of freshness, so many working people purchase fresh or cooked foods on their way home. Those who do not work often shop before each main meal. Their seriousness about subtle distinctions in cooking techniques carries over to concerns about subtle differences in the freshness of the food.

COOKING EQUIPMENT

Chinese homes had and still have very few pieces of cooking equipment. Stoves are often simply single charcoal braziers. For burials and to assure food in the afterlife, stoves seem complex, but they are not. Restaurants have more heat sources, but theirs were and are more sophisticated and clearly much larger. Most families cooked on wood or charcoal, and still do. Recently, some families, particularly those in the three largest cities in China, have begun to cook on gas. With or without it, homes have one or maybe two burners to cook on. Careful planning is required; time considerations and the high cost of fuel are paramount. Lots of families use one, two, or at most three main items of equipment when cooking their food. An ordinary pot to cook liquids in is one; another is a *guo* or pan for stir-frying, frying, or steaming; and if there is a third, it could be a grill-like metal plate.

For steaming, a specialized steamer works best in restaurants. At home, food is put into a bamboo basket or the newer plastic or metal ones. These have holes in the bottom to allow the steam to circulate. They are put on the wok or in a pot and set above boiling or simmering water. A leaf, pieced of oiled paper, or damp cloth—even a carrot or other vegetable slice—sits inside the steamer basket to separate the food from it and prevent the food from sticking. One to four baskets can be stacked over the bottom container, pot, or wok and below the steamer cover. In restaurants, hospitals, hotels, and places that feed large numbers of people, it is not uncommon to see 6 to 12 huge steamer baskets stacked over the bottom wok that sits with rapidly steaming water, and under a huge cover.

Woks and Tools

The main cooking pot, the wok or *gao*, usually has a conical bottom, somewhat akin to an upside-down Chinese hat used in the fields. This shape is important because the cooking vessel sits directly in or over a heat source. The best woks are made of fast-heating metal, usually thin steel. A metal or bamboo cover is used infrequently, certainly never for initial stir-frying, but always for steaming. Some woks come with a rack that attaches on the side. This wire shelf is useful for draining fried foods placed on it, as the drained fat returns directly into the pan. A wok is best for stir-frying and can be any size from 14 inches in diameter, a typical home size, to 3 feet wide, a common restaurant size. Because a family or a

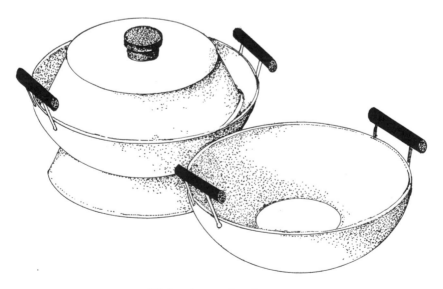

Woks, ring, and wok cover.

restaurant chef can deep-fry, simmer, boil, or steam foods in this equipment, the number of needed cooking items is greatly reduced.

Besides the cover, other metal and/or bamboo items are used to cook
foods in a wok. An important one is a *guachan* or spatula. This tool is used
to stir the foods as they cook and to remove them from the pan when
done. A strainer basket is useful; most have a handle made of bamboo and
a basket made of twisted wires. This long-handled device is used to drain
and then remove foods from a wok or pan. Another item is a large, flat
metal strainer with holes that can also remove large amounts of food from
boiling water or from hot oil. Sometimes both the wire and the flat
strainer are used in tandem to shape foods to be fried. They can be used to
shape noodles, for example, into a basket that can hold other foods. Tools
such as these make cooking fast and efficient.

The Chinese use other large and small pots for boiling or simmering
foods. However, with but one or two burners, most foods are cooked in or
on a wok or in a pot. A few other items are used, though less frequently, such
as a ginger grater to do what its name says, and a plate grabber to remove

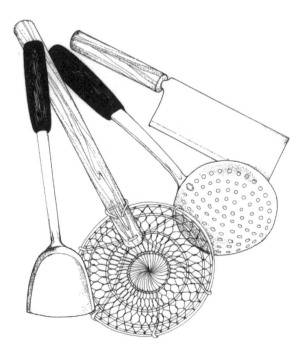

Wok tools (wok spatula, strainer basket, and
strainer ladle) and a cleaver for cutting ingredients.

steamed dishes from wok or pan. These are most often found in restaurants or the homes of the affluent.

Rice Cookers

Most rice cookers are electric, and they are becoming commonplace. This is the modern tool to prepare rice, rather than the traditional way of making rice in a bowl placed in a steamer. Rice and water, with or without salt, go in this electric device; a button is pushed; and automatically this pot cooks the rice and stops when the rice is cooked to perfection. An electric rice cooker can double as a pot to steam foods in, and it is a particularly effective way to reheat leftovers.

Chopsticks

Chopsticks are the implement of choice for cooking and eating food. Longer ones are used to cook, shorter ones to eat. The word for chopsticks, whether for cooking or for use at the table, is *kuaizi*. It means quick-quick or quick-boys. These two equal-sized utensils can remove a specific item from any dish and can be used for stirring or even piercing a food. Most are made of bamboo. Those made for cooking use are 4 to 10 inches longer than those used at the table. Chinese chopsticks are longer than Japanese ones; they are a little thicker and are usually square at the top and round at the bottom, which is the part used to retrieve food and put it into the mouth.

Cutting Board

Most homes have one large, heavy cutting board. Traditionally, it was made from a horizontal slice of a large tree trunk about 4 to 6 inches thick and 12 to 20 inches in diameter. This circle was used for chopping, cutting, and pounding foods before cooking them. Nowadays, very few homes have such a tree slice, but restaurants still do. Theirs are thicker, up to 10 to 15 inches, on legs, and at a convenient height for cutting. Newer cutting boards for homes or restaurants are made of hardened plastic. Older rectangular wooden ones and those cut directly from trees are still in use.

Tea Kettle and Pot

Homes and commercial kitchens have a kettle to heat water for making tea and other purposes. For tea, when the water gets very hot or boils (black tea needs boiling water, green teas need water about 10 to 20 degrees cooler), the water is poured into a clay or ceramic teapot to make and serve tea. These clay or ceramic teapots can be very stylized or simple. Kettles are simple and utilitarian, and their sizes are related to size of the family or restaurant.

Cleavers and Other Small Cooking and Storing Items

The common Chinese household cleaver is about eight inches long and three to four inches wide, and most have wooden handles. Those for chopping bones are heavier and thicker than those used for meats and vegetables. In restaurants, they can be any size, smaller to mostly bigger, thinner or thicker, and much longer, too, particularly to cut large melons or squash. A cleaver is the preferred item for cutting food before cooking it. The blade is used to cut, the side of it to pound, and the end of the handle for tasks such as smashing garlic. A square whetstone, oiled or with water, is used to keep the cleaver sharp. Good cooks like very sharp cleavers, so they sharpen them frequently. Most Chinese homes and commercial kitchens use only one or two cleavers and rarely use knives. Neither cleaver nor knife ever appears on a Chinese dining table. The Chinese believe that cleavers and knives are weapons and are inappropriate for table use.

Serving ladles are common, particularly in restaurants. They are used to stir and to move hot liquids such as soup to individual bowls. Bigger metal ones can be reserved for kitchen duty and large ceramic ones used at the table.

Chinese food requires a lot of cutting and pre-preparation before cooking. Homes and restaurants use several platters or trays to put cut foods on before cooking. A good cook needs the food all cut and ready before starting to cook, and uses bowls of any size to marinate the foods. It is common to use rice bowls and serving-size bowls, even teacups, for marinating foods.

For making dumplings and other dough foods, hands and a small rolling pin are the items of choice. Chinese rolling pins are about eight or nine inches long and an inch or inch and a half in diameter. There are small crimping tools, primarily used in restaurants, to shape dumplings into fruits, vegetables, and even small animal shapes. A scissors with rounded half-circle handles is used for cutting dough into shapes and for other things as well.

Rare is the Chinese home with an oven. Most roasted and baked foods are eaten in restaurants or purchased from them or from street vendors, then taken home to eat. Microwave oven use is catching on, but the microwave is still not a common household item. The Chinese prefer cooking their food immediately before eating it; markets now sell foods precut to help.

In addition, earthenware or pottery jars are used to store pickled foods. Many homes keep them handy, under the table where foods are prepared. Near the stove are bottles and jars of homemade or purchased fermented sauces, and cloth bags or small saucers of different seasonings. Bottles and jars can be taken to markets to be refilled with soy and other sauces and various other condiments, which are available in bulk amounts.

EATING EQUIPMENT AT THE TABLE

Fancy homes and fancy restaurants use rests to set soup spoons and chopsticks on. Affluent homes and ordinary restaurants may have wooden or ceramic ones. Besides these, table settings include ceramic rice bowls, teacups, small saucers for dipping sauces, and individual soup spoons, usually ceramic. Every person has one of each. While plastic bowls, teacups, and soup spoons are easily available, most Chinese prefer ceramic ones because they claim plastic or metal gives food a funny taste.

The individual service bowls and teacups often double as measuring utensils when preparing foods. Chopsticks are used to mix foods and pick them up to coat them. There are flat plates and platters to put foods on in their pre-preparation stages. The Chinese use these same large platters and bowls to bring foods to the table. Most tableware, therefore, doubles as items to use when preparing foods before cooking.

SPECIALTY ITEMS

There are a few unique items, including the chrysanthemum firepot, Mongolian grill, and clay pot that a few homes and some restaurants have. A firepot is known as a hot pot, a Mongolian pot, or a Mongolian hot pot, and it is popular in the north of China and used most in winter. It is a communal cooking pot. Some restaurants give each diner or family group one for its own use, putting it on the table on a thick metal tray. In this metal device, people cook their own food in liquid that sits in the donut-shaped ring resting on its chimney. That ring gets filled with water or stock. People take raw ingredients from platters of raw meats and vegetables sliced thin and set on the table. Diners have, besides chopsticks and soup spoons, a long-handled small wire basket to cook and retrieve foods they put in the liquid.

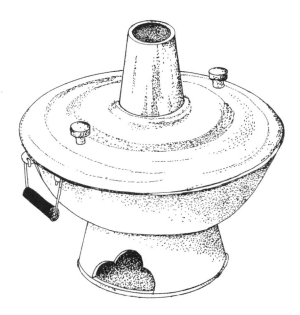

Mongolian hot pot.

To cook in a Mongolian hot pot, also called a firepot or a chrysanthe-mum hot pot, only a small amount of raw food goes into an individual wire basket. One or a few pieces at a time are submerged in the hot liquid. When the food is believed to be done, the strainer basket is removed and the food put on a person's plate or in their bowl. Most Chinese cook their vegetables crisp or slightly crisp and their meats medium rare. They do this in the liquid in the ring heated by direct contact that is sitting on and near the middle of the chimney. The chimney serves as the flue for the charcoal. Nowadays, electric firepots are available, and people are en-couraged to use them because cooking indoors with charcoal uses up oxy-gen and pollutes the air.

Another specialty item, also northern in origin, is the Mongolian grill. More common in restaurants than in individual homes, this griddlelike metal plate is slightly elevated in the center. When put over charcoal out-doors or another heat source indoors, foods grill directly on its elevated sur-face, the liquid running off or boiled away in its grooves. Animal and vegetable products are cooked on this grill, which is best oiled first to prevent sticking. The foods are turned and removed when believed to be done, and here too vegetables are preferred crisp and meats with some pink remaining.

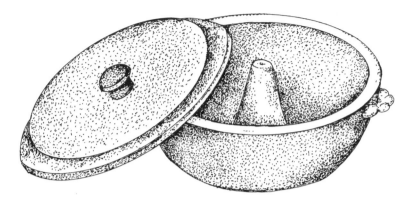

Yunnan pot.

There are many types of clay pots or *niantuguo* used in steamers or directly on a heat source. Some have wire around and under them to prevent scalding a user should they break apart when heated. Those that are sandy go by the name of sand pot, and others are just called clay pots. Both kinds are smooth and usually glazed on the inside. Sand pots are sandy on the outside, giving them their name.

People in the southeast cook and steam together in a pot called a Yunnan pot or *qiguo*. It has a short, upside-down, funnel-shaped chimney in the center with a narrow aperture at its top. This donut-shaped container can be 10 to 14 inches wide and about 4 to 6 inches deep. When filled with food and covered, it is put over steaming water or half submerged. It never sits on the bottom of a pot. The chimney produces steam that condenses in the pot and circulates, so foods are heated and cooked from the steam around them and from liquid in the pot itself.

There are other, less common items of equipment, but rare is the Chinese family that uses them. Restaurants have them if they specialize in foods that need them, but few do.

RECIPES BY COOKING TECHNIQUE

The most ancient Chinese cooking technique was heating food on hot rocks or in hot water to grill, boil, or simmer them. Later, the Chinese steamed some of their foods, and then they learned to bake them. Roasting, braising, and deep-frying were known long before stir-frying, the last major technique and one unique to Chinese cooking. Here are a few recipes using some of the main cooking techniques.

Steamed Pork with Seasoned Rice Flour

- 1/2 pound pork loin, cut into half-inch slices or boneless pork chops
- 1 tablespoon rice wine or dry sherry
- 1/2 teaspoon Chinese black vinegar
- 1 tablespoon thin soy sauce
- 1/4 teaspoon salt
- 1/4 teaspoon mixed fine ground white and coarsely ground black pepper
- 1/4 teaspoon ground Sichuan pepper
- 1/2 cup glutinous rice flour (if unavailable, use Cream of Rice cereal)
- 2 scallion tops, the green part only, thinly sliced

1. Mix pork with rice wine, vinegar, and soy sauce, and marinate for 15 minutes. Then drain, but do not dry the slices.
2. Mix salt, all three peppers, and rice flour, and put into a flat soup bowl.
3. Coat the drained pork slices with rice flour and put in a shallow bowl.
4. Place in a steamer, and steam over boiling water for 50 minutes, then serve with scallions scattered on top of the pork.

Stir-Fried Shrimp with Chinese Vegetables

- 1 Chinese dry mushroom, soaked for 20 minutes in warm water, stem removed
- 1/4 pound silk squash (Chinese okra), peeled
- 1/4 pound large white radish (daikon)
- 1 tablespoon corn or peanut oil
- 1/2 pound fresh shrimp, peeled, veins removed, and cut in half the long way
- 6 small dried shrimp, soaked in hot water for 15 minutes, drained, and boiled for 1 minute
- 1 tablespoon Chinese rice wine or dry sherry
- 1/2 teaspoon sugar
- 1 tablespoon thin or mushroom soy sauce mixed with 1/4 teaspoon cornstarch
- 1/2 pound baby bok choy, leaves individually separated
- 1 teaspoon sesame oil

1. Cut mushroom into thin slices, and cut silk squash and white radish into strips about the same size.
2. Heat oil and fry all shrimp for one minute. Add rice wine, sugar, mushroom soy mixture, and the slivered vegetables, and stir-fry this mixture for 2 minutes. Then add bok choy leaves and fry another minute or just until they wilt. Toss with sesame oil, and serve immediately.

Braised Shanghai-Style Soybean Sprouts

- 1 tablespoon thin soy sauce
- 1/2 teaspoon sugar
- 1/2 teaspoon salt
- 1 tablespoon corn or peanut oil
- 1 scallion, white part only, minced
- 1/2 clove garlic, minced fine
- 1/4 cup Yunnan or Virginia ham, slivered
- 1 pound soybean sprouts, tails removed

1. Mix soy sauce, sugar, and salt, and set aside.
2. Heat wok, add the oil, and fry the scallion pieces and garlic for a half minute, then add ham and stir-fry for 1 minute more.
3. Add soy mixture and a half cup of cool water, bring to the boil, lower the heat, and braise for half an hour, stirring every 5 to 10 minutes. Drain, should any liquid remain, and serve.

Boiled and Baked Peanuts with Red Bean Curd

- 2 cups shelled raw peanuts, halved and their paper skins removed
- 1/2 cup cool water
- 2 tablespoons mashed fermented red bean curd
- 1 tablespoon sugar

1. Put peanuts, red bean curd, sugar, and water in a pot and bring to the boil, continuously stirring this mixture. Reduce the heat slightly, and continue to stir until all the liquid is absorbed. This can take from 3 to 5 minutes.
2. Preheat oven to 300 degrees Fahrenheit. Spread the peanuts on a cookie sheet, and bake for three-quarters of an hour, stirring them after 10 minutes and then every additional 5 minutes.
3. Cool completely. Any leftover nuts can be stored in a jar in a cool, dark place for up to a month.

Lotus Root Chips

- 2 fresh lotus roots, peeled
- 2 cups corn or peanut oil
- 1 teaspoon very coarse salt

1. Slice the lotus roots thinly crosswise. This is can be done with a potato peeler, but the slices are best slightly thicker than that, perhaps 16 to 20 to the inch.

2. Heat oil to 375 degrees Fahrenheit, and deep-fry half of the slices. Remove them from the hot oil, drain well, and sprinkle with half the salt. Repeat with the second half. Then toss the two batches together, and serve.

4

Regional and Provincial Foods

Chinese people struggle to define where a dish originated, whether it is typical, how it may have changed as it moved from place to place, or if indeed it changed at all. Everyday cooking principles and the results they produce are reasonably similar from one end of China to the other. So as recipes move, their final products might be affected by local ingredient use and minor taste changes. However, as there are few differences, this begs two questions: Are there regional differences? And if so, what defines a food of a specific region?

The Chinese word to cook, *pengtiao,* means to cook and to season. Most Chinese cooking and seasoning is similar. Regional cuisines, to be different, need to be defined by certain dishes, cooking styles, ingredients, and tastes. A recipe may have started in one specific location, but is it different when cooked in another place? To define what is regional is akin to taking a motion picture of food changes and discussing it frame by frame. Does that mean that the concept of regional foods that use the same ingredients is, by its very nature, vague and blurred? Some think so, and others disagree.

What makes a food regional, other than its origin? The Chinese and those who study their foods learn about differences place to place as foods travel, and they say that regional differences play a minor role. A few agree that when looking at these small differences, it is possible to assign them compass points or cities of origin. That is how they generalize about regions and Chinese cooking styles. Others categorize foods by origin, dialect, and language group. Still others assign a recipe to a region based upon history, taste, and cooking technique. For example, the north is often associated with salty dishes, brined foods, and soy sauce. But are all foods with these ingredients northern? Most would say no. Foods from the south are thought to be, as the French might say, *au natural*. Are all foods that are cooked that way considered southern food? Of course not. Near Shanghai, in what is considered China's east, people say the foods favor the sea and are somewhat sweet. Does that mean that the tastes of people in Guangzhou, which is in the south and also favors foods of the sea, are eastern? Not always. As a matter of fact, all attempts to specify regions of Chinese cooking are subject to debate inside and outside of China. Cooking styles, ingredients, tastes, and even where foods belong and how they are named overlap.

It is hardly surprising to find food consumption differences in a country about the same size as the United States. It has been argued that these differences are best explained by geography and climate, both of which impact food and farming. While Chinese cooking has been differentiated by region, there are national traditions that override these considerations. Most of them are based upon cuisines of China's imperial court, and many believe that these cuisines are the most important considerations.

CHINESE FOODS ARE EVOLVING

The movement of food in China began when early nomads helped individual and local culinary worlds meet and mix. Foods certainly moved along what we now call the Silk Road; they even moved long before that. Foods move when people in local homes and local eateries meet travelers and townspeople, when they eat and drink together or within sight of each other. Some local Chinese traditions mixed with foods related to their Muslim, Afghani, or Turkic neighbors. They saw or tasted some prepared foods, but made them with familiar tastes. They could have had foods indigenous to the region they lived in and mixed them with foods brought in by diverse nomadic populations.

Movements of people, food, and goods were and are continually taking place. An early example of movement can be seen in Chinese silks. They can be found as early as 1500 B.C.E. in what is now Afghanistan. Food, no doubt, was brought in with these silks and other merchandise. People who transported them there experienced a host of new food tastes and probably brought some back to China when they returned home.

After the founding of the Chinese Empire in the third century B.C.E., there was considerable territorial expansion. That brought even more movement and exchange of foods. The first Chinese history was completed in 90 B.C.E. It mentioned new foods and their coming and going. More than a thousand years later in the Yuan Dynasty (1276–1386 C.E.), the ruling Mongol court and its leaders came from the north. They used southern cooks, local cooks, and their own cooks who, together and individually, incorporated new ingredients. These cooks refined Chinese food to meet the tastes of the new rulers.

The Mongols were succeeded by Ming Dynasty rulers who were not northern, but were instead ethnically Han Chinese. They deemed northern foods un-Chinese, of lesser value, and were repulsed by some of them. This example shows continuing change in what was accepted and eaten or rejected as Chinese food. Before and since, codifications define what is, was, and even should be considered Chinese food. Not everyone agrees with these; as a matter of fact, some can cite foods to fit them, and others cannot.

Restaurants are rapidly changing what the Chinese eat and what is considered Chinese food. They have also changed what the Western world believes Chinese food to be. What Chinese people actually eat is often very different from what restaurants serve. It is also different from the Chinese food people read about in cookbooks and newspapers, or hear about or see on radio and television. These sources most often speak about the foods of the elite. They are related to economics and local thinking about food, and they do not necessarily represent what the majority of Chinese people in or outside of China actually eat.

Some say that Chinese food is a combination of soy sauce, rice wine, and fresh ginger. Further simplifying things, others specify that foods in or from the north of China add soybean paste, garlic, and/or sesame oil to soy sauce, rice wine, and ginger. In the south they claim that Chinese food adds garlic, stock, and/or fermented black beans to the first three ingredients to be deemed southern Chinese food. In western parts of China, they say, adding hot chili pepper and/or sweet and sour flavorings gives western Chinese flavor.[1]

Generalizations about Chinese cuisine lead to inaccuracies. Time-honored divisions represent food consumption of the elite along with opinions of a few, be they Chinese or not. They are not based on surveys of what the Chinese are actually eating. Surveys indicate the Chinese eating more similarly than differently, no matter where they live or what their regional heritage may be.[2]

Nonetheless, divisions of Chinese food can be a good place to begin understanding specific tastes and Chinese cuisine. Using them requires understanding that Chinese food is very diverse and includes more than ten thousand different dishes. It requires knowing that main differences at meals are based upon what is called the wheat-rice divide or what is served with these dishes.

North of the Yangzi River, the main food consumed was and still is wheat. South of it, the largest number of calories, and therefore the main grain, was and is rice. This divide is the most critical regional difference in Chinese food. It is important because grains and other staple foods make up 70 percent or more of the calories the average Chinese person eats each day.[3] Other foods flavor the grain or staple foods, and that varies by what is available and affordable. Only foods of the onion, cabbage, and radish families are quite similar almost everywhere in China; how they are used can be less so.

The Chinese eat a huge variety of foods, perhaps the largest variety of any culture in the world. Food made with Chinese taste can be made with any number of ingredients. Prepared food with the same name may not taste the same in different places or even in different homes in the same location. It is not easy to place a dish simply by name, or to locate its origin by ingredients or flavor. Before technology made it possible to transport foods over long distances, climate, culture, and contact impacted what the Chinese grew, hunted, fished, and ate. Now differences are less easy to elucidate because foods and the people who prepare them travel from place to place, and there is radio and television to move these ideas.

EARLY REGIONAL DIFFERENCES

There are many ways to look at Chinese food differences. Relating food to provinces or administrative districts can be a useful beginning. There are 22 provinces, 5 autonomous regions, 31 autonomous prefectures, and 3 municipalities (Beijing, Shanghai, and Guangzhou). Add Hong Kong, which became part of China in 1999, and that makes 62 distinct political subdivisions. Does each have a cuisine?

Regional differences were not important in early China, when the country was smaller. Ancient Chinese cuisine was very different from Chinese food today. Was ancient cuisine a simple cuisine with mostly boiled or simmered foods? Does that mean that cuisines with dishes that are steamed, braised, stir-fried, or made using other cookery methods are not Chinese because they were not part of early Chinese food culture?

Stir-frying, though different from today, began during the Han Dynasty (202 B.C.E.–220 C.E.). It was not well-developed until hundreds of years later and really did not blossom until after the beginning or perhaps nearer the end of the Song Dynasty (960–1279 C.E.). The Chinese food most people think of today did not exist until the Ming Dynasty (1362–1644). Foods in the Zhou Dynasty (1122–221 B.C.E.) were Chinese long before stir-frying. They used at least 44 plants, with the most important staple grain being millet. Was that not Chinese food?

Early books about these times mention common domestic and wild game and do not mention food differences from one place to another. Was eating mostly millet eating Chinese food if it was prepared to look and taste the same as millet made in other countries? Was this common millet or foxtail millet? Was it prepared similarly in the north and in the south? In the east and in the west?

FOOD BY COMPASS POINTS

The simplest regional divisions might be four styles based upon compass points. Can China's culinary styles in its 62 administrative districts be reduced to four neat categorizations? Chinese chefs and their culinary organizations continually discuss regional differences, but what are these differences? They agree that a cuisine is considered great only if it has a wide range of dishes. Chinese food certainly has that, but regional foods have far fewer. Are they less great and therefore less important? Looking at cuisines within China, is dividing them by provinces and/or political district too fine a system? Not all of those places have a large range of dishes. Still, many are mentioned as regional cuisines. Does that make some of them great Chinese cuisine and others less than great?

The following generalizations or groupings consider the main or important culinary regions of China. Omitted are the foods of the autonomous regions, even though these regions make up close to 60 percent of China's landmass and are where most of the government-recognized minority populations live. The foods of these places are different from the food the Han majority eats. Their foods are not the focus of this book. Does that mean foods from most of China are not Chinese?

There are many jurisdictions with respected Chinese culinary influences. Major ones are Anhui, Beijing, Fujian, Gansu, Guangdong, Guangzi, Guizhou, Henan, Hainan, Hong Kong, Hubei, Hunan, Inner Mongolia, Jiangsu, Jiangxi, Liaoning, Qinghai, Shaanxi, Shandong, Shanghai, Shanxi, Sichuan, Tianjin, Xinjiang, Xizang (Tibet), Yunnan, and Zhejiang. This section addresses some but not all the important culinary or regional differences in China. It is a broad-brush view that does not allow for subtle differences. Chinese food resists being organized into one or even into a few groupings, and one can not divide all cooking styles that existed before and those that exist today. While Chinese food is united by geography and ethnicity, it is divided by climate, agriculture, and tradition. Furthermore, no regional or local styles are mutually exclusive. There are more similarities than differences between them.

In spite of many similarities, the land in China is not all the same, so different regions produce different foods. China's northeast is where the soil is yellow, silty, and fertile, its weather varied by seasons. The southeast, a rich agricultural area, has lots of coastline, is semitropical and full of fertile valleys, and produces several crops a year. The northwest has scrubby grasslands, some desert, and some fertile land. It supports a nomadic way of life that still prevails for some, and many ethnic groups live there. The southwest is mountainous, heavily forested, and with many minority populations, most living in and around Yunnan Province.

Chinese Culinary Styles

Some say that within China there are eight popular and different styles of cuisine. Did they choose eight because eight is a lucky number for the Chinese? In the Chinese numerology the life of man is ruled by the number eight. Or did eight get selected because culinary aficionados consider

Outdoor restaurant in an area where many minorities live, Kashgar. Photo © Art Directors/TRIP/Warren Jacobs.

foods great in these eight places? These eight areas are the provinces of Guangdong, Shandong, Sichuan, Jiangsu, Zhejiang, Fujian, Hunan, and Anhui. For some, this is their order of culinary importance, and for others it is not. They deem this list subjective and personal.

The finest cuisine begins where most agree one can obtain the best food in China. That means the south, particularly Guangdong, and more specifically the capital city of Guangzhou. This great food is known in the Western world as Cantonese cooking. In China, they see the finest cuisine on a broader basis as including not only foods from Guangzhou but also from Chaozhou, Dongjiang, Guangxi, west of Guangzhou, and other nearby places. Some even include the foods of Hong Kong and Macau. Others expand it to include the foods of the nomadic Hakka people who settled in the south.

Cantonese and Other Southern Foods

Over the years, there have been many ways to say, write, and spell *Cantonese*. *Kwangchou* is one name for the city that used to be called Canton. In ancient times, this area was part of what was known as the Baiyue region. Its cookery was known as *Yue* or *Yuecai* cuisine. Some say it is a great cuisine because people of this region have always stressed food and drink. To them, eating is very serious business; they relish all kinds of food. A Chinese proverb says it best: one should be born in Suzhou, grow up in Hangzhou, eat in Guangzhou, and die in Liuzhou. The rationale is that people in Suzhou are considered beautiful, Hangzhou is thought a gorgeous place, people in Guangzhou eat and enjoy the very best food available, and wood from Luizhou is considered the best for coffins.

Cooks from other regions do not excel in as many different cooking techniques as do those from this region. Here they are said to be experts in deep-frying, stir-frying, baking, steaming, curing meats, preparing foods to be eaten from a common pot such as the hot pot, and garnishing foods such as needed for appetizer platters. In addition, many of these techniques are used to make foods that go with tea and are called *dientsin*, *yumcha*, or dim sum foods.

Guangzhou is the birthplace of dim sum dishes. Dim sum loosely translates to "dot the heart," and people think that these small snack-type sweet or savory foods cooked in many ways do just that. They like to eat them in the morning, middle of the morning, or middle of the day. When prepared with special ingredients or in special ways, these "dot the heart" foods can be served before or in between courses at a banquet.

There are no agreed-upon foods representative of the southern region. What is agreed upon is that meals emphasize foods of the sea and include a wide combination of flavors. Southern or Cantonese cuisine stresses attention to freshness of ingredients, lightness, crispness in cooking, texture, taste of each ingredient, and eating foods in season. Its chefs use virtually everything that grows or moves. Their cooking emphasizes stir-frying, steaming, and poaching and includes all other techniques. Southern meals include a wide variety of foods, with roasted meats a regional specialty. People in China's south care about the color of each food and its presentation. They have always incorporated ingredients new to Chinese cuisine such as peppers, peanuts, tomatoes, and corn. They use many other foods introduced by foreigners who visited or lived in this region.

The long southern coastline affords a huge variety of foods from the sea, many made into seafood sauces such as oyster sauce, an ingredient particularly adored here. Multiple growing seasons allow farmers to produce a variety of fresh vegetables throughout the year. Local orchards send an abundance of fruit to market, all at the peak of ripeness. Cooks here use all these foods, preserve each food's natural color and flavor, and appreciate having a plethora of different foods to chose from.

Common flavorings in all southern foods include garlic, fresh ginger, scallions, oyster sauce, wine, chicken broth, and fermented black beans. Cooks of the region prepare many tonic foods that incorporate different herbal items; they believe in their healthful properties. Southern cooking is home to sweet and sour dishes and exotica such as shark's fin, snake, and black chicken. In addition, southerners are known to prepare and enjoy many vegetarian foods made with minimal seasoning. Most southerners can make more different dishes than cooks in other regions.

Typical southern dishes include roast suckling pig, roast duck, soya chicken, barbecued suckling pig, roast goose, salt-baked chicken, crystal chicken, bird's nest soup, steamed fish, crispy skin chicken, and small steamed or pan-fried dumplings. Others are crabs in aromatic oil, red-cooked pork with dried squid, pork and watercress soup, beef in oyster sauce, lychee pork, abalone with fish and pork balls, oysters in black bean sauce, steamed carp, stewed fried pork, braised chicken liver with sliced snake, red orange pudding, duck with caterpillar fungus, eel soup with angelica root, milk and meat with white yam, and eight treasure chicken.

Beijing, Shandong, and Other Northern Food Regions

Beijing is the current capital of China. Earlier pronounced and spelled *Pekin* or *Peking*, its cuisine represents fine food from all over the country.

It is known not just for the best of the capital, but also for fine tastes from all other regions. How to divide its and the rest of China's culinary can be problematic, particularly for northern foods.

Some call foods from Shandong the best in the north, while others say it is the best in the country. Northern and northeastern regional cuisine includes not only foods of Beijing but also those of Jinan, Shandong's capital city. It also encompasses the foods of the neighboring provinces of Hebei, Henan, Shanxi, Shaanxi, Ningxia, and Gansu. They all are known for braising, baking, deep-frying, stir-frying, grilling, and stewing.

People in this region use sea and land foods cooked with soy sauce, vinegar, scallions, and garlic. Stews are popular, as are steamed breads, steamed and baked buns, noodles, and other foods made with wheat. Dishes here use many nuts, including chestnuts, peanuts, olive nuts, and pine nuts. The delicate, mildly seasoned, fragrant foods of this region include vestiges of Manchu and Mongol cooking; two styles popular since the Yuan Dynasty (1276–1368 C.E.).

To the people of Beijing and surrounding areas, pork, duck, and mutton are three favorite meats. Mutton is not liked much in the rest of China but is appreciated here, probably because of China's initial contacts with the Mongolians. Yellow fish from the Yellow River is a favorite in this region, as are yellow wines. Foods here delight when made with vinegar and pepper, are coated with flour paste before cooking, or incorporate stiffly beaten egg whites. The latter is a technique sometimes called velveting. Noodle dishes are particularly popular in the north. People like them from midday to well past midnight; they like steamed breads as well, and both are consumed at meals and as snack foods.

Some southern parts of the northern region are fertile, but climate here allows for but one growing season. Other arid areas are not desirable for crops. They are fine for grazing, so animal foods are popular. In the north, wheat grows better than rice, as does sorghum and millet, so people eat lots of foods made with these grains.

This culinary region produces quite a few wines, some made from grapes and in the European style, and lots of beer. Beer, which originated in Germany, is produced and consumed here—and all over China and the world—since it was first made in Qingdao in the 1800s. Up through the Song Dynasty, people were fond of drinking alcoholic spirits. Ancient writers were immersed in wine and rhyme, and northern Chinese people, in particular, consumed a lot of it.

Typical and popular dishes in Beijing and throughout northern China include Peking duck, braised conch in brown sauce, and sautéed clams. Citrus is a common flavoring used in dishes such as orange beef, which is made with the dried peel of special tangerines. Popular lamb dishes include mutton hot pot and lamb in tea sauce. The latter is made with *sacha* sauce, best translated as barbecue sauce even though the second syllable, *cha*, can mean tea. In this instance the two syllables were mistranslated as tea sauce; *sacha* sauce does not have a drop of tea, is made from fermented sea creatures called krill and brill, and is mixed with spicy ingredients.

Adored in the north are also *shaomai*, a steamed, stuffed snack food; *jiaozi*, a Chinese-type ravioli; and pot stickers, which are boiled and then pan-fried. Also popular are stewed oxtail, steamed shrimp in egg whites, shredded pigs' ears, grilled meatballs with cloud ear fungus, sour pork and bean sprouts, and braised onion cakes.

Sichuan, Hunan, and Other Western Foods

In the west and elsewhere, many agree that Sichuan cuisine is the best. An earlier name for foods from this region was *Bashu* because foods were from what were called the states of Ba and Shu. These states later became counties in the Sichuan Province, and their foods and those of nearby areas are labeled southwestern food.

This semitropical region represents foods not only from the province of Sichuan (also transliterated *Szechuan*), but also from Hunan, where foods were called *Hsiang*. Foods here are quite different from those prepared elsewhere in China. Most of the dishes are piquant, currently made with chili peppers. They used to be made spicy with other spices, herbs, and flavorings because chili peppers did not come to China until sometime in the sixteenth century.

Today, whole chili peppers and red oil, made when chili peppers are cooked in and then removed from oil, are used along with brown Sichuan pepper. Before, Sichuan pepper (also known as brown pepper) and artemisia, along with other items, made the foods piquant. Early Chinese texts speak of Hunan's spicy and herbal foods. They may have been hotter then, but these days Sichuan food is considered the hottest, and the cuisine that uses many more spices than virtually any of the others. In the Sichuan Province, hot summers and mild winters make these *mala* or hot and spicy foods important.

Foods in the southwest are also sour and salty. A goodly number incorporate cured meat or pickled vegetables. For generations, salt was extracted from local wells in the Sichuan Province. It was revered and hard to get in some parts of China, but the folks in Sichuan and the rest of the southwest used lots of it. Besides the salty taste, many foods here are made sour with lots of vinegar.

Some foods in the southwest are prepared with fish-flavored sauce or a sauce typically used on fish. Fish is not a common food, even though four rivers—the Ming, Tou, Jialing, and Yangzi—run through this landlocked province. The region has many freshwater foods swimming in its rivers and lakes. The rivers gave rise to the name of the Sichuan Province; the Chinese word *si* means four, and the word *chuan* refers to river.

Cooking methods in the southwest are more complicated than elsewhere in China. In many recipes one or more ingredients are double- or triple-cooked, some dry-fried with spicy ingredients and then cooked again before being added to the cooking process. Most dishes are both spicy and with strong flavorings. These can include lots of soy sauce, ginger, onions, chili peppers, and the local brown Sichuan peppers botanically known as *Xanthoxylum piperitum*. Many call them *fagara*, while others just call them Sichuan peppercorns, even though they are not true peppers. People in the Hunan and Sichuan Provinces use them and different fermented broad bean pastes and spicy fish pastes along with lots of rice, sweet potatoes, sorghum, soybeans, peas, barley, wheat, and smoked and cured foods.

Hunan has many mountains, rivers, and lakes, and its cooking is not only piquant but also oily. Some say it is more oily than the foods of Sichuan. Here they like fat juicy ducks and a plethora of good-sized lake and river fish. Goats roam local mountains, and goat stew is adored.

Tea plants dot hillsides in both the Sichuan and the Hunan Provinces. People like their tea made black and into tea bricks, an older form of tea, and they drink it strong. The brick is used by breaking off chunks of hardened compressed leaves, then brewed stronger than in most regions of China. This makes a somewhat bitter beverage that goes well with heavily spiced, oily food. They also make a special tea called *pestle*. Its tea leaves are mixed with salted and diced ginger, oil, sugar, ground sesame seeds, fried peanuts, and soybeans. Sometimes people add ground cooked rice.

Many ethnic minorities live in some parts of western China, particularly in Yunnan and the autonomous regions, counties, and prefectures nearby. Quite a few of them enjoy dairy products and follow the Islamic religion, which forbids the eating of pork. Beef and mutton are popular meats for them and the many Han who live there. So are thick soups and hot-pot and crock-pot cooking. The western region also does considerable herbal cookery, with many dishes incorporating medicinal ingredients for their flavor or texture, such as cordyceps, jujubes, and lycium berries.

Typical dishes in Sichuan and surrounding southwestern provinces include hot and sour soup, ma po doufu, twice-cooked pork, diced chicken with chili sauce, strange flavor dishes (often without fish, these dishes are cooked in the style of fish dishes), dan dan noodles (a spicy, oily noodle dish topped with minced pork and bits of chilies), pork family style, dry-fried long beans, kung pao chicken (made with lots of chili peppers), ants climbing trees (a dish of ground pork and cellophane noodles that looks a described), smoked duck, bean curd family style, and ribs wrapped in lotus leaves. Popular in Yunnan are crossing-the-bridge noodle soup and other dishes (given that name for being the foods a scholar's wife took over a bridge to bring her husband his lunch and other meals), Yunnan steamed chicken, and a heavy digestive tea called *puer*, the only tea that is aged in China. In Hunan and Hubei, typical dishes include stewed shark's fin, crystal chicken, steamed meat and sausage, spiced beef, willow lamb, minced pork and pickles, stuffed spareribs, dry-cooked freshwater eel, Hsiang- (or Hunan)-style prawns, and steamed pigeon eggs.

Shanghai and Other Eastern Cuisines

In the east, the best-known cookery is Shanghai cuisine. It depends upon delicate flavors and lots of red-cooking, which means cooking in soy sauce. Many foods have a somewhat sweet taste from small amounts of brown rock sugar. There are a small number with a sour taste because in this region they use a special black vinegar called and from Qinjiang. Foods are salty too. Many of them use Zhejiang ham, cured like and tasting similar to Smith-field ham. These many flavors combine well and mellow in the plethora of long-cooked foods prepared in eastern culinary regions.

South of Shanghai, and often considered an eastern region, are foods of the Fujian cuisine. There and on the nearby island of Hainan off the southern tip of the Guangdong Province, dishes are heavily based upon foods from the sea. Eastern cuisine stresses sweet, sour, salty, and savory tastes not just at every meal but often in every dish. Foods from this region are light and not oily or greasy.

Soups are popular in Fujian and eastern provinces, and two or more can be served at every meal. The foods of Taiwan have roots in Fujian, as the island of Taiwan is just across the Taiwan Straits. Foods also have tastes from Japan because Taiwan was a Japanese colony for 50 years. Japan also ruled parts of eastern China, so raw fish is popular in Taiwan and some eastern provinces.

Sweet potatoes are also eaten a lot here, especially in Fujian. The Chinese prepare them fresh or dried and use their flour. Typical foods from Fuzhou, the capital city of the Fujian Province, and the surrounding areas are dishes made with red wine lees. These dregs of rice are found at the bottom of barrels of wine made with red rice. They color and flavor many eastern dishes.

Typical dishes from Shanghai, Fujian, and nearby regions include Wangpo crab soup, white cut pork, ham with honey syrup, date-paste pancakes, spareribs with sweet and sour sauce, eel with leeks, shredded pears with crystal fruit, fish ball soup, hairy crabs (a local specialty), West Lake carp, pork with dragon well tea, and pressed duck casserole. Those from Fujian, its capital city of Fuzhou, and places near it include chicken with red lees, Hainan rice (named after the island of Hainan), Fuzhou fish soup, steamed pork in ground rice, quick-fried duck in red wine paste, pork kidney in sesame sauce, and shrimp in egg whites. In Taiwan, foods from Fujian are adored, and foods from elsewhere in China are also liked and served frequently. The Taiwanese and the Fujianese also like foods made with pressed bean curd, foods cooked in tea and soy sauce, and those made with fresh and dried soy milk skin.[4]

Lesser-Known Culinary Styles

Other cuisines can be put in one or another of the above regions. Several are important components of the Chinese culinary; all have origins in one or another particular area; all are known, respected, and loved. One important cuisine is the Jiangsu cuisine, which uses many freshwater ingredients from its many lakes and rivers and concentrates on stewing, stir-frying, braising, roasting, and deep-frying. Typical dishes include a special lion's head made here with crabmeat and many steamed herring dishes.

Another respected and loved cuisine is the Zhejiang cuisine, which has roots in cities such as Hangzhou, Shaoxing, and Ningpo. Some call these foods eastern, and others do not, but all agree they are fabulous. Many of their delicious dishes are cooked with tea, and many include foods of the sea. Each of these cities is at the edge of a large body of water. Typical dishes include West Lake fish, West Lake soup with watershield (a slippery sea-type vegetable collected from Hangzhou's West Lake), shrimp with Longjing tea, and oyster soup.

Another popular style of cookery is Anhui cuisine. It has many game dishes, uses a lot of mountainous vegetables and local herbs stewed, steamed, or roasted. Typical dishes include Fuli roast chicken and *popia*. The latter are pancakes rolled with meat or vegetables, an especially popular food taken along when visiting ancestors' graves. The pancakes have origins in what was called Amoy. Anhuians also like many dishes made using game, including stewed deer tail and braised bear paw.

Lesser known, but nonetheless popular, are foods of the Hakka people. These people preserve their meat in wine, soybean paste, and other seasonings, eat frugally, and like different kinds of rice and rice dishes at each meal.

Their foods are characterized by stews, often made with pickles and salted vegetables, and many one-dish meals including a most famous one called salt-baked chicken. Others include steamed eggs, pork with preserved vegetables, and Hakka-style stuffed bean curd; their *doufu* is filled with meat, fish, basil leaves, and scallions. Originally a more central mountain population, many Hakka wandered south in and near Song Dynasty times. Somewhat later, the people of Guangzhou dubbed them *Hakka*, which in their language means guest people, because they were strangers.

Still another popular culinary style, more national than regional, is the vegetarian cuisine known as *su*. Eating no meat was popular before the Song Dynasty. It was adopted by Buddhists and others who wished to exclude all animal foods. *Su* dishes are often light and named after their imitated meat counterparts. They make extensive use of gluten, tofu, and vegetable ingredients. They mimic the look, taste, and names of their animal counterparts; such names were adopted to make guests staying at Buddhist monasteries feel comfortable and at home.

Other Cuisines

There are many other cuisines, too many to detail, but a few should at least be mentioned. Hainan cuisine is somewhat similar to Fujian cuisine with its many soups and broths. Muslims populations have a special cuisine that makes food taste Chinese while following all the tenets of their Islamic religion. Manchu cuisine has dishes that mimic those served during the tenure of the Manchu court. The Confucian cuisine follows the tenets of Confucius and does very careful cutting, cooking, and so on. There is a Song Dynasty banquet cuisine that mimics that dynasty's multiple-course meals. Not to be left out are foods prepared with traditional Chinese medicines in mind. Some call this tonic cuisine (see chapter 8).

RECIPES BY REGION

There are thousands of different regional and provincial dishes. Their names can be a window on where they are from. Those that follow are a small sampling.

Hakka-Style Stuffed Salt-Baked Chicken

- 1 two- to three-pound chicken
- 4 tablespoons soy sauce

- 3 tablespoons Chinese rice wine
- 1 teaspoon table salt
- 1/2 teaspoon five-flavor powder
- 1 star anise
- 2 scallions, minced
- 2 slices fresh ginger, minced
- 4 shelled shrimp, veins removed and minced
- 2 tablespoons minced Smithfield or other smoked ham
- 2 tablespoons minced bamboo shoots
- 4 dried lotus leaves, soaked for one hour
- some thick twine
- 3 cups coarse (or kosher) salt
- 1 tablespoon sesame oil

1. Clean and dry the whole chicken and make a pocket between the skin and the flesh.
2. Mix soy sauce, rice wine, table salt, five-flavor powder, and star anise, and marinate the chicken in this for half an hour, then drain, remove the chicken, and discard the marinade.
3. Mix the scallions, ginger, shrimp, ham, and bamboo shoots, fry for one minute, then cool.
4. Stuff this mixture between the skin and the breast meat, wrap the chicken in the lotus leaves, and tie with the twine.
5. Line a small baking pan with aluminum foil and put half the coarse salt on it, then put the chicken on the salt and cover it with the rest of the salt. Do not leave any chicken with less than half an inch or more of salt. Then bake the chicken in a 350 degree Fahrenheit oven for two hours.
6. Remove the chicken and encrusted salt to a heavy cutting board, and using a rubber mallet gently crack the salt open and carefully untie and unwrap the lotus leaves. Be careful and avoid getting the salted crust on the chicken.
7. Remove the chicken to a serving platter, cut it into serving pieces with poultry shear, drizzle the sesame oil over the chicken, and serve.

Hangzhou's West Lake Sliced Fish and Watershield in Soup

- 1 pound any white-meat fish fillets, sliced into half-inch-thick slices
- 1 bottle watershield, drained or half pound of cooked and then sliced okra, or any other green vegetable
- 4 cups chicken stock

- 2 tablespoons minced Smithfield or other smoked ham
- 1 teaspoon sesame oil
- 1/4 cup Chinese rice wine

1. Put all the ingredients in a pot, and slowly bring this to just below the boil.
2. When hot and the fish is opaque, pour into a soup tureen and serve.

Sichuan Mapo Doufu (Tofu)

- 1 pound firm bean curd, cut into half-inch squares
- 2 tablespoons corn oil
- 1/4 pound minced or ground beef or pork
- 4 garlic shoots or 2 scallions, minced
- 1 tablespoon sesame oil
- 1 glove garlic, minced
- 1 tablespoon (or less) spicy bean sauce with garlic
- 1 teaspoon chili powder
- 1 teaspoon thin soy sauce
- 1 teaspoon cornstarch mixed with 1 teaspoon cold water

1. Put bean curd and oil in a hot wok and fry for two minutes, then remove the bean curd and set aside.
2. Heat the remaining oil, and fry the meat and the garlic shoots or scallions just until the meat loses its color. Set this aside with the bean curd, and discard any remaining oil or other liquid.
3. Heat the sesame oil, add the garlic, bean sauce, chili powder, and soy sauce, and stir-fry for half a minute or until fragrant, then add the reserved bean curd, greens, and meat, and lower the heat and simmer this mixture for five minutes.
4. Add the cornstarch mixture, bring to the boil, and stir until thickened and the starch clears somewhat, then serve.

Velvet Shrimp Beijing-Style

- 2 tablespoons corn oil
- 1 pound shrimp, shells and veins removed
- 2 slices fresh ginger, minced very fine
- 3 scallions, minced very fine
- 1/2 teaspoon salt
- 1 tablespoon Chinese rice wine

- 1/2 tablespoon thin soy sauce
- 4 egg whites, beaten lightly (do not beat them stiff)
- 2 tablespoons cornstarch
- dash ground white pepper
- 2 tablespoons Smithfield or other smoked ham, minced very fine
- few sprigs of cilantro, for garnish

1. Heat oil and stir-fry shrimp, ginger, and scallions for half a minute, then add salt, rice wine, and soy sauce and stir-fry another half minute.
2. Add egg whites and gently stir-fry to mix well, then add cornstarch, white pepper, and ham, and stir in completely. Fry two minutes and no longer, then put the shrimp mixture into a preheated bowl, garnish, and serve.

Hainan Fried Rice

- 1 tablespoon peanut oil
- 1/4 cup broken pieces of peanuts
- 1 small onion, diced
- 2 eggs
- 4 cups cooked rice
- 1 slice fresh ginger, minced
- 1 clove peeled garlic, minced
- 1/2 fresh chili pepper, minced
- 2 teaspoons thin soy sauce
- 1 teaspoon hoisin sauce
- 6 clams, minced
- 3 peeled shrimp, veins removed, minced
- 1 salted egg yolk, optional

1. Heat oil, and fry peanuts just until they start to brown, then remove with a slotted spoon.
2. Add onion to the oil and stir-fry until it is wilted, but not browned, then add eggs, ginger, garlic, and the chili, and stir-fry until the eggs begin to set, then add the rice and stir thoroughly until every grain of rice is coated with egg and oil.
3. Add soy sauce and hoisin sauce and stir well, and then add clams, shrimp, and salted egg yolk, if used, and stir-fry about two minutes until the shrimp turn pink.
4. Fold in the nuts, and serve.

NOTES

1. P. Rozin, "The Socio-Cultural Context of Eating and Food Choice," in *Food Choice, Acceptance, and Consumption*, ed. H. L. Meiselman and H. J. H. MacFie (London: Blackie Academic & Professional, 1996).

2. J. M. Newman and R. Linke, "Chinese Immigrant Food Habits: A Study of the Nature and Direction of Change," *Royal Society of Health Journal* 106 (2): 286–271 (1982); V. Mah, "Chinese Food Traditions," in *From Cathay to Canada: Chinese Food in Transition*, ed. J.M. Powers (Willowdale, Ontario, Canada: Ontario Historical Society, 1998); E.K. Ludman and J.M. Newman, "Yin and Yang in Health-Related Food Practices of Three Chinese Groups," *Journal of Nutrition Education* 16: 3–5 (1984).

3. J. M. Newman, L.H. Sirota, and X.Y. Lei, "Chinese Food Habit Perspectives," *Journal of the Association for the Study of Food and Society* 1: 31–38 (1996).

4. J. M. Newman, "Fujian, the Province and Its Foods," *Flavor and Fortune* 6 (2): 13, 20 (1999).

5

Meals

Chinese and Western meals are different. Differences include the food it-self, how individual food items are cut and cooked, and how dishes and meals are served. This is true in family settings at home and when a meal is eaten in a restaurant. In China today, main meals are lunch and dinner. For those who can afford it, they almost always consist of several dishes and at least one main staple food. For those with little, a meal can include the staple and perhaps one other dish.

Each dish is served on its own platter or bowl. Food is not put on an in-dividual's plate, except for the staple, and that is almost always served in a bowl. Using chopsticks, people help themselves to food on the serving dishes. They select one or a few morsels at a time and take them in any order they please. Another difference is that dishes are made to accom-pany and flavor a large amount of a staple or *fan* food. That *fan* can be rice, noodles, or another grain food. People eat the staple food alone or be-tween items selected from the serving dishes of *cai* foods that might be plant, animal, or a mixture of both. There is usually more staple food in a large bowl available should they want more, and many do.

Chinese and Western beverage consumption is also different at main meals. The beverage at most Chinese meals is soup. A secondary beverage can be the liquid that vegetables or noodles were cooked in. Soup can mean just one soup or several at any one meal. In the home, the bowl or tureen of soup is set on the table. Diners help themselves when they want some and almost always have some at the end of the meal. Rarely do they have it when the meal starts. In restaurants or when there are guests, soup is usually served and the remainder is set on the table for diners to help themselves should they want more. Accommodating Westerners, Chinese restaurants outside of China and those expecting foreign guests in China serve the soup first.

Wine, beer, and/or hard liquor can accompany a meal. Beverages such as soda or tea rarely do, except at formal meals such as banquets. Tea is usually served before or after meals. In and around Guangzhou, it always accompanies dim sum, is available at other snack times, and is available at meals in a few homes and restaurants.

Like meals, snack dishes come on their own plates. Diners help themselves to the one or ones they desire. Snacks can be one or more items, some served with a dipping sauce or two; and at snacks, beverages can be whatever the diner wants. This might be boiled and cooled water, boiled water still hot or warm, tea, and recently coffee, soda, or any other beverage. Rarely are alcoholic beverages served with snack foods.

Another difference between Chinese and Western meals is that in homes all cooked dishes and soups are placed on the table before anyone sits to eat them. The number of soups and main dishes is not fixed, and soup numbers vary by region. Most often there is one hot soup and perhaps a cold and sweeter one at the meal's end. At banquets, two or more hot soups are commonplace. In the Fujian Province, two or three hot and cold soups or more can be had at each meal.

The number of main dishes is often determined by a family's affluence. Generations ago, when food was less plentiful, a family would have but one or two *cai* dishes with or without soup. Now many more dishes are served at a single meal to accompany the *fan* or grain food. The number is now usually three or four dishes and soup. If a family includes five or six persons, then five or six main dishes are usually served. It is not uncommon for the number of dishes to be close to the same number as there are diners. No matter the number, *cai* dishes are always served with one or more grain foods. The quantity of grains almost always exceeds all other dishes combined.

In affluent families, meals can start with four or five small plates of savory hot or cold appetizers. Their purpose is to provide variety and stimulate the appetite. These small dishes, also known as small plates, are in addition to soup, main dishes, and staple foods. Small plates are less common at ordinary family meals. No matter the income, they are provided when a friend or guest joins the family. They are becoming less common in families where all adults work away from home and no one is there to help prepare them.

In China, another important difference from Western meals is that foods are almost always cut in small pieces, mostly before being cooked, and a few like steamed chicken afterward. They are cut because no knives are available at a Chinese dining table. The Chinese considered knives to be weapons. Food is eaten with chopsticks or a spoon, rarely with fingers. Other differences include the use of very little fat and no or many seasonings. Most dishes mix animal and vegetable items. While preparation takes a long time, most cooking is fast because foods are in small pieces.

Only a few implements are needed to eat Chinese food. These include chopsticks, a soup bowl, a short-handled deep soup spoon, and sometimes a teacup or small wine cup. Some Chinese drink soup from the bowl and use the spoon for other liquids and taking foods from serving dishes. Chopsticks and a spoon are used together for thick soups and noodle dishes. For serving others, additional serving spoons and chopsticks are provided. People of northern heritage, if they have tea, use a glass rather than a teacup, an influence probably of Russian origin.

Chinese soup spoons are different from Western ones in size, shape, and material. They hold about twice as much and have higher sides, and most are ceramic. Recently, they have become available in plastic, but most people do not like that taste or mouth-feel. Teacups and wine vessels also differ from Western ones. The teacup has no ear, and it holds less than two ounces of liquid. Wine cups look like tinier teacups and hold about half an ounce of liquid. Saucers are different, too, and usually do not go under teacups. They are smaller, have low sides, hold about half an ounce, and are used for dipping foods into soy sauce or other condiments. Yet another difference seen at meals is that individual grain food bowls can look like large Western serving bowls for soup.

WHEN EATING BEGINS

A meal begins when everyone in the family comes to the table and is seated. Certainly no one eats a morsel of food until an honored guest and the eldest or elders have something to eat. That is changing; respect for elders in China and all over the world is diminishing. After elders or guests take their first chopstick full of food, then the host or senior family member signals that others can eat, and he or she starts to eat too. Large families and restaurants use a lazy Susan in the middle of the table. It eliminates passing serving platters and bowls, and speeds up each person's opportunity to help himself or herself to food.

BREAKFAST

Breakfast is less formal than either lunch or dinner, and it has fewer dishes. Breakfasts in southern China include a thick rice gruel called congee or *juk*. Northern breakfasts center around hot soy milk and fried crullers called *yaotai*. Eaters dip the crullers into the milk and sometimes into granulated sugar. Breakfast can also be a large piece of steamed bread, plain or stuffed. These items can be eaten plain or with other small dishes, many more savory than sweet.

SERVING AND EATING FAMILY STYLE AT MAIN MEALS

Lunch and dinner eating occasions are considered main meals; breakfast is not. At these main meals, lots of *fan*, or grain foods, accompany lesser amounts of *cai*, or vegetable and meat dishes that are to flavor the *fan*. At the main meals, each place setting has a bowl filled with or ready to be filled with rice or noodles. At breakfast, this bowl can have rice gruel (*congee* or *juk*). In very few families, one might find the food pre-plated; more commonly, individuals help themselves from the serving bowls and platters set out for all to share. And, if economics allows, there is additional grain food available in a large serving bowl for those who want more; many people do help themselves to more *fan* during the meal.

With ingredients cut small and each person taking them, often one at a time, and eating them intermittently with their staple food, the Chinese see this as sharing their food. That is because they take what they want and, before doing so, share some of the best in each dish with their elders and guests. They are trained to do this from early childhood. In restaurants and at formal meals, they help others, using serving chopsticks and spoons set there for this purpose.

With chopsticks in the right hand, individuals pick up their food. In the other hand, they hold the rice (or noodle) bowl near their mouth. The food is transported from serving platter over the bowl of staple food and into the mouth. It goes there alone or with some grain food. Many folk, particularly older ones, eat several mouthfuls of rice or noodles and only an occasional item or two from a main dish. This process is repeated, later in the meal interspersed with mouthfuls of soup, more grain food, a taste or two of vegetables or meat, and so on. The Chinese take some soup at the end of the meal to "fill the cracks," as their expression goes. That is why extra soup is almost always available.

Individual family members do not pile food from platter or bowl on their own plates before eating, should they have individual plates. They do not eat one vegetable, then all meat or poultry or fish, as many Westerners do. Most main dishes are mixtures of foods: a small amount of animal protein and many vegetables. This makes it difficult to know exactly how much of any one particular food any one individual eats. Some people have flat, small, salad-plate-sized individual dishes that are six or seven inches in diameter and are used primarily for bones and other discarded items such as shrimp tails. When no plate is provided, they put this waste in a pile next to their other individual dishes.

TABLE MANNERS

Chinese people believe manners at the table are important. They consider it courteous to select the best or most special item with the extra chopsticks and offer it to the eldest person or the guest. It is considered rude to take those special items for oneself. Eating at a Chinese table is never a grab what you want affair. In general, rules are adhered to with or without guests or elders, and at home and when dining out.

A most important rule is that elders begin to eat before younger folk do. After them, senior family members usually help themselves, or younger ones help the seniors to food from platters and bowls. Young folk, be they 4, 14, or 40, allow the eldest, then other elders at the table, to take and taste first. Everyone waits before helping themselves until encouraged by an elder. A young person is thought especially polite if he or she puts a special item on the plate of someone older. Young children are taught not to grab before helping others garner the best morsels.

Manners, the Chinese believe, begin with eating and drinking. They believe that both are basic needs and activities that must be done properly. Thus, Chinese exercise good table manners with due diligence and take pride in practicing proper ways of eating. The rules adhered to at the table are not new. *The Book of Etiquette*, written about four thousand years ago, lists many proper food behaviors, more about what not to do than about what to do. They have been practiced at every home and away from the home table for eons. Some of them include the following:

Do not eat audibly.
Do not bolt your food.

Do not roll the rice into a ball.

Do not spread out rice to cool.

Do not crunch bones with your teeth.

Do not grab what you want.

Do not replace fish and meat that you have already tasted.

Do not draw items of food in the soup through your mouth;
    use chopsticks for this.

Do not stir or add condiments to the soup in the common bowl.

Do not throw bones to the dogs.

Do not pick your teeth.

Those whose behavior at the table or elsewhere is less than proper are called foreign devils. The Chinese believe that non-Chinese do not know the rules and, therefore, eat differently. They do not want to be such devils. People who eat impolitely are considered foreign because the Chinese know not to eat in a manner deemed rude or impolite. Therefore, each Chinese person takes a first bite of food when correct to do so and not before any elder and/or guest.

There are things that the Chinese rush to do at the table. These include rushing to give someone else special items from the service dishes before helping themselves. Another important behavior is, when appropriate and polite, to take food from the closest side of the common platter or bowl. Getting up and reaching is considered rude. Stretching or standing to get something for oneself is absolutely forbidden. It is preferred that only the host stand to acquire a special tidbit, and then to give that to an elder or honored guest.

There are several other polite or impolite things different from in Western cultures. It is polite and considered acceptable to make slurping sounds when consuming soup. That is deemed acceptable because making noise sucks in air, cools the soup, and avoids burning the mouth. In addition, slurping indicates that the item is liked. It is impolite to stand chopsticks upright in a food or dish. If that is done, they look like incense sticks used for funerals. That action is interpreted as wishing someone dead. Another rule says to never lick chopsticks, a behavior that is also considered exceptionally rude. There are others—more don'ts than do's; they can be found in any Chinese book of etiquette; they can also be seen and practiced when following the behaviors of others at mealtime.

Mother and child eating, Beijing. Photo © Art Directors/TRIP/Keith Cardwell.

ONE HAND, TWO CHOPSTICKS

Dexterity and one-handedness are needed to use chopsticks. If chopsticks are held too tightly, fingers cramp. Dexterity also means that chopsticks are used only in the right hand. Children are taught that left-handed use is inappropriate. It is a lot easier when everyone at the table uses the same hand. Not doing so can knock someone else's chopsticks or food out of that person's hand. This use of right-handedness is similar to eating rules in other countries. For example, in the Arab world and in India, people do not eat with the left hand, although for a different reason.

BEVERAGE FORMALITIES

Tea, while not common at a main meal, is always served, as are alcoholic beverages, at formal meals. Note the word *served*. When people want tea, they do not help themselves. A good thing to do is to take the teapot and pour some for one or more others at the table, and then pour some for oneself. The same rule applies to other beverages. When ready or wanting to drink, one needs to wait for one or more persons whose beverages were just poured to take their sip first. This requires paying attention and being responsive to others before rushing to satisfy oneself.

Other rules include not filling teacups (rice bowls, too) to the top and never setting down teapots with spouts pointing at anyone. A teacup filled to the brim can burn the person who tries to pick it up. Not pointing the spout is similar to the Western custom of never pointing a finger at anyone.

Just as one does not initiate tea drinking, one does not take a glass of wine or liquor alone. Wine and liquor are more common at banquet times, but are consumed at some family meals, particularly when one or more guests joins a family at home. To take a drink requires paying attention. The polite thing to do is to toast someone else. One should lift the glass or cup with the right hand and toast that person slowly and clearly. The left hand is not idle; its three middle fingers touch the bottom of the cup or glass, palm open and facing upward. Some people say that this custom started so that everyone sees that the person making the toast has no weapon. Those being toasted lift their beverage and everyone drinks together, saying *gambei*. That means bottoms up, and the Chinese empty the glass or cup when someone says *gambei*.

In the south of China, when someone serves tea, the recipient says thank you not with words but with the pointer and the tallest finger. The person taps the fingers on the table, bending them as he or she does so. This action represents a bow of thanks known as a kowtow, which in China is spelled *koutou*. This old custom probably originated in a legend about an emperor raised by common folk. He supposedly told them not to kowtow when he poured tea. The bending fingers were his expected respect, a thank you without interrupting conversation.

Tea is always served between meals and when a guest arrives. To be polite, the host or hostess offers it immediately after a guest arrives. Correctly, the cup is handed to the guest with both hands. The guest should receive it in both hands. If seated, a guest rises before accepting tea, then sits down to drink it. This giving and accepting a beverage, with two hands exposed, probably relates to the way glasses are held when giving a toast. It shows both hands and no hidden weapon, an action probably important in ancient times.

SEATING ARRANGEMENTS

Where one sits is not determined by grabbing a chair and sitting down any more than eating is done grabbing a piece of food. Among family at home, there are usually no rigorous rules. Away from home or with guests, seat selection can be formal, and the host or hostess seats everyone. In most countries, formalities are practiced less often, but at formal meals the Chinese still believe seating to be an important issue. The honored guest is usually asked to sit on the north side of the table or facing the door. This custom began because north emulates earlier emperors whose thrones were on the north, facing south. Facing the door, in ancient times, made guests feel comfortable as they could see anyone entering the room. This was their assurance of safety.

There are variations on where honored guests sit. In Western countries it is an honor to sit opposite the honored guest, but not so for the Chinese. In ancient times, anyone seated in that position was deemed of little importance. The host or hostess sat there to show humility and to indicate that others were more important. Not everyone follows these rules, and there are regional differences. For example, in the south of China, an honored guest sits two seats to the left of the host. The next most important person is seated two seats to the right. Couples often do not sit together as is common in many other countries, and no one goes to the table until told to or escorted there.

INVITATIONS AND RESPONSES

In ancient China and in some places today, wine is warmed and then served. That custom may explain why Chinese formal invitations say "Wine glasses are ready and await your arrival." Ancient Chinese traditional invitations to meals, wine shops, or eateries were hand-delivered on folded red paper. Today, some still come on red paper, but modern invitations more often use the post, phone, fax, or even e-mail. Guests may wonder who else will be in attendance. To make them comfortable, the Chinese used to list all of them on these red notes. This is less common today. It is still polite to render an immediate response to every invitation.

Arriving promptly is the proper thing to do because not until the last guest arrives can anyone be ushered to the table or toasting begin. Honored guests should never be the last to arrive. While toasting begins a formal meal, more toasting is interspersed during it. And often, near the end of a meal, finger games can be played. One is similar to the game known as rock, scissors, paper. After each round, the loser needs to take a drink and *gambei* it down quickly, bottoms up. These games and others were excuses for drinking at meals and in wine houses, as early restaurants were called. Ancient poetry speaks of many inebriated people at formal and informal meals in the wine houses.

There are regional differences, family differences, and economic differences in the many Chinese rules for invitations, responses, eating, and drinking. They do not differ for informal and formal occasions. Most rules are less formal than before, but they have not totally disappeared and differ less by region nowadays than by tradition and culture. There are fewer northern, southern, eastern, and western differences, some localized ones, and many differences practiced by minority populations.

NATIONALITY AND FAMILY DIFFERENCES

The foods and food behaviors of ethnic nationalities in China are different from those of the Han majority. Many Turkish influences date back to early trading days and Middle Eastern, Russian, and Asian influences from culinary connections in early times or on the Silk Road.

People talk about regional differences in food and food habits, but they are difficult to trace. Many nationalities have lived in China for thousands of years, and many Chinese people have lived only in one region or another for like amounts of time. While differences might be generalized by specific behaviors, compass points, dishes, cooking techniques, condiments, and spices, nowadays they are more limited to individual and small groups of families.

To explore regional and ethnic food behaviors, the Chinese like to invite others for meals. The guests most often return the favor; doing so is a Chinese custom. At these and other meals, the Chinese like to talk about food. When they invite people whose background is different, they learn about heritages other than their own. From these occasions, and from meals at work and elsewhere, they learn how families and other groups practice and change food habits.

EATING THEN VERSUS NOW

To understand food, place, and time differences, a compass can help. To the Chinese, north is *bei*, south is *nan*, east is *dong*, and west is *xi*. Many dishes indicate origins in their names or tell about type of cooking used to make them. For instance, *Beijing* means north capital, and *Nanjing* means south capital, as it was the capital city in the time of the Eastern Jin (317–420 C.E.). So Beijing duck represents the north's love of roasted meat and Nanjing duck the south's love of salty foods. One could make similar characterizations for Guangdong in the east and Guangzhou, its capital city, from which most early Chinese immigrants went to the United States. Xian, a large city in the virtual center of China today, was in earlier times west of the central core of China. Today, people associate

Xian with the hundreds of terra cotta warriors found buried there. Only a
few know it was called Chang-An and was China's capital during the
Tang Dynasty (618–907 C.E.). Fewer still realize it was at the western end
of what we now call the Silk Road before and after Tang Dynasty times. It
was a place where Asian and Middle Eastern foods made their way into
Chinese cuisine, so foods with these names can indicate eastern or western places of origin, with few spices or many in their dishes.

Today, the Chinese eat many more and different foods than did their
grandparents or great-great-grandparents. Cooking methods have also
changed. Chinese ancestors ate less food at virtually every meal and ate
fewer times in a day. Some ate only two meals, and the very poor were
lucky to eat once a day. In ancient times, when people did eat, sharing
food was not common. Each ate from his or her own bowl of food. Sharing from communal dishes came into being during the ninth to the
eleventh centuries.

No matter where one's ancestors hailed from, they ate more like each
other than they do these days. Before imperial dynasties and before 1600
B.C.E., people prepared fewer dishes, ate fewer meals, and ate fewer kinds
of food. They ate a lot less animal food except during festival times. Even
then, they ate it sparingly. Today, those who can afford to eat meat during
and between festival periods and consume more calories than did ancient
peoples. Fewer people eat what was considered a common amount of food
each day. That is, fewer eat only one stuffed steamed bun each morning,
lunch on soup and rice, maybe with a piece of a vegetable or two, and
have dinner with only a few vegetables over rice or noodles and maybe
another soup.

Differences, when they did exist, centered around the specific grains
they ate. Most people, in ancient times, consumed 85 percent of their
calories from grain foods. Today only about 60 or 65 percent comes from
grains.[1] In some families, years ago, people ate four bowls of rice a day and
little else, except maybe a few tablespoons of vegetables. As time went on,
with more and more food available, they ate more. Today, many people
eat too much; about 10 percent of China's children are obese.[2]

Of course, not everyone in early China ate poorly. About the time of
and after the Zhou Dynasty (1122–221 B.C.E.), people of high rank ate
more and better foods, sometimes even better than today. Their elders ate
even more. In these early times, older men were served more dishes than
were younger men. At 60 years of age they could have three dishes to flavor their grain food if they were part of the emperor's army or entourage
of some ten to twenty thousand persons. At age 70, four different main

dishes were served daily by imperial decree, five main dishes at age 80, and six main dishes to flavor grains each and every day at age 90.

What these dishes were is uncertain, but they were served with wine or boiled water. The *cai* or vegetable and meat dishes were mixtures of ingredients, just as they are today. This serving of staple foods, meat and vegetable dishes, and something to drink began then and continues today. Drinking is *yang*, eating is *yin*, and a person needs both to be well-nourished. What one drinks and eats is less prescribed, but there is little doubt that everyone's ancestors drank more alcoholic beverages than people do today.

Ancestors and Chinese people today do not stuff themselves. They stop eating before they get full, and parents teach children to leave the table when 70 percent full.[3] They do not exercise this restraint at holidays, birthdays, or special occasions. Elders abide by these old-fashioned rules, particularly at home. They like wine first, stewed meats and vegetables next, then wine again with other dishes. Stews, called *kengs*, still are eaten by all classes of Chinese people; the amount of meat varies from none to lots. Scallions flavor these stews, even if they have no meat. This was something learned from their ancestors, who also flavored their stews with garlic and leeks.

Previous generations were lucky to attend a banquet or two each year. At them, grain foods were served last, and fruits were served after the grains. Banquets today are different because they have fewer dishes, take less time, might be more sophisticated, and are enjoyed more often than ever before.

Grain dishes available during the Han Dynasty (202 B.C.E.–220 C.E.) included various types of millet, rice, wheat, barley, soy and lesser beans, and hemp. How refined they were was and still is a class distinction. Everyone may want to eat completely milled grains with their husks completely removed. They look and taste better. The affluent can afford this luxury, and rich people eat more of them and more steamed and stir-fried foods with these refined grains. They also eat more foods imported from other countries, mostly from Asia, as they did years ago.

In Beijing and other cities, food stalls did and still do serve foods and snacks. Popular were and are candies, dried pork, pastries, salted meat, drinks, hot dishes, dumplings, steamed sea scallops on their shells, greens of many kinds, salted eggs, and more. Eating street food, an ancient and still an existing practice, continues, but vendors now sell more in small shops than on the street.

The foods they sell changed little, but the purchasers changed a lot. Servants of the affluent used to buy and bring these foods to their houses.

Ordinary people hearing vendor bells singing out their wares in the neighborhoods went to buy them, too. Gone is the monkey on a chain ringing bells to attract attention. More men and women work and share shopping on the way home. They purchase foods raw, and they purchase cooked ones more often than ever before, almost daily. When food needs cooking, many adults help prepare and cook it together after work.

What has not changed is telling children never to leave a grain of rice or a noodle in their bowl. Some tell children that, for every grain of rice left, they will marry a person with that many facial pockmarks. Others tell their offspring that the sweat of workers in the fields made these grains, so they need to heed their efforts and eat them all. Fewer parents tell children and grandchildren not to speak at meals and to listen to others so they can grow up smart. Nowadays, adults listen to their children, whose conversations dominate home meals.

In ancient times few places had restaurants, and many set up markets every few days. If one could not cook, hawkers sold hot and cold foods and beverages such as tea and alcohol. Now people buy drinks such as orange soda, which became available in the 1940s. It did take a while for the Chinese to get used to drinking anything but previously boiled water, liquids from making noodles or vegetables, wine, and tea. Now they drink lots of beer, soda, wine, and even bottled, not boiled water.

CURRENT TASTES IN FOOD

Now southerners enjoy more *cai* or vegetable and meat-flavored dishes that are milder, have fewer seasonings, and are cooked less. They also eat more foods of the sea, use more unusual ingredients, take longer to eat a meal, and seem more relaxed than do Chinese in the north. In contrast, northern Chinese, when eating at an outdoor vendor, often keep one foot on a stool or bench. That may be because their weather is colder, and they eat faster and dawdle less. Northern foods are thought bland and without foods such as water chestnuts, so popular in the south. People in the north prepare foods with many nuts. Eastern foods are more acidic because they use more vinegar; eastern people eat many seafoods and many dishes that are a bit sweeter than elsewhere in China. In the west, foods have more peppers, more piquant flavorings, and many nuts, too.

No matter the region, banquets with their fewer dishes rarely start with a gorgeous appetizer platter in the shape of a phoenix or panda. They are made with less attention, and banquet tables are set with a simple flower or two, soup bowls, and Chinese soup spoons. These formal affairs are still enjoyed at birthdays, weddings, and funerals and during visits from honored guests, and people today eat many more of them, occasion or not.

Many banquets today have one, two, or three special dishes, using nourishing dishes made with sharks' fins, birds' nests, sea cucumbers, abalone, pom pom mushrooms, and even bear paw and camel toe. During the time of Mao Zedong, these dishes were out of fashion. Mao thought them classdistinctive food and worked toward a classless society. Everyone is pleased that they are back in fashion and more popular than ever.

SOME EXAMPLES OF MAIN MEALS

While it is impossible to select a meal by compass point that everyone agrees is representative and typical, a few examples can emphasize foods of different locations.

A typical northern lunch or dinner might include

Radish soup made with pork
Crispy duck
Stir-fried shrimp garlic, and leeks with gailan, a Chinese broccoli
Lamb sweet like honey
Boiled rice
Steamed fruit with silver mushrooms

A typical southern lunch or dinner meal might have

Winter melon, abalone, and loquat soup
Fried shrimp-stuffed bean curd
Braised sliced abalone
Soy sauce chicken
Steamed whole fish
Boiled rice
Almond float with dried fruit
Tea

A typical eastern lunch or dinner meal could include

Chicken with cucumber soup
Stir-fried shrimp and walnuts
Red-cooked ham knuckle

Lemon chicken

Drunken crabs with ginger

Steamed rice

Tea and litchi dessert

Tea

And a typical western lunch or dinner meal might include

Hot and sour soup

Preserved mustard greens with chicken and sesame oil

Fish with fermented broad bean sauce

Ma po dou fu (bean curd) with beef

Family flavor fried pork

Boiled rice

Kumquats in syrup

TYPICAL BREAKFASTS

Breakfasts are often eaten quickly. They differ from lunch and dinner meals, and also can have many small dishes. These items provide flavoring to the rice gruel or soy milk that is the basic component of the meal—rice gruel in the south, soy milk in the north. On non-workdays, many families go out to eat and socialize, catching up on family news. This helps retain their cohesive family structure. Breakfast is not considered a meal because most breakfasts do not have lots of rice, noodles, or other grains. The small dishes served at breakfasts vary by season, region, and taste. They can include salted or pickled vegetables, fish, or meat and/or any foods left from the day before. Some breakfasts include a large piece of steamed bread, plain or stuffed with a little bit of sweetened pork. These can have small plates with them and/or boiled peanuts, even a favorite food or two. Families do like to eat breakfast in a restaurant and have dim sum, a meal type that originated in the south of China.

DIM SUM

Families that go out for dim sum in a restaurant can eat it any time before two or three in the afternoon, which is when these places no longer serve dim sum. It is usually the first eating time that day. A favorite dish is called pocket soup. It is one large dumpling in a bowl; it can be in a bowl

Dim sum. Photo © TRIP/A. Tovy.

of soup, and the dumpling itself is full of liquid. It spurts into the mouth with a first bite. This specialty is filled with many seafood goodies, and it is an eastern treat. The filling is mixed with gelatinized soup before being sealed into its pocket-cum-dumpling wrapper. When steamed, the gelatin melts and becomes the soup that spurts on first bite.

A very good pocket soup dumpling is filled with strands of shark's fin, small pieces of shrimp, sea cucumber, crabmeat, even little bits of scallop, and maybe some minced pork. Less expensive pocket soups only have minced or ground pork and maybe small pieces of crabmeat. When made small and served from a steamer rack, this dish is simply called soup dumplings. Made that way, it is a specialty in and around the city of Shanghai. There it is served at a breakfast, lunch, and dinner.

Other dishes at dim sum eateries allow diners to select as many dishes as they want from trays or wagons circulating in the restaurant. They are small dishes, and one can eat several, even if alone. Commonly, restaurants prepare anywhere from 20 to 60 different kinds of small dishes and serve noodle and rice dishes and plain or special types of congee or thick rice gruel dishes, and other snack foods. Some of these small dishes have two or three dumpling-type items on them. Listed alphabetically, the small dishes might include

Baked roast pork pie

Bean curd skin with shrimp stuffing

Chinese sausage bun

Crystal bun

Curried chicken roll

Egg custard

Egg or spring roll

Jaozi (sometimes translated as Chinese ravioli)

Mango pudding

Pan-fried fish cake

Pan-fried stuffed pepper or eggplant

Pan-fried turnip cake

Red bean cake

Rice noodle beef roll

Round Chinese chive dumpling

Shu mai (wonton skins filled with minced pork)

Special rice-cruller roll

Steamed chicken finger

Steamed chopped beef ball

Steamed plain bread

Steamed ribs in black bean sauce

Steamed roast pork bun

Steamed shark's fin and pork package

Steamed shrimp dumplings

Taro or turnip cake

Slightly larger and more expensive items for dim sum might include

Baked scallops on shell

Chicken feet in black bean sauce

Clams in black bean sauce
Curried beef triangles
Lotus root cakes
Mango pudding
Mixed beef tripe
Preserved egg congee
Shark's fin-seafood soup dumpling
Shrimp-stuffed bean curd
Shrimp toast
Snails with salt-pepper sauce
Stewed duck web with oyster sauce
Tripe in superior stock

These typical dim sum dishes roll around restaurants on wagons or are carried around on trays. They are offered to everyone seated at tables. Some families order large noodle and rice dishes made dry, that is, without a sauce or with sauce. Those come on large platters brought to the table straight from the kitchen, as any ordered large bowls of soup. Some of these might include

Black mushroom vegetable crabmeat soup
Braised noodles with crabmeat and vegetables
Dry-fry beef chow fun
Frog congee with hundred-year eggs
Noodle and seafood vegetable soup
Rice noodles with shrimp and scrambled egg
Seafood with e-fu noodles
Two-color fried rice: chicken in red sauce and egg white with beef
Yang chow fried rice

Dim sum restaurants, particularly those in the south, serve a large selection of barbecued meats such as

Barbecued ribs
Country-style squid
Honey-roasted chicken wings

Nanjing-style salt-pressed chicken
Roast duck
Roast pig
Roast pork
Roast suckling pig
Soy sauce chicken
Steamed chicken

Many also serve many types of congee in clay pots or ordinary bowls, including those already mentioned and others made with chicken, pork, sliced fish, or frog, and they also make them plain.

Always available, particularly at large dim sum eateries, is a good selection of different types of tea, special ones costing more. Choices can include green, oolong, black, litchi-black, jasmine pearl, chrysanthemum, tung-ting, and ever so many more different teas. More modern places can have a recent Taiwan favorite, bubble, also called buba, tea. It is black pearl-sized balls of tapioca added to any hot or cold tea or any beverage. They are popular in fruit drinks, milkshakes, flavored drinks, coffee or commercial beverages such as Postum, Sanka, and Ovaltine, or a mixture of honey and lemon. These balls are made from a tan-colored mixture of ground cassava, the root tapioca is made from, with sugar and caramel coloring added. Newer varieties are made in pastel colors; original ones start out dry, hard, and tan and when boiled for about two hours turn soft, shiny, and somewhat translucent. This new rage began in Taiwan and has spread to Hong Kong, southern China, and Western countries.

BANQUETS

These are always formal meals, almost always eaten in restaurants. They are discussed in chapter 6, Eating Out. Others are discussed in chapter 7, Special Occasions. Some banquets represent particular places or serve regional dishes. Some of those regional or provincial foods are mentioned in chapter 4, and additional information follows.

REGIONAL FOODS

Meals discussed may be typical, but not every Chinese person eats typical foods. Nor do they eat foods from their region of origin or where they currently live. They may have been born or raised in another part of

China. Dishes they like might be different because an adult in the family came from another region of the country. Perhaps they like a food they ate at a friend's home or in a restaurant that featured food from elsewhere. Maybe they read a book or watched television or a movie and saw foods of other places. Books, movies, television, videos, and travel bring outside influences into Chinese homes and onto their tables.

Typical meals may become an item of the past, perhaps faster for family meals than formal meals. In no country is food standing still. Outside influences are changing Chinese foods just as they change foods in other countries around the world. In several generations, people may not recognize foods as coming from China or from the regions where they grew up.

RECIPES FOR TYPICAL MEALS

Typical home meals are cooked and placed on the table before the family sits down. When seated, people take some rice, noodles, or other grain from the serving bowl and put it into their own bowl. Using their own chopsticks, they take morsels of meat and/or vegetables or whatever is served from the main platters or bowls and either put that into their mouths or, more often, get some grain to go with it and then put it into their mouths. Soup is consumed during or at the end of the meal, or both. If guests join, it is common to serve the platters and bowls with serving utensils for everyone's use, so that they can put the food on their individual flat plates and from there use their own chopsticks to eat. The recipes here can be used for one meal or individually; most often these dishes are served at main meals, lunch or dinner.

Meatball and Cellophane Noodle Soup

- 1/4 pound minced or ground chicken
- 1/2 teaspoon minced ginger root
- 1 tablespoon thin soy sauce
- 1 tablespoon Chinese rice wine or dry sherry
- 1 tablespoon cornstarch
- 1/2 teaspoon salt
- 1 ounce package of dried cellophane noodles, soaked half an hour, then drained
- 1/2 teaspoon Chinese rice vinegar
- 2 tablespoons fresh coriander, minced

1. Gently mix chicken, ginger root, soy sauce, rice wine, cornstarch, and salt. Form into about 16 to 20 very small meatballs.
2. Bring one quart of water to the boil, gently lower the meatballs into it, reduce heat to simmer, and cook for three minutes.
3. Add cellophane noodles and vinegar, and cook an additional five minutes.
4. Serve in a warmed soup tureen or large bowl, and garnish with the coriander.

Stuffed Pork Omelets with Oyster Sauce

- 1/4 pound ground pork
- 2 slices fresh ginger, minced
- 2 scallions, minced
- 1 tablespoon thin soy sauce
- 1/2 teaspoon sugar
- 1 scant teaspoon cornstarch
- 1 teaspoon corn or other light vegetable oil
- 4 eggs, each one beaten separately
- 2 tablespoons oyster sauce
- 1/2 tablespoon cornstarch

1. Mix pork, ginger, scallions, soy sauce, sugar, and cornstarch. Divide into four parts, lightly and slightly flatten each part, and set aside.
2. Heat oil in an six-inch fry pan and fry one egg until just set. Put one batch of pork mixture just to one side of its center and fold the other half of the egg over, pressing the edges of the half circle together. Set this omelet in a heat-proof flat-bottomed bowl such as a glass pie plate. Then repeat until the other three stuffed omelet packages are made and placed into the bowl.
3. Put the bowl in a steamer over rapidly boiling water and steam for 15 minutes.
4. Mix oyster sauce, cornstarch, and one-quarter cup of cool water, and pour this mixture over the omelet packages, then serve.

Sacha Beef Lo Mein

- 1/2 pound fresh noodles
- 1/2 pound flank steak
- 3 tablespoons *sacha* sauce (Chinese barbecue sauce)
- 1 slice fresh ginger, minced
- 2 cloves garlic, minced

- 1 scallion, minced
- 2 teaspoons cornstarch
- 1 tablespoon dark soy sauce
- 1 cup shredded cabbage
- 1 cup bean sprouts
- 1 carrot, peeled and shredded
- 3 tablespoons corn or peanut oil

1. Cook the noodles in boiling salted water until just tender; do not overcook.
2. Cut the meat into two-inch pencil-thin strips, and mix it with *sacha* sauce, ginger, garlic, scallion, cornstarch, and soy sauce.
3. Mix the vegetables together.
4. Heat wok or pan and add oil; when it is hot, add the meat and stir-fry until half cooked. Add vegetables and stir-fry two minutes more. Mix with the hot noodles and serve.

Corn Kernels and Red Nuts

- 1 cup corn oil
- 1 cup pine nuts or Chinese olive pits
- 2 cups corn kernels
- 1/4 teaspoon coarse salt
- 1 Chinese chive, minced

1. Heat wok, add oil and the pine nuts, and fry the nuts until light reddish-brown. Then remove and set aside.
2. Reheat oil and fry the corn kernels for three minutes. Then add salt and return the pine nuts to the oil. Stir-fry for another minute or until totally reheated.
3. Add Chinese chive, stir three or four times. Drain and remove to a serving bowl.

Golden Tofu

- 1 pound firm tofu, cut into three slices, then each one quartered
- 1 cup corn or peanut oil
- 1 teaspoon sugar
- 2 cups chicken broth
- 1/4 teaspoon finely ground black pepper

- 1/4 teaspoon coarse salt
- 1 teaspoon Chinese black vinegar
- 1/2 teaspoon sesame oil
- few sprigs fresh coriander

1. Stack six layers of paper towels on a three-sided cookie sheet. Put the tofu on half of this, and fold paper over the tofu pieces. Put a sardine or another thin can under the cookie sheet on the closed end, and have the open end hang over the sink. Press gently on the tofu and extract some of the water.

2. Heat wok or deep pan and add the oil. When it is hot, deep-fry half of the tofu pieces, pouring oil over any parts of tofu not submerged in the oil, until they are nicely crusted on the outside. Remove to a double layer of paper towels, and repeat with the rest of the tofu. Set oil aside for another purpose, and clean wok or pan.

3. Put wok or pan back on the heat, add 1/4 cup water and the sugar, and stir until the sugar starts to turn light brown, stirring it all the time. Just as soon as it does, add the chicken broth, salt and pepper, vinegar, and tofu, and simmer uncovered for 10 minutes.

4. Add the sesame oil and cook another minute, then put onto a heated plate, garnish with coriander, and serve.

Two-Way Hot Cabbage

- 1 1/2 pounds celery cabbage
- 1/4 teaspoon fine-ground salt
- 4 slices fresh ginger, peeled and finely slivered
- 1/2 teaspoon hot pepper flakes
- 1/4 teaspoon coarse salt
- 1/4 teaspoon finely ground Sichuan pepper
- 1 teaspoon sugar
- 1 teaspoon sesame oil

1. Cut cabbage in half lengthwise, then across into one-inch pieces.

2. Bring one quart of water to the boil, add the fine-ground salt and the celery cabbage pieces, bring the water back to the boil, let it boil for one minute, then drain.

3. Mix ginger, hot pepper flakes, coarse salt, Sichuan pepper, sugar, and sesame oil, and mix with the drained hot cabbage, tossing it well. Serve while still hot.

NOTES

1. E. N. Anderson, *The Food of China* (New Haven, Conn.: Yale University Press, 1988); P. G. Kittler and K. P. Sucher, *Food and Culture in America*, 2nd ed. (Belmont, Calif.: Wadsworth Publishing, 1998); J. M. Newman, L. H. Sirota, and X. Y. Lei, "Chinese Food Habit Perspectives," *Journal of the Association for the Study of Food and Society* 1: 31–38 (1996).

2. J. Jun, *Feeding China's Little Emperors* (Stanford, Calif.: Stanford University Press, 2000).

3. K. C. Chang, *Food in Chinese Culture* (New Haven, Conn.: Yale University Press, 1977).

6

Eating Out

The Chinese eat more meals at home than away from home, though most workplaces did and do provide meals in the middle of their employee workday, no matter the hour. Workers expect this job perk. Most get it, though some employers minimally deduct funds from their salaries. In earlier times, people worked for themselves or for the family, so this facet of eating away from home did not exist, and there were few other opportunities to eat out.

FORERUNNERS OF RESTAURANTS

When workplaces expanded, there were small, then larger places to go to eat. However, eating a meal away from home was not always desirable. Some people ate snacks from street vendors; others went to teahouses; and still others found a small spot for a quick bite. There were wine houses, too. Snack shops and teahouses stayed open until the wee hours, as did wine houses, but tiny places to eat and teahouses were more convenient and more socially acceptable than wine houses. The wine houses were major forerunners of restaurants, but many people would not go to them. Teahouses did serve a little food but not meals to accompany their many teas. They became places where music, poetry, and play readings took place while people had tea and small bites to go with it.

People went to wine houses for wine and other entertainment, poetry included, and for women. Most wine houses did serve meals, primarily to men and some older women. Besides drinking, dawdling, dining, and conversation, people played drinking games. Getting tipsy was a popular activity. That was one reason they were not always respectable places. Excessive use of opiates was another. Years ago, restaurants, teahouses, wine mansions, and wine houses could be full of inebriated folk who indulged in alcohol, opium, or both. Dark, dank wine houses no longer exist; the current Chinese government outlawed them.

In the Song Dynasty, specifically the Southern Song (1127–1279 C.E.), wine houses were popular, and common phrases about them included "respectable people do not go to such places" and "those places are not very high class." Therefore, eating in the forerunners of what we now call restaurants was not desirable for women and young children. Going to them was not a high-class thing to do.

There were some small general eateries, most filled with large numbers of lower-class workers. Clientele were often bothered by the bawdy customers. The elite, military, and other upper-class citizenry avoided them. These lower-class eateries and the wine houses, in addition to drunkenness, proffered prostitutes and drugs. The wine houses were never intended as places to go just to eat out, though small eateries were.

When these places concentrated more on food and less on alcoholic beverages and loose women, they became respectable and popular. A few even became first-class eateries, opulent places with gorgeous decorations and illuminations and fine food. Many then had tablecloths to eat on and yellow flags to hang outside. These two items became recognizable markers of good places to enjoy fine food.

Hundreds of years ago, these finer wine mansions and restaurants had something virtually nonexistent now—private alcoves off their dining rooms. They were for men who indulged in wine or women or those who needed a nap after dinner. They were popular when traveling home meant a long and arduous trip. Less fancy places had no such reclining alcoves; many were in basements, served food with no pretensions, and serviced lower-class patrons. Except for the first-class eateries, restaurants did not consider service an important part of their business. Chinese customers then and now prefer emphasis on food, not amenities.

Besides good food, sharing food was and still is exceptionally important to the Chinese. In their culture, sharing comes with rules, some known, others learned through practice and observation. Eating at a restaurant meant that after everyone sat down, the dishes arrived. Unless specified otherwise, they came when each was cooked and at the discretion of the kitchen. At formal meals such as banquets, dishes arrive one by one immediately after the preceding one was finished and cleared away.

There were many long-established rules that are still in common practice. For example, at home, smaller quantities of meat and other animal foods accompanied larger servings of grains and vegetables. The reverse was true in a restaurant or a meal at someone's home. Eating out meant that grain foods were of lesser importance and eaten in lesser quantities than at home. This was even more true at banquets, when prestige animal foods were most important and often the only item in a particular dish. Prestige foods are discussed in chapter 7; they are eaten on special occasions. While animal foods were dominant at meals away from home, they were not just any animal foods. Seafoods predominated, and pork, the main animal food at home, was absent.

Emphasis on animal foods differed and still does when eating snacks away from home. Snacks could be grilled meats and organ foods served on skewers, intended for consumption while walking down the street or when stopping and sitting just a few minutes. Most often snacks were grain foods such as dumplings and noodle dishes, intended to be eaten quickly. Speedy consumption was not the rule.

WHY EAT OUT, AND WHERE?

The majority of Chinese people live in rural areas, not in cities or larger towns. They have limited access and opportunity to eat away from home, and many have limited funds. While there are no taboos about eating out and only a few rules, many Chinese do so rarely. This may be due to cultural values, location, economics, and tradition. Eating a meal away from home used to be rare, perhaps due to adherence to the Chinese saying that "frugality is the beginning of family success." Though eating out was rare and expensive, it was and is an activity the Chinese take seriously.

While eating away from home was rare, the long Chinese tradition of celebrating special occasions was not. Celebrations could be for major life-cycle events, honoring special guests, or celebrating religious or cultural festivals. Celebrations were festive meals set in places to enjoy them. Nowadays, ordinary Chinese often have festive meals just for these and for less auspicious occasions. Doing so away from home is important, as most used to and still live in small, crowded rooms, places inappropriate and inadequate to celebrate with food and drink.

Affluent people have had homes for these events. They might celebrate in their homes or in a restaurant where more people can be accommodated. Such places have adequate dishes and tables and know-how. Some affluent people rent places and workers for events, but such places used to be almost impossible to find in China. In the countryside, people celebrated out-of-doors in a garden or even in the street, a practice that used to be commonplace. At these outside events, sometimes there were tables, but more often people sat on their haunches. The food was set out before them on tables or on tablecloths placed there for the food. Weather and other factors impacted that practice. With places more readily available now, fewer events are held outdoors.

Urban areas always had places for celebrations, and at various economic levels. People, be they peasants or gentry, could and still order individual dishes or special meals for these celebrations. They select restaurants based on quality, locations, types of food served, and price ranges. The special occasion can be a newborn's one-month birthday. That is when the child, by Chinese standards, is considered one year old. Or a celebration could be held when Westerners consider the child one, which the Chinese call the second birthday.

Gathering for other birthdays is common now. It was not years ago, when most Chinese only celebrated a person's entering a new decade of life at and after the age of 60. Other life-cycle occasions at which to rejoice and share food were and are weddings, to honor the deceased after a funeral, and when a special guest comes to visit. These important times are planned with great detail, except for the funerals, though some funerals have been planned in advance. At a funeral meal, people help the widow, widower, or other survivor, by giving money to defray an extravagant meal believed to help the deceased get to the next world.

Special occasions can be honored with a family meal in a restaurant or a banquet meal. The latter costs considerably more. For many Chinese the cost is less important than the foods served. The Chinese spend more for these meals and other eat-away-from-home occasions than do other cultural groups. They believe when doing any entertaining that there needs to be food and at least one special dish. They think all foods served need to be carefully selected. Doing so brings honor to those making the choices. Ordinary restaurant meals can cost a lot or a little. Meals for celebrations can be among many economic choices restaurants provide. The Chinese take seriously the making of these decisions.

BANQUETS

Banquets are formal meals, and most are eaten in restaurants. The food served at them is recorded in many cookbooks; food served to the various emperors is documented in imperial historiographies. Every dish at a banquet can be made to local or personal tastes. When Chinese people go to a restaurant to plan a banquet, they spend dozens of minutes discussing how each dish should and will be made. Sometimes they want a particular chef to make a dish; other times they want assurances that the restaurant will make it the way they want it to taste.

Banquets are almost always eaten at tables of 8 or 10, and some people squeeze in an eleventh person. They are special meals and usually have several expensive dishes made of very special foods considered haute to the Chinese. When families go out to eat, they usually order family meals, not banquets. A family meal is less formal and less expensive. They only rarely order shark's fin, bird's nest, sea cucumber, abalone, or any other prestige food. One reason is price; another is that these foods take a lot of time to prepare. While Chinese families honor a special birthday or life-cycle event, they need not only select the food, but also decide where to have this event.

Some formal family meals can be banquetlike. At them, foods can be ordered from preselected set menus and may include a dish requiring lengthy preparation time. Usually, family affairs require dishes with minimal pre-preparation, though sometimes they do have one prestige dish. On a very special occasion, those doing the ordering might ask to replace one or more of the preselected items. Some restaurants have more expensive preset banquet-type menus to choose among. Differences exist in number and expense of ingredients, culinary efforts, quality and location of the restaurant, and the expertise of the number one chef. Banquet menus are more extensive and yet more universal than regional. There are some special banquets, usually emulating imperial ones, such as a Song Dynasty banquet, a Confucian banquet, and so on.

A typical banquet might include the following

Stars around the moon (five to seven cold appetizers, one centered, others around it)

Three to five hot appetizer-type dumplings or dishes

Bird's nest soup

Abalone with snow pea leaves

Peking duck with *shao ping* (a cooked dough to enclose duck skin, scallion, and hoisin sauce)

Shark's fin with shredded chicken

Asparagus, sea cucumber, and stuffed bamboo pith fungus

Eel with taro and black beans

Steamed Shanghai cabbage with a Conpoy white sauce

Squab with steamed mushrooms in oyster sauce
Red-cooked bean curd-wrapped carp
Buddha's delight
Eight precious rice pudding

Famous television personalities in China, Taiwan, the United States, and elsewhere, and those who have written Chinese cookbooks, discuss a few banquet meals. One entire cookbook is about menus of formal meals.[1] It includes recipes and pictures of completed dishes in eight different locales, a vegetarian banquet, and a buffet. Using them and others as models, with variations, here are four regional meals.

A northern banquet might begin with several appetizer dishes plated and on the table, such as

Stir-fried chicken with jellyfish
Quick stir-fried gizzard and kidney
Sliced fish with wine sauce
Sautéed scallops with bamboo shoots

These would be followed by all hot main dishes, served one at a time, with no grain food served with them because banquet meals usually have one staple food such as a special noodle or rice dish, and it is served at the end of the meal. Northern dishes popular at banquet meals might include

Stewed shark's fin with brown sauce
Prawns Peking-style
Bird's nest soup with ham
Braised sea cucumber with shrimp eggs
Roast Peking duck with noodle doilies
Braised abalone with chicken and tripe
Shredded assorted meat soup san-ton style
Sweet and sour fish with pine nuts

This northern banquet could end with

Deep-fried sweet rice balls
Sweet silver wood ear with peach and cherry soup

Several of the above dishes originated or were served at an imperial court in the northern capital city of Beijing. Others have origins in the nearby province of Shandong.

A southern banquet might be Cantonese-style and from that city, now known as Guangzhou. It might begin with a phoenix-shaped cold-cut platter made up of cooked but cold abalone, roast of barbecued pork and duck, ham, sausage, tongue, liver, cashew nuts, white asparagus, cucumber, carrot, olives, and more. All of these foods would be cut and shaped to look like this mythical Chinese bird.

Main dishes, many with Western food and spice influences from this city where many foreigners lived, particularly in the 1800s, could include

Scrambled egg with crabmeat
Stuffed chicken wings with shrimp
Shark's fin and assorted seafood soup
Deep-fried prawn cutlets
Bird's nest soup
Steamed and smoked chicken
Braised black mushrooms and asparagus
Stir-fried boneless pomfret
Flower steamed dumplings

A southern banquet could end with

Baked Chinese tapioca pudding
Minced lotus seed soup in pineapple cup

An eastern banquet might feature Shanghainese or Fujianese food. One using many dishes from the province of Fujian could begin with

Stuffed chicken wings with ham
Deep-fried crispy eel
Steamed dried scallops with cream sauce
Stir-fried jellyfish and kidney

For main courses it could have

Braised shark's fin with seafood
Deep-fried prawns with green seaweed

Assorted seafood and sweet potato soup
Stewed spareribs with sea cucumber
Meatball soup Fujian style
Sliced crispy duck with red wine sauce
Stuffed bean curd in soup
Steamed glutinous rice with crabs
Sliced fish with sweet and sour sauce

Sweet dishes to end this meal might include

Taro pudding with red dates
Peanut dumplings in almond soup

A western banquet featuring foods of Sichuan or Hunan with appetizers from this region of China might include

Squid rolls with hot dried peppers
Dry-cooked bamboo shoots
Coin-shaped shrimp cakes
Stir-fried squid with hot sauce

Main courses could include

Braised abalone with assorted meats
Cold-sliced prawn with five kinds of sauce
Deep-fried duck cakes
Steamed chicken and spareribs in pumpkin
Liver and quail eggs soup
Stewed beef with hot bean sauce
Assorted vegetables Chen-tu style
Braised baby eel with red hot pepper

This western banquet could end with

Turnip tarts
Mashed sweet walnut and green peas pudding

These meals and banquet foods are typical, found not only in books but also in selected set meals and banquets available in restaurants. While quite a few restaurants have preset menus at different prices for family meals and special banquets, it is not mandatory to use them. Some people prefer selecting all or most menu items from dishes they know and want. Others ask for a change in one or more preset menu selections. Some restaurants do not allow changes in family meal suggestions, but will welcome them for banquets. Some will swap only one dish for another; others charge accordingly and will make any changes requested.

Many people do make changes because not every Chinese person eats typical foods or banquets selected by a restaurant or one from the region they grew up in or currently reside in. They may have been raised in another part of China and want those foods, or they may be honoring guests from elsewhere. In addition, they might want more or fewer dishes, though 10 plus or minus 1 does seem a common current number.

NOWADAYS

In cities and larger population centers, even in the countryside, elite restaurants and fine cooking can be had. Large and small places serve meals with no alcoholic beverages; some only serve banquets, and others only dim sum. Eating out has changed and become a respectable and desirable activity. In fine Chinese restaurants one can dine well, and in a private dining room.

Eating out means different things to different people. It is important to know that many Chinese prefer a cavernous, popular, even noisy place. They like the idea that everyone can watch what, how, and with whom they are eating. Not every one agrees. Upper-class and business patrons prefer taking their meals in private places or rooms, where they will not be seen or watched. Some eateries can accommodate them in such rooms or with screens that offer some privacy. The elite and the affluent do not eat on the ground floor. They prefer upstairs and away from view. Those who have visited China may have wondered why they needed to climb flights of stairs for their dinner. That was granting status, an honorific for them as foreign guests.

When the Chinese eat out, they deem it an important event if many people are in attendance. When going to eat out, where and how many dishes to have comes after attention to the foods to be served. Next comes price, total number of dishes served, and who will share them. There are other signs of a meal's importance. Eight is a lucky number to the Chinese, so at least eight main course dishes are served at a banquet or fancy family meal; but there can be more. Main dishes should include seafood and special foods that speak of the meal's value. For some, so does the amount and variety of alcoholic beverages served. Examples of foods considered of high status, which the Chinese call nourishing dishes, are bird's nest, shark's fin, bear paw, camel toe, monkey-head mushroom, and other expensive items. If several of these are served, the meal is even more important.

Nourishing dishes are more important philosophically than for nutrients provided. Many are gelatinous items like bird's nest and shark's fin; a few are special herbal dishes or dishes made with special wines. Most important is that they are made with expensive and/or hard to get items that speak to their value and also speak to the consideration of the host who selected them.

COMPLEXITIES OF EATING OUT

Meals have many unwritten rules. An important one is that rarely do they happen quickly or occur just to satiate hunger. Meals eaten away from home are for entertainment or special occasions; they emphasize food and sociability. If at home, someone can be employed to prepare and serve the meal. Some people borrow staff or places to enjoy a meal, leaving themselves free to host properly. Less-affluent people may not have these luxuries, but they do entertain as best they can afford, but do so rarely.

Most family meals are less sociable and take less time than spent at life-cycle meals or banquets. The latter can take several hours. Years ago, people ate holding bowl or plate while sitting on their haunches; it was often a quick eating occasion. This is still common, but now homes and less-expensive eateries use low stools and simple benches and some put food on low tables. These encourage longer eating times. Becoming commonplace are standard-height tables and chairs; furthermore, meals today can be and often are more leisurely.

GUEST RESPONSIBILITIES

Those who attend a Chinese banquet or an important family dinner need to know what is and is not considered polite. In general, the first responsibility is to answer the invitation promptly. Celebration meals are important, and hosts are honored when guests attend. Attending such an event after acceptance is a must. It matters not if the event is an ordinary birthday or a funeral, at a restaurant or home, or family style or an expensive banquet. Attending is a sign of politeness and caring; not doing so is extremely rude; this is important to the person hosting it.

Restaurant Alley of Wangfujing, a shopping street, Beijing. Photo © Art Directors/TRIP/Tibor Bognar.

The second responsibility is to arrive on time. No one can eat, often cannot be seated, until everyone is there; that makes tardiness particularly rude. Fancy facilities may have places to gather before a meal. Guests should arrive early and wait there, or at informal meals wait at the host's assigned table. While waiting, it is not polite to nibble or drink. This is true even if one is seated and nuts and other nibbles or tea or other beverages are on the table. When the host is ready, diners are advised where to sit. Guests need to watch for clues as to when to begin eating, course by course. Conversation while waiting should be minimal and light. For formal meals, guests do not enter the dining room until so advised. They wait, then sit where and when told to. In less formal situations, if seated and waiting at a table, guests should rise when the person hosting arrives and wait until told where to sit. The person hosting sits at the most important table. At formal meals the host serves special tidbits first to the important guests. Everyone needs to pay attention, watch, use special chopsticks provided when serving others, and determine when it is proper to help themselves.

Another guest responsibility is to taste every dish served. One should show positive emotion when taking the so-called nourishing ones. Taking a modest amount of any one food item at any one time is considered correct. Taking too much of any one item is thought rude. Reasons vary; the primary concern is for others at the table, and a secondary one is not to upset balance in one's own body. Should that happen, the person hosting the event would consider it his or her responsibility, even if it were not.

Other responsibilities vis-à-vis table behavior are to never toast another person until the host has toasted everyone, never drink an alcoholic beverage alone, and always toast others, including the person hosting the affair. At the end of a meal, guests should leave promptly after the host stands up and says a general good night or good-bye. Lingering is rude because the host cannot settle the bill or leave the restaurant until all guests have left. Be sure before leaving to compliment the host or hostess about how good the dishes were and how generous he or she was to provide them.

Affluent people usually serve more food because they can afford to. Their meals, if fancier, last longer, and guests need to plan on staying until the meal ends. At a fancier meal, a guest is offered a larger number of dishes. Guests need to plan to taste this greater variety and the large number of alcoholic beverages served. At these very fancy meals, libations begin earlier in the meal. A considerate host presses guests to eat and drink more. A guest needs to refuse after every two or three encouragements, or he or she will overeat and drink too much. Furthermore, the guest will seem greedy if he or she does not proffer some refusals. The more formal the meal, the greater the restraint needed when selecting items from serving pieces or accepting those offered directly. There is no way to know how many dishes will be served, so restraint is always important.

Guests have additional responsibilities. They need to compliment the host or hostess often about the quality of the food and its elaborate preparation. They need to keep in mind that each dish was carefully selected, its culinary techniques and contents considered and chosen with great care. Where and how foods are served, their cost, and their delicacy of preparation communicate importance and provide honor to the person hosting an event. Appreciation should reflect these issues, and not expressing appreciation says volumes about the guest.

CONVERSING ABOUT FOOD

Talking about food is important, no matter where or when. The Chinese spend a great deal of time discussing menus. They do this amongst themselves and with waitstaff before ordering a regular or banquet meal. Doing so, the waitstaff provides status and respect to them in return.

While waiting for food to arrive, discussions occur about food eaten at previous meals. Not doing so shows lack of interest and makes others think one does not care about the food served. Common things to discuss include where the chef is from, how fresh the food is, how it is made, the last time one ate a similar dish, and other topics.

These days, the Chinese like to meet and eat out frequently with friends and family. They always discuss food, their favorite topic, in a positive fashion. It is considered exceeding rude to speak negatively about food. Acceptable conversations include different styles of restaurants, no matter what their specialty, ordinary places serving the foods of one province or another, and the foods of an expert chef or an ordinary cook.

SNACKING

Snacking can mean consuming foods of great complexity, such as those at a dim sum meal, or it can mean going out for a simple bowl of noodles. All types of snacking are on the rise in China, as worldwide. However, snacking is not new to the Chinese; they have always purchased light bites from itinerant peddlers. To the Chinese, snacking is not and never was considered eating a meal. A meal means grains or staple foods with dishes to flavor them.

In the morning, it is common to eat snack foods at home or on the way to work. They might be purchased from a street vendor, a tiny eatery, or a larger one with or without tables and chairs. It is also common to go to places that serve dim sum, gathering there with families and friends. It is common for one person to go early and hold the table, and others to come when convenient. Some stay the entire time; others do not. These behaviors are considered acceptable because this is a snacking occasion and not a meal.

Snacks can be eaten anytime, day or night. Those who like to eat out late often stop for a bite on the way home from work or play. They might frequent a noodle shop, a hot pot restaurant, a congee eatery, or any other specialty place. They snack when hungry or just to socialize, and they go for a small bite or a big snack. They stop by places that sell soup, fried dough products, or steamed cakes. They go more often in the morning, less often late at night. People snack or eat at night markets and everywhere food is sold. Acceptable places to snack are selected because of the quality of food they serve.

Interest in food remains high whether snacking at home or eating away from home. The quality and variety of food, the expertise of the chef, the reputation of the facility, and value received attract the Chinese. Beverages and ambience are of lesser importance. Their interest in snacks and food at them and at meals are close to obsessive.

TEA SHOPS AND THEIR FOOD

Tea shops were in vogue in the Song through the Tang Dynasties (960–1279 and 618–907 c.e., respectively). They are popular again and deemed desirable places to go for social occasions and for snacking and drinking tea. They are places where men and women meet to chat or do business. Many are in beautiful settings; their ambiance is appropriate, even classic. No one is rushed; the tables are beautiful; and the varieties of tea and snacks are considerable. Most tea shops do not serve meals. Many provide entertainment, including plays, poetry readings, and other similar activities, usually in the evening. Those that produce small plays might have short music recitals or offer other forms of entertainment, including singing, acting, and poetry contests. Though there are fewer such places than a thousand years ago, they are popular and becoming more so and are joined by many simple outdoor places to take tea.

In the south of China, elderly gentlemen used to begin their days taking their birds in covered cages to a tea shop or a dim sum eatery. They would stay for long periods of time, chatting with friends while their birds sang to them and each other. Most were pensioners who spoke about whatever pleased them. They were pleased to share time and food with each other. Modern health laws do not allow birds, caged or otherwise, in an eatery. Their birds are no longer welcome. Some places have put hooks outside to hang bird cages while their owners go in to chat, talk business, or make other arrangements. Some stay outside and just enjoy the birds. And nowadays older women can and do join them.

CHINESE FOOD ABROAD

Within the last quarter century, Chinese restaurants have become important eating and gathering places for Chinese and non-Chinese people outside of China. Years ago there were only a few well-known Chinese restaurants in foreign cities. Most were where there were large Chinese populations. Now American-born Chinese and Chinese in every country are eating out more, as are people of almost every nationality.

Couple at simple teahouse, Chengdu. Photo © TRIP/T. O'Brien.

Eating out is so pervasive that everyone, Chinese included, now eat billions and billions of meals away from home each year. These meals are enjoyed in restaurants, schools, and workplaces. The Chinese and the more than million first-generation immigrants and their offspring everywhere in the world eat out often. It is an expression of increased affluence, inadequate or limited facilities, and/or disinclination to expend time or energy cooking at home.

Chinese food facilities are growing, as are Chinese populations outside of China. These food facilities are places to taste and learn about the foods of this culture. They are places to taste authentic Chinese cuisine. They satisfy the growing number of non-Chinese people who want real Chinese food. They are also places to taste what Chinese restaurateurs think others really want to eat. Food at these eateries tell tales about what Chinese people eat in China and what they eat abroad. They express the transnationalization of this ancient culture. They are also places where Chinese immigrants and later generations of Chinese maintain cultural eating and drinking traditions.

Europe, Asia, and the rest of the world have discovered McDonald's and other fast-food emporia. The Chinese have too, both in and outside of China. While Westerners sample foods with different ethnic flavors and enjoy exotic dining experiences, so do the Chinese. Affluence, education, the availability of fewer people to prepare foods at home, and an increase in food availability increases influences on Chinese food. In places like Hong Kong and Guangzhou, and elsewhere in and outside of China, Chinese foods are changing. Some eateries use mayonnaise in traditional Chinese dishes. In others, fried potatoes serve as a new bed for a cooked Chinese dish. In yet others, uncooked salads are appearing on Chinese menus.

In the United States, there are tens of thousands of Chinese restaurants, the most of any ethnic population in that country. Why so many? Perhaps more Chinese people have settled there and everywhere around the world and opened them. In the United States, the Chinese are one of the largest immigrant populations. Perhaps American customers have traveled a lot and tasted Chinese foods elsewhere and liked them. Perhaps the Chinese foods are tastier and more affordable.

Restaurant owners and their customers can find Chinese ingredients, Chinese cookbooks, and Chinese chefs on television. Some people gravitate to Chinese restaurants after watching chefs such as Ken Hom, Martin Yan, and others prepare Chinese food on television. In and outside of China, the Chinese continue to observe dietary and health practices of their mother country. Second- and third-generation Chinese abroad join the throngs in every country who seem to want to know about and eat Chinese food.

Chinese restaurants outside of China are small, middle size, and mammoth structures that feed up to five thousand diners every day. Some are humble with no decor; others are opulent and glitzy. All reflect their clientele. Each offers Chinese food appreciated by its clients; when it fails to do so, it goes out of business.

CHANGING CHINESE FOOD

New and different foods and how foods are served change what Chinese people eat. Many of these changes are reflected in Chinese restaurants. Reasonably new is the Chinese buffet concept of serving Chinese food. There are Chinese buffets all over the world. This idea has recently come to China. There they also serve dozens of prepared Chinese foods put out for diners to select. Most items are deep fried or have been previously stir-fried. They sit cooked and ready for patrons to select soup, starch, and the many different kinds of foods that entice them. Most often diners can return and select more or others at will. At some buffets, tea or other beverages are included in the total price; at some they cost extra. With increasing globalization of the world's food supply, greater food availability, and more intermarriages, Chinese buffets still serve mostly Chinese dishes. In the United States they also include sushi or other Japanese food, some Italian items, and Greek, Korean, and/or Thai foods in addition to the Chinese foods.

There are more and more food courts, which started in Singapore. They regulate and attend to sanitary concerns of their mostly Chinese food vendors. There and in other countries, people purchase foods from a variety of individual vendors. They take these foods to a table belonging to all of the vendors. Like buffet facilities, Chinese and foods of other nationalities are available.

Food courts have come to China, too. There, people can buy one or any number of different Chinese ethnic foods, or foods popular in other Asian and Western countries, to eat or to take home. Recently, one food vendor at a food court preparing many ethnic foods made his place look as if had individual and different ethnic vendors; all his foods were made in his own kitchen.

Other new food ideas are Chinese fast-food, sort of McDonald's-like or à la Kentucky Fried Chicken. Both franchises are very popular in China, the latter serving more chicken and having more customers every day than any of its other worldwide franchises. Some of the sauces provided by Western franchises in China have Chinese tastes. Other eateries in and outside of China are remaking Chinese foods into fast foods. These meet the needs mostly of young people, who eat fewer and fewer regular meals and enjoy more and more snack-type eating occasions.[2]

MEALTIME GAMES

The Chinese can play games at formal meals, particularly at weddings and other banquets. They do not consider it rude to be involved in two or more games or in conversations among three or more people at any one time. Any person can enter or leave a game or conversation at will, and interference or interruptions are commonplace. While this was acceptable behavior, it is becoming less so.

Fun at Chinese meals does include these multiple conversations and the table games. One game of forfeit called *cai mei* or *mu chan* sometimes is played at dinner tables. It is common at feasts and wedding celebrations, more among men but recently somewhat equalized among the sexes, and very popular among young adults. This finger game includes shouting out the number of fingers pointed or flung out at competing players. The object is to have a total of 10 fingers pointed into the center of the table. While many can play, only one person plays caller and shouts a number. At that moment, players show their fingers and shout the number they are projecting into the center of the table. Making an error requires taking a drink of whatever alcoholic beverage is on the table, and in China that means bottoms up or *gambei* and emptying the glass with one swallow.

There are many drinking games, all with the same consequences. In *duize*, the first player says a complete sentence. The second player needs to say another sentence in the same grammatical order as the first. That means noun, verb, article, compound word, or whatever needs to be duplicated. In addition, if the first player uses a famous quotation in his or her sentence, then the second needs to insert a quote in the same location in the sentence. Furthermore, the sentence must be the same length, with the same grammatical components, and so on. Needless to say, there is lots of drinking for losers. Games and those playing them do get more boisterous, and the players more inebriated, as each game continues.

RITUALS

The Chinese are a culture of people quite habitual in their tastes, games, and diet. Even though there are thousands of possible dish combinations, it is common for Chinese people to order the same favorite dishes over and over again. Perhaps this is because many rarely go out to eat, but perhaps not. It may be because they love what, when, and how they eat. Those who play games always want to play the same ones; others never indulge in them. Those who eat a particular menu like to order the same one each time they eat out. This is true except when some foods are better in a particular season. They will never order a dish out of season—that is, no summer food would be ordered in winter, and vice versa. No ordinary food should be served at a banquet. Foods, dishes, and games have appropriate times and places; all are worth talking about, all worth eating, and all to be enjoyed.

Formal meals are even loaded with traditional equipment. The place setting at one can include a small plate, chopsticks resting on a holder called a chopstick rest, a serving spoon, and several empty glasses. Here the spoon is intended for taking food from the serving plates. If there are three glasses, one is for China's most famous alcoholic beverage, *maotai*, a second for wine, and the third for beer. The Chinese do not drink cold or ice water at a main meal and until recently did not serve or consume soda either. Now some formal meals have soda available at each table; it is always there when children are expected.

One ritual is that formal family meals and banquets begin with cold appetizers on small dishes sitting on individual plates set around a larger one (called stars around the moon), or that they have a gorgeous appetizer platter designed like a basket of flowers, a special bird, or even a panda. This is considered auspicious. Another ritual is that each plate have the right number of food items; guests must take just one of each. Still another is that, at a very formal meal, these foods be served by those hosting or the waitstaff. What is not ritualized is whether hot appetizers will follow the cold ones or vice versa.

At a banquet, after appetizers are cleared away, a clean plate is served to each person. After that, main dishes can be served. Protocol demands that guests taste each dish and make an appropriate comment then or sometime thereafter. Less compulsory these days is that soups be interspersed with main dishes, and if only one soup is served that it be at or near the end of the meal, or that hot and then cold sweet dishes follow the final soup. A newer practice is that fruit, cut into small pieces, follows the final sweet soup.

Chinese do consider it their duty to keep putting food on the plates of honored and important guests. Less practiced is that a guest's empty plate be refilled whether the guest wants more or not. The same is true for tea, beer, soda, or *maotai*. Empty plates and glasses did say that more food or drink was requested, even if the opposite was expressed orally. No longer are refusals polite behavior and not what is wanted. In most Western cultures, finishing food or drink and saying no more is wanted is accepted. This was not so in the Chinese culture, as an empty plate or teacup was a silent ritual waiting for things to be added to it. Therefore, it was polite to leave a little food or drink so that more would not be offered. Knowing that particular ritual when with more conservative persons or when visiting a Chinese person's home can make for less discomfort at a meal.

Behaviors make for different rituals. To the Chinese, ambiance was not important; dimly lit facilities made them question what management was trying to hide, and quiet places told them that people were not having a good time. Chinese families take children, elderly parents, and others out to eat with them. They expect kids to be noisy, and it was and is acceptable for them to wander about. With seniors in attendance, raising voices so that they hear what is said is likewise acceptable.

All rituals and behaviors are changing. Some are still very important, others less so. Knowing what was done and practicing that will always be accepted behavior to the Chinese; theirs is a culture that, for the most part, still appreciates rituals, even if they themselves do not practice them.

RECIPES FOR INFORMAL OR FORMAL OCCASIONS

These dishes are commonly ordered in Chinese restaurants for informal and formal family occasions. The steamed dumplings, beef and water chestnut packets, and sweet potato balls are typical for dim sum. The steamed shrimp with garlic sauce, red-cooked duck and daikon, and steamed sea bass in black bean sauce are popular dishes for lunch and dinner. Because formal and informal meals often have one or two snack-type foods, the Chinese would deem it appropriate to add a few dim sum dishes to a main meal. Except for rice and noodle dishes, the reverse is rarely true. No formal banquet dishes follow because they use ingredients not always easy to obtain and use techniques difficult and time-consuming for most home preparations.

Steamed Dumplings (*Shumai*)
- 1/2 pound ground pork
- 1/2 cup minced raw shrimp
- 5 water chestnuts, finely minced
- 2 scallions, finely minced
- 1 teaspoon each thin and dark soy sauce
- 1 egg, separated
- 1/2 teaspoon cornstarch
- 1 pound wonton skins, at room temperature

1. Mix pork, shrimp, water chestnuts, scallions, both soy sauces, egg yolk, and the cornstarch.
2. Put one and a half tablespoons of this mixture on a wonton skin, lift the sides around it until they meet at the top, but do not seal the dough. Brush the top with some egg white.
3. Put the dumplings on a piece of parchment paper, and put that on the slats of a bamboo steamer basket. Cover with a bamboo steamer top, and put this into a large steamer. Let it steam half an hour. Serve in the basket, alone or with soy sauce, plum sauce, or any other sauce dip.

Beef and Water Chestnut Packets
- 1 cup wheat starch
- 1/2 cup tapioca flour
- 1 teaspoon peanut oil

- 1/2 pound finely chopped or ground beef
- 1/4 cup water chestnuts, chopped
- 1 teaspoon preserved kohlrabi or preserved cabbage
- 1 teaspoon thin soy sauce
- 1/2 teaspoon sugar
- 1/4 teaspoon coarse salt
- 1 teaspoon water chestnut flour
- 1/4 teaspoon corn oil

1. Sift wheat starch and tapioca flour into a bowl. Add one cup boiling water, stirring with chopsticks or a fork. Then add two tablespoons cold water and gently combine into a ball of dough.
2. Rub hands with some of the peanut oil, turn dough out on to a board, and knead for 5 minutes, then let dough rest for 15 minutes before dividing into 30 to 40 parts, and roll each into a ball.
3. Rub rolling pin with some peanut oil. Roll each ball into a three- to three-and-a-half-inch circle.
4. Mix beef, water chestnuts, preserved vegetable, soy sauce, sugar, salt, and water chestnut flour.
5. Spread corn oil on a heat-proof plate, and thoroughly dry hands, removing all traces of the oil.
6. Put one teaspoon meat mixture on a circle of dough, fold dough in half, seal edges by pressing lightly with a fork, and place on the oiled plate.
7. Put plate in steamer over rapidly boiling water for 20 minutes. Lift the dough packages to a clean lightly greased plate, and serve.

Sweet Potato Balls

- 1 pound sweet potatoes, peeled and diced
- 2 tablespoons sugar
- 1/2 cup sweet potato or yam flour, sifted
- 3 tablespoon sweet potato or yam flour, unsifted
- 2 cups corn or peanut oil

1. Boil sweet potatoes until soft, about 25 minutes, remove from water and mash well.
2. Add sugar to hot potatoes, slowly incorporate the sifted potato flour, and allow to cool.
3. Roll sweet potato mixture into one-inch balls, roll these into the unsifted flour, and set aside for half an hour or until exterior flour is moist.

4. Heat oil to 350 degrees Fahrenheit and deep-fry half of the sweet potato balls 2 minutes or until they are golden brown. Repeat with rest of them, then serve.

Steamed Shrimp with Garlic Sauce

- 10 jumbo raw shrimp still in their shells
- 1/2 teaspoon corn oil
- 4 large cloves garlic, minced
- 1 scallion, green part only
- 1 tablespoon mushroom or thin soy sauce
- 1 tablespoon Chinese rice wine or dry sherry
- 1/4 teaspoon ground white pepper
- 1 teaspoon peanut oil
- 1 small piece of parsley sprig, for garnish

1. Prepare the shrimp by removing the swimmerettes, if there, with a scissors. Use a small knife and cut open the shrimp shell from that very same side. Next, carefully cut the shrimp flesh but do not cut the outside shrimp shell or the tail section. Remove the black vein. Then press gently to flatten the shrimp and the shell, not breaking it or removing it from the tail section.
2. Put flattened shrimp, tails to the outside, in a circle on a heat-proof flat plate.
3. Heat corn oil in a wok or small fry pan, add garlic and scallion, and stir-fry for half a minute. Then add soy sauce, rice wine, and pepper. Pour this mixture over the plated shrimp and steam over rapidly boiling water for three minutes.
4. Heat the peanut oil, and after removing the plate of shrimp, pour this hot oil over the shrimp and serve garnished with the piece of parsley in the center.

Red-Cooked Duck and Daikon

- 1 four-pound duck, fat removed and cut into eighths
- 1 cup corn or peanut oil
- 4 slices fresh ginger
- 2 cloves garlic
- 1/4 cup thin soy sauce
- 2 tablespoons dark soy sauce
- 2 tablespoons Chinese rice wine or dry sherry
- 1 teaspoon sugar
- 8 whole cloves
- 1 star anise

- 1 large white radish (daikon), about one pound, peeled and cut into one-inch chunks

1. Dry duck with paper towels.
2. Heat wok, add oil, and fry ginger and garlic for 2 minutes, do not let them burn, then discard both and fry duck, half at a time, stirring frequently, for 5 minutes each. Drain and put into a large heavy pot.
3. Add soy sauces, rice wine, sugar, cloves, and star anise, and one cup water. Bring to the boil, and rapidly reduce heat to a low simmer. Cook for 90 minutes, stirring every 15 minutes. If not enough liquid remains, add another half cup of water. Check to see if duck is very tender; if not cook another 15 minutes. Remove duck. Add one cup of water and daikon and boil for 15 minutes. Drain and mix with the duck, leftover liquid included, and serve.

Steamed Sea Bass in Black Bean Sauce

- 2 pound sea bass, scaled, cleaned, and gutted
- 1/2 teaspoon coarse salt
- 2 tablespoon salted black beans, very lightly mashed
- 1 tablespoon Chinese rice wine or dry sherry
- 1 scallion, sliced fine
- 1 large clove garlic, minced
- 3 slices fresh ginger, peeled and minced
- 2 tablespoons thin soy sauce
- 2 tablespoons peanut oil

1. Dry fish with paper towel, make three gashes on an angle in flesh on both sides halfway down to the center bone. Rub with salt and set aside for 10 minutes.
2. Mix black beans, rice wine, scallion, garlic, ginger, and soy sauce.
3. Rub heat-proof platter with a little of the oil and put fish on it, then pour black bean mixture over the fish and put it in the steamer over rapidly boiling water. Steam for 20 minutes.
4. Heat remaining peanut oil, pour it over the fish, and serve.

NOTES

1. Pei Mei Fu, *Pei Mei's Chinese Cookbook*, Vol. 3 (Taipei, Taiwan: Author, 1979).

2. J. A. G. Roberts, *China to Chinatown* (London: Reaktion Books, 2002).

7

Special Occasions

The Chinese enjoy many holidays and festivals. Only a few are religious, and not everyone celebrates all or any of them, religious or not. Discussed here are holidays and festivals of the Han. Many of these respect and remember ancestors; others celebrate important times in the lunar calendar that relate to their agricultural heritage; a few honor important heroes; and there are others. Most are traditional; a few more modern. Some have unique elements that do not relate to specific foods, but every occasion is celebrated with food or feast. Holidays and festivals are times to gather and eat, even though only a few of them boast a specific food intended for a particular day.

The most important annual celebration is readying for and celebrating the Lunar New Year. Less important is honoring the concluding day of these festivities, known as the Lantern Festival. New Year's Eve and the first day of the Lunar New Year start a very special holiday, while the Lantern Festival, which occurs 15 days after the first day of the Lunar New Year, ends it. Second to the Lunar New Year holiday are celebrations for the Dragon Boat Festival, the Qing Ming Festival, and the Moon Festival. At or after every one of them, Chinese families and friends gather to eat.

At Lunar New Year's Eve, only immediate or household family members get together. Rarely does their meal include outsiders. At all other celebrations, sharing an eating occasion is not limited to family. That is true on days celebrating flying kites or flowers as well as honoring and visiting specific tombs of one's ancestors. Though every celebration can include a meal, most are not associated with specific foods. They are opportunities to share food and honor the day. Some celebrations—such as the Double Ninth Festival, the day to send Winter Clothes to the Ancestors, and days to offer thanks for good harvests, to the heavens, and so forth—have lost importance over time, but often they are still occasions to gather for a meal celebration with family and friends.

Additional celebrations most Chinese still honor include specific life-cycle events such as the birth of a child, particularly a baby boy. And there are birthdays, marriages, and funerals when family and friends gather for a meal. There are also newer festivals that honor people, places, and things and the older events most often associated with nature, the spirits, and/or respect for the ancestors. Some celebrations are based on the solar or lunar calendar; newer ones are scheduled with respect to the Gregorian calendar.

CALENDAR DIFFERENCES

The Chinese use three calendars. The first two calendars were based upon close observation of the sun, moon, and stars. They celebrate seasonal change and honor ancestors. The third calendar is the Gregorian calendar. Most holidays are associated with the lunar calendar; a few are based on the solar one; and day-to-day life and newer holidays use the Gregorian calendar, which is more familiar to the Western world. Holidays based on the lunar or solar calendars do not fall on the same day every year on the Gregorian calendar.

Chinese lunar calendars often have 12 months, each with either 29 or 30 days. Some years there is an additional month; called intercalary. Seven intercalary months occur every 19 years. They are needed to match the Chinese lunar and solar calendars and to make sure that the winter solstice always falls in the eleventh month, the summer solstice in the fifth month, the spring equinox in the second month, and the autumn equinox in the eighth month. The Chinese word for these extra months that make the calendar match the rising and waning of the moon is *jun-yueh*. The extra months were calculated and added when, as an agrarian society, seasonality, accuracy, and appropriate placement of festivals were necessary. In both regular and extra months, minor lunar holidays occur every first and fifteen day. There are also auspicious days such as the fifth day of the fifth lunar month, the ninth day of the ninth month, and so on. Clearly, Chinese calendars can be complicated.

ANNUAL HOLIDAYS

A quick overview of major holidays and some of lesser importance throughout the year is presented here. Then the most important Chinese holidays, particularly those involving food, are discussed in more detail and in order of their importance. Delineated one by one, they are not necessarily in calendar order.

January 1 is New Year's Day in the Gregorian calendar. This Western holiday comes before festivities of the Chinese Lunar New Year and Lantern Festival. These two occur on the first and fifteenth days of the first month of the lunar calendar, respectively. Then comes the *Tiancang* Festival on the twentieth day of the first lunar month, celebrating filling the granary and looking forward to a bountiful harvest in the coming year. Following it is *Guanyin* or the Goddess of Mercy's birthday, celebrated mostly in Daoist temples on the nineteenth day of the second lunar month. Qing Ming Festival, another lunar holiday, is in spring. Then the Chinese visit the graves of their ancestors. For those who live in the Yunnan Province, there is Water Splashing Festival, also in early spring, usually in mid-April.

On the fourth of May in the Gregorian calendar, the Chinese celebrate Youth Day, and the first of June is Children's Day, a national holiday. After these auspicious days comes Dragon Boat Festival, celebrated during the fifth lunar month, and the Ghost Festival, which occurs near the end of summer. The Moon Festival follows during the middle of the following lunar month. Double Ninth comes next, celebrated on the ninth day of the ninth lunar month. It is a day to drink wine, write poetry, and leave home to avoid disaster. Sometime thereafter on September 28 comes Confucius Festival, celebrating his birth. National Day is three days later on October 1 to honor the founding of the People's Republic of China.

The next-to-last major holiday is the religious celebration of Christmas on December 25. Then Christian faithful honor the birth of Jesus. The next week is New Year's Eve according to the Gregorian calendar, and New Year's Day begins the year once again.

Lunar calendar years do not end when Gregorian ones do. They wind down on the twenty-fourth day of the last or twelfth lunar month. Then the Kitchen God, also called the Prince of the Oven, goes on his own holiday; he visits Yu Huang, the Jade Emperor in Heaven. His task is to report on the merits of people in his household the past year. He returns anywhere from the eve of the Lunar New Year to the end of New Year festivities, which is Lantern Festival day. These days are close to the beginning of spring. They are near the end of January or the beginning of February on a Gregorian calendar. The week before Lunar New Year, activities taking place include thoroughly cleaning house, buying new clothes, settling debts, and generally getting ready for the festivities. They also include making food for the New Year holiday.

Chinese New Year

To prepare for this most important holiday, people celebrate and count the days before the very first month of the Lunar New Year. This period is celebrated by most Chinese people everywhere in the world, who think about and do things to auspiciously end the old year. Families pay respects to elders and friends; they get ready to welcome the God of Joy to whom they kowtow when the year begins anew.

Lunar New Year occurs before anyone needs to prepare for spring. It is a time when agrarian people can be together and celebrate. In the traditional family, the husband's duty was to provide for the family, and the wife's responsibilities were to run the household, worship the deities, pay homage to ancestors, maintain family shrines, and see that festivals were celebrated appropriately.

This most important lunar holiday for Han Chinese and many other Asian populations is also known as Spring Festival because it comes just before the beginning of spring. However, it did not always occur on the first day of the first lunar month. Therefore, a major reform was completed in 104 B.C.E. to fix it to always fall on the day of the first moon after the sun enters Aquarius. That means it is never celebrated before January 21 or after February 20. There were other early fixes to accommodate something called solar sections. Elders still use this somewhat newer lunar calendar, while China officially adopted the Gregorian calendar in 1912. The 104 B.C.E. fix did reduce confusion, but it did not change lunar holiday celebrations. Nor did it alter Spring Festival's being determined on the lunar calendar. The Chinese call their New Year both *Chun Jie* and *Xin Nian*, the latter literally meaning New Year.

Custom dictates that women prepare traditional and special holiday foods for the Lunar New Year. It advises them to seek counsel from fortunetellers, spirit mediums, and religious folk. As a woman tends preparations for the festivities, she is to consult the almanac to be sure of the date, remind her husband to settle their debts, visit elder relatives, and help with the giving and exchanging of gifts. One task is to prepare red envelopes of money, called *angpau*, for the children. Another is to make donations to relatives, the poor, and others who are needy. Monies go in red envelopes because that color symbolizes luck and assures that all evil will be exorcised. The money wishes luck to recipients and to the family that gives it.

The woman also sees to it that branches of flowering trees such as peach or pussy willow come into the home to decorate it for the New Year. The fragrances call attention to their presence and to the home. Other tasks include making offerings to the ancestors and thinking about life that restarts in the year ahead. It is a woman's time to turn over a new leaf and encourage others to begin a new lease on their lives. She arranges for the writing of good luck signs on strips of red paper and sees to it they are put up on the front gates. This practice, called door signing, began when a Ming Dynasty emperor issued an edict requiring them on the doors of all homes. All of these efforts assure that New Year is time to clean the slate and wish for better economics and better times ahead.

New Year's Eve is when many Chinese eat a vegetarian meal to honor Buddha. For those who can afford it, New Year's Day dinner is time for eating bird's nest soup and for offering family members a cup of tea containing a dragon's eye fruit, a red date, and sometimes a piece of ginseng. People also offer this tea to those who visit, and they give some to the children's grandparents and other elderly family members to wish the elders a vigorous healthful life, more grandchildren, a good death, and their return to their ancestors.

Some wonder why every house needs to be very carefully cleaned. One saying explains that houses are cleaned so that "specks of dirt neglected do not fly into eyes and blind someone in that home." Cleaning and all other activities have a rationale. The money is for good wishes for giver and receiver; the edible gifts such as candies, other sweets, and oranges are for a sweet year; and so forth. When the Kitchen God's mouth is smeared with thick sugar paste or honey before his image near the stove is burned and sent on its celestial trip on or near the twenty-fourth day of the twelfth month, it assures reporting to the Jade Emperor only nice sweet things. Some families dip the Kitchen God's portrait and that of his wife, or their name papers, in wine or other spirits to make him tipsy and in good temper before he tells the Jade Emperor about the family he watched and protected. Firecrackers are set off when he goes to report to the God of the Heavens. They are to sound like horses hooves pulling his chariot, as does rice thrown onto the fire. The straw thrown on his image is said to feed his horses. Some families put a cup of tea near the spot where his image burned. They pour it out midway through that process so that he drinks something thought valu-

The Kitchen God.

able and necessary on the way and before reporting on merits of the home's daily life. Igniting firecrackers also has other purposes. The firecrackers keep evil spirits away, humor the immortals with noise, and please onlookers who get to see, hear, and delight in the festivities.

When the Kitchen God returns between Lunar New Year's Eve and the Lantern Festival, a new picture or name paper replaces the one that sent him on his way. The new one will be honored, too, so the elderly who revere him are assured clear eyesight and fast-moving limbs. He keeps the younger folk who honor him energetic. The wife's devotion assures all in the family health and peace for the coming year.

Little New Year

Days between the times the Kitchen God leaves and returns are called Little New Year or *Xiao Xin Nian*. During these days and New Year's Eve, a great deal of food is prepared. Most important are the dozens, if not hundreds, of dumplings called *jiaozi*. Some are made with a coin inside, particularly if small children reside in the home. Everyone eats dumplings on New Year's Eve and New Year's Day. They are made in advance; no sharp instrument such as a knife is used on the eve of and on all Lunar New Year day. The Chinese believe that if they cut something, then their luck in the coming year will be cut.

New Year's Eve is when the entire family gathers. Family members try to stay up late to welcome the coming year. At midnight they wish each other well and feast on the dumplings that were filled with black sesame seeds and sugar. The next day they eat those made vegetable fillings and other vegetarian food. In ancient China, elaborate meat foods, including chicken with wine or pig's head and pork, were consumed for the Lunar New Year's Eve meal. However, when the Kitchen God, thought to be a deity of Confucius, was elevated to a *Fu* or Buddha, many families replaced meats with vegetarian dishes to honor his new incarnation.

Before feasting at midnight, people pay respects to their ancestors, making three kowtows to each of them in front of each ancestral tablet. These tablets are kept in an auspicious place in the home. They also light incense in front of these tablets and offer the ancestors ceremonial foods. In ancient times, it was the duty of the man of the house to pray to the returned Kitchen God to show that he was head of his household, and after that women and children could show devotion to the Kitchen God. Nowadays, it is the woman who does that devotion.

The New Year's Eve feast has foods of symbolic value. Those who are not Buddhists might serve a whole fish because the word for *fish*, which is *yu*, sounds similar to words for *surplus* (*yukuan*, *yingyu*, and *shengyu*). The steamed or fried *jiaozi* represent and look like ingots of gold. The written character for these New Year dumplings also sounds like the word for *many sons*, something most Chinese families would like to have. At the New Year's Eve meal, some have made and eat spring rolls. They look like rolls of gold. A *niangao* or New Year's cake is served that night, again the next day, and many times throughout the two weeks, until there is no more. The Chinese word for that cake means sticking together and going high. These two ideas portend success in families and at work.

The New Year's breakfast is set out before going to bed. Like all meals during this holiday, it must be overly abundant. Size is said to foretell the amount of food the family will have in the coming year. Later this day and during the next few, people set aside time to visit relatives and friends, eldest to youngest. They bring them sweets for a sweet year and items that wish for abundance. They also bring red envelopes for their children and those thought to be needy.

A person who comes to visit and pay respects is offered tea, small sweet foods, and some dumplings prepared but not cooked in the days before New Year. Sweets are also offered in an eight-sided dish or box. Eight is a symbolic of prosperity. These can be and often are the same sugared fruits and nuts offered to the ancestors on New Year's Eve. The foods in this eight-sided container, called a prosperity dish, can include candied melon for good health, red-dyed melon seeds for joy and happiness, sweetened dried lychees for strong family relationships, sweetened coconut symbolizing togetherness, and candied kumquats representing golden riches. Visitors also are served peanuts, called the long-life nut, lotus seeds wishing for many sons, and the previously mentioned New Year cake called *niangao*. When guests eat these symbolic foods, family members say, "May you have much satisfaction year after year."

On New Year's Day, everyone wears new clothes. The streets are full of revelers and people going visiting. Firecrackers go off everywhere. Businesses are closed, but their owners stand in the doorways giving money to the lion dancers whose drums are said to ward off evil as they dance around.

When visiting during Little New Year, foods with special meanings are brought as gifts. Most common are oranges for good fortune and tangerines with leaves still attached that say their relationship will remain secure. These and the other foods are appropriate gifts at this season or any other, as are pomegranates, whose many seeds wish for many offspring. Black moss, also known as hair seaweed, is given to wish the recipient exceptional wealth. Dried bean curd wishes personal fulfillment; bamboo shoots wish for strength; a chicken with head, feet, and all its parts symbolizes completeness; noodles or long beans portend a long life; and any whole foods symbolize a proper beginning to the New Year.

Other gift foods, when in season, are peaches that stand for immortality or at least a very long life, apples because they say "peace be with you," green olives representing ingots of gold, and pears to say "may there be no separation from friends." These and round cakes resemble ingots of gold; they are popular at the New Year or any other occasion.

Lantern Festival

The Lantern Festival is 15 days after Lunar New Year. It used to be second in importance to the Chinese New Year, but not everyone celebrates this ancient holiday—at least people do not celebrate the way it was done years ago. Then its Han origins deemed it a time to light the way when closing New Year festivities. Not everyone believes Lantern Festival to be an old holiday. Some wonder about its importance and its age. One tale is about a Ming emperor who ordered ten thousand candles set afloat to make a small holiday into an important one. Another says this Ming emperor set the candles on a lake so that Buddha would come, see them, and honor him. Still others believe it was not until the Tang Dynasty that the custom of illuminating the countryside took hold. Which is true is anyone's guess. However, ancient China, as an agrarian culture, did celebrate spring after the first full moon of the year. People thought heavenly spirits were flying around. They believed that lanterns made by adults and children lit the way for them and those not yet gathered into heaven's place of judgment. They also thought that the lanterns assured the spirits perpetual luck and aided wandering souls and those who were trying to find them.

Popular lantern shapes nowadays are of the 12 animals who sought out Buddha, the same animals used on some Lunar New Year cards, for whom each year in China's 12-year cycle is named. They are the rooster (also translated as cock), dog, pig (also known as boar), rat, ox, rabbit (sometimes called hare), serpent (which can be called snake), sheep (or ram, goat, or lamb), tiger, dragon, horse, and monkey.

In early and modern times, lanterns were round, and some looked like trees, plants, and/or other animals. Later, some were made in people's im-

Lantern wishing double happiness.

ages so that Buddha would be enticed to come to see them. Candles were set on crossed pieces in their bottom. Nowadays flashlights are attached there. Some people carry lanterns aloft at the ends of long poles and walk around town or in the park. Others place them outside their homes. Some write poems or riddles on them. Those who go out of their way to walk with lanterns might be saying *tsanteng chiao* as they wish for many sons. Wishing to get married and have children, unmarried girls used to take their lanterns and go into the fields to steal scallions. This act was to assure finding a good husband.

One emperor held a large feast on Lantern Festival Day. He had hundreds of firecrackers set off, and he put out hundreds, if not thousands, of lanterns. People hung their own colored silk, glass, gauze, and even horn lanterns. Markets sold fresh and dried fruits and fresh flowers. People purchased precious things such as gold, jade, and other jewels. Children bought goldfish and put them in small jars; they carried them and their lanterns everywhere that night. Nowadays many municipalities do special things in their parks. Some have stages lit with scenes from famous stories. Some have citywide competitions; others have flower festivals. No longer a day off from work for everyone, this holiday is still celebrated in some cities and towns. There, people purchase or make lanterns, carry them to these parks, enjoy the well-lit scenarios, symbolically light the way for lost souls, and eat homemade or purchased sticky sweet rice filled with bean paste called *tangyuaner*. More recently people enjoy ice cream, sodas, sweets, crispy sugared crackerlike foods, and other cold treats.

Penghu, in Taiwan, has a special event on this day. Hundreds of fishing boats in their Waian Harbor light up the nighttime sky, and tourists and locals come to see them and the local *qigui*, which stands for "appealing to the turtle." This somewhat new event has become a Lantern Festival ritual that expresses hope for peace and prosperity in the coming year. People pray to the turtle for longevity and good fortune. One turtle used is solid gold, weighing almost 20 pounds; another is made of about ten thousand pounds of rice weighing close to eight hundred pounds. It is made annually of pineapples and mandarin oranges. The oldest turtle is very small, made of hardened glutinous rice paste and sugar, and used for a three-day temple *qigui* ceremony that ends with a massive display of fireworks. This celebration also uses buns piled high, in the shape of a tall, thin triangle, called offering buns.

A month after the Lantern Festival is the birthday of the Goddess of Mercy, called *Guanyin*. Lanterns can be prominent on this day. Some

ticularly if small children reside in the home. Everyone eats dumplings on New Year's Eve and New Year's Day. They are made in advance; no sharp instrument such as a knife is used on the eve of and on all Lunar New Year day. The Chinese believe that if they cut something, then their luck in the coming year will be cut.

New Year's Eve is when the entire family gathers. Family members try to stay up late to welcome the coming year. At midnight they wish each other well and feast on the dumplings that were filled with black sesame seeds and sugar. The next day they eat those made vegetable fillings and other vegetarian food. In ancient China, elaborate meat foods, including chicken with wine or pig's head and pork, were consumed for the Lunar New Year's Eve meal. However, when the Kitchen God, thought to be a deity of Confucius, was elevated to a *Fu* or Buddha, many families replaced meats with vegetarian dishes to honor his new incarnation.

Before feasting at midnight, people pay respects to their ancestors, making three kowtows to each of them in front of each ancestral tablet. These tablets are kept in an auspicious place in the home. They also light incense in front of these tablets and offer the ancestors ceremonial foods. In ancient times, it was the duty of the man of the house to pray to the returned Kitchen God to show that he was head of his household, and after that women and children could show devotion to the Kitchen God. Nowadays, it is the woman who does that devotion.

The New Year's Eve feast has foods of symbolic value. Those who are not Buddhists might serve a whole fish because the word for *fish*, which is *yu*, sounds similar to words for *surplus* (*yukuan*, *yingyu*, and *shengyu*). The steamed or fried *jiaozi* represent and look like ingots of gold. The written character for these New Year dumplings also sounds like the word for *many sons*, something most Chinese families would like to have. At the New Year's Eve meal, some have made and eat spring rolls. They look like rolls of gold. A *niangao* or New Year's cake is served that night, again the next day, and many times throughout the two weeks, until there is no more. The Chinese word for that cake means sticking together and going high. These two ideas portend success in families and at work.

The New Year's breakfast is set out before going to bed. Like all meals during this holiday, it must be overly abundant. Size is said to foretell the amount of food the family will have in the coming year. Later this day and during the next few, people set aside time to visit relatives and friends, eldest to youngest. They bring them sweets for a sweet year and items that wish for abundance. They also bring red envelopes for their children and those thought to be needy.

A person who comes to visit and pay respects is offered tea, small sweet foods, and some dumplings prepared but not cooked in the days before New Year. Sweets are also offered in an eight-sided dish or box. Eight is a symbolic of prosperity. These can be and often are the same sugared fruits and nuts offered to the ancestors on New Year's Eve. The foods in this eight-sided container, called a prosperity dish, can include candied melon for good health, red-dyed melon seeds for joy and happiness, sweetened dried lychees for strong family relationships, sweetened coconut symbolizing togetherness, and candied kumquats representing golden riches. Visitors also are served peanuts, called the long-life nut, lotus seeds wishing for many sons, and the previously mentioned New Year cake called *nian-gao*. When guests eat these symbolic foods, family members say, "May you have much satisfaction year after year."

On New Year's Day, everyone wears new clothes. The streets are full of revelers and people going visiting. Firecrackers go off everywhere. Businesses are closed, but their owners stand in the doorways giving money to the lion dancers whose drums are said to ward off evil as they dance around.

When visiting during Little New Year, foods with special meanings are brought as gifts. Most common are oranges for good fortune and tangerines with leaves still attached that say their relationship will remain secure. These and the other foods are appropriate gifts at this season or any other, as are pomegranates, whose many seeds wish for many offspring. Black moss, also known as hair seaweed, is given to wish the recipient exceptional wealth. Dried bean curd wishes personal fulfillment; bamboo shoots wish for strength; a chicken with head, feet, and all its parts symbolizes completeness; noodles or long beans portend a long life; and any whole foods symbolize a proper beginning to the New Year.

Other gift foods, when in season, are peaches that stand for immortality or at least a very long life, apples because they say "peace be with you," green olives representing ingots of gold, and pears to say "may there be no separation from friends." These and round cakes resemble ingots of gold; they are popular at the New Year or any other occasion.

Lantern Festival

The Lantern Festival is 15 days after Lunar New Year. It used to be second in importance to the Chinese New Year, but not everyone celebrates this ancient holiday—at least people do not celebrate the way it was done years ago. Then its Han origins deemed it a time to light the way when closing New Year festivities. Not everyone believes Lantern Festival to be an nations to relatives, the poor, and others who are needy. Monies go in red envelopes because that color symbolizes luck and assures that all evil will be exorcised. The money wishes luck to recipients and to the family that gives it.

The woman also sees to it that branches of flowering trees such as peach or pussy willow come into the home to decorate it for the New Year. The fragrances call attention to their presence and to the home. Other tasks include making offerings to the ancestors and thinking about life that restarts in the year ahead. It is a woman's time to turn over a new leaf and encourage others to begin a new lease on their lives. She arranges for the writing of good luck signs on strips of red paper and sees to it they are put up on the front gates. This practice, called door signing, began when a Ming Dynasty emperor issued an edict requiring them on the doors of all homes. All of these efforts assure that New Year is time to clean the slate and wish for better economics and better times ahead.

New Year's Eve is when many Chinese eat a vegetarian meal to honor Buddha. For those who can afford it, New Year's Day dinner is time for eating bird's nest soup and for offering family members a cup of tea containing a dragon's eye fruit, a red date, and sometimes a piece of ginseng. People also offer this tea to those who visit, and they give some to the children's grandparents and other elderly family members to wish the elders a vigorous healthful life, more grandchildren, a good death, and their return to their ancestors.

Some wonder why every house needs to be very carefully cleaned. One saying explains that houses are cleaned so that "specks of dirt neglected do not fly into eyes and blind someone in that home." Cleaning and all other activities have a rationale. The money is for good wishes for giver and receiver; the edible gifts such as candies, other sweets, and oranges are for a sweet year; and so forth. When the Kitchen God's mouth is smeared with thick sugar paste or honey before his image near the stove is burned and sent on its celestial trip on or near the twenty-fourth day of the twelfth month, it assures reporting to the Jade Emperor only nice sweet things. Some families dip the Kitchen God's portrait and that of his wife, or their name papers, in wine or other spirits to make him tipsy and in good temper before he tells the Jade Emperor about the family he watched and protected. Firecrackers are set off when he goes to report to the God of the Heavens. They are to sound like horses hooves pulling his chariot, as does rice thrown onto the fire. The straw thrown on his image is said to feed his horses. Some families put a cup of tea near the spot where his image burned. They pour it out midway through that process so that he drinks something thought valu-

The Kitchen God.

able and necessary on the way and before reporting on merits of the home's daily life. Igniting firecrackers also has other purposes. The firecrackers keep evil spirits away, humor the immortals with noise, and please onlookers who get to see, hear, and delight in the festivities.

When the Kitchen God returns between Lunar New Year's Eve and the Lantern Festival, a new picture or name paper replaces the one that sent him on his way. The new one will be honored, too, so the elderly who revere him are assured clear eyesight and fast-moving limbs. He keeps the younger folk who honor him energetic. The wife's devotion assures all in the family health and peace for the coming year.

Little New Year

Days between the times the Kitchen God leaves and returns are called Little New Year or *Xiao Xin Nian*. During these days and New Year's Eve, a great deal of food is prepared. Most important are the dozens, if not hundreds, of dumplings called *jiaozi*. Some are made with a coin inside, par-

Tower of buns.

younger Chinese make them to honor her. Others paint pictures of her to carry on this holiday. No one is sure why.

Qing Ming and the Cold Food Festival

This holiday has many names, including Qing Ming, the Festival of Pure Brightness, All Soul's Day, Spring Festival for the Dead, the Feast of the Dead, Sweeping the Graves Festival, and the Cult of Ancestral Worship Day. Older Chinese people think it an important holiday, but younger ones are less apt to celebrate, at least not in traditional ways. Traditionally the whole family went to visit and clean the graves of their ancestors. There they worshiped them and showed them great respect.

This day has been confused with an ancient holiday called the Cold Food Festival. That was a day when lighting fires was prohibited. Actually, the Cold Food Festival occurs on the day before Qing Ming. One tale says it was started to celebrate a Zhou Dynasty patriot who chose to die rather than accept gratitude for feeding his ruler some of his own flesh when both of them were starving. Years later, this patriot was living in the forest and would not come out or accept being honored by his ruler. The ruler tried to force him out by setting the forest ablaze. A related story about the Cold Food Festival says that the ruler of the state of Jin had to flee because of civil unrest, and when he did, his friend followed and stayed with him for 17 years. When reinstated as king, he offered this loyal subject an official post. He refused and retired to the hills. In a fit of frustration, the king set fire to the woods, then was even more frustrated to learn that his loyal subject was burned to death. To honor him, the king decreed that no fires be set on the anniversary of his friend's death. Still another story tells that fires were put out to conserve fuel. Then a rice gruel dish became popular because it was tasty even cold. Any of these tales can be the reason people eat only cold foods, mostly cold rice gruel, before the Qing Ming holiday. Incidentally, Qing Ming was a week-long festival now celebrated but one day.

For the Qing Ming festival, people prepare and bring tea eggs, egg tarts, and in some places the fixings for *popia* to ancestor grave sites. *Popia* are meat-and-vegetable-filled pancakes. They are rolled to look like spring or egg rolls. At the gravesite after the appropriate homage to the ancestors, people fill them with shrimp, crabmeat, radish or carrot sticks, bean sprouts, and slices of omelet and roll the pancake. Any number of different sauces can be served with this cold rolled food that resembles rolls of money. Some people bring cold roast pork or duck, offering cakes along with oranges, tangerines, and other fruit, wine, tea, other vegetable dishes, nut mixtures, cold fried fish, and sometimes the favorite foods of the deceased for their spiritual pleasure.

With the food comes incense and flowers to honor the ancestors. Before eating, people clean the grave area. The food is set before the ancestral tablets. Each family member in turn, eldest to youngest, lights some incense, bows three times, and pours some wine, liquor, or tea on the ground to give the deceased something to drink to accompany the foods set before them. A proper bow or kowtow, which the Chinese call *jugong*, requires bending down three times, head touching the ground, knees on the ground. After the requisite kowtows, the family eats and drinks everything, including items set before the ancestors. Then they tear sheets of fake money or incense paper, put them on the graves, and burn them. If firecrackers are allowed, lots of them are ignited to make sure the ancestors know they are there.

At this festival, elders, who are always concerned about health, and women, whose charge it is to keep festivals such as this one, wear a small piece of willow in their hair to guard against sickness. It also prevents evil spirits from doing them harm. Should no family member be able to pay these respects, a nonfamily member can be sent to tend to these activities and invite the ancestors home to where the family's ancestral tablets rest.

There are new reasons to celebrate the Qing Ming, also called the Festival of the Tombs Day. One is to plant trees, and another to remember and practice an ancient ceremony that welcomes increasing light and additional warmth from the sun. In ancient times, this ceremony may have also included a wish to induce rain for spring planting, but that tradition seems to be lost.

Moon Festival

All full moons are times of celebration. However, the night of the full moon on the fifteenth day of the eighth month is the most important one. Perhaps it began as a mid-autumn harvest festival when people honored the moon and put melons and fruits in their courtyards. In ancient times, rich and noble families gave presents to one another on this occasion. They gave various fruits and moon cakes called *yuehbing,* and at the end of the holiday they burned a poster, a rabbit's effigy.

The items in the courtyards were for the Goddess of the Moon, a lady called Chang-E. Her husband, an archer named Yi, saved the earth from the scorching sun. He is said to have shot down nine different suns. Next to her offerings of yellow beans were set out for the Jade Moon Rabbit. He is said to sit under a cassia tree pounding gold, jade, and jewels into precious elixirs of immortality. It was his picture that was burned.

At early harvest festivals, before the common practice of making moon cakes, officials sent gifts of mirrors resembling the moon to more senior officials. Eventually, they made dew-collecting basins and fill them with something called flirting with the moon broth. Its ingredients are not known. Both of these are prayer symbols for the delay of wet weather. With good harvests, ordinary people could feast and rejoice over their good fortune— that is, until the Mongol rulers decreed that every 10 families had to support one of their officials. This made the people quite angry.

Modern origins of this holiday began in the fourteenth century, when people baked moon cakes and put a small piece of paper in those intended for loyal Chinese. The paper indicated the time and place to meet and start a rebellion to overthrow the garrison in Beijing. Many obeyed. The overthrow succeeded and eventually rid the country of the Mongolians then ruling China. It also ended the Yuan Dynasty and began the dynasty called Ming in the year 1368.

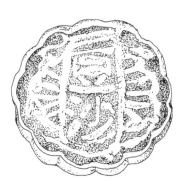

Moon cake.

Women adore celebrating this festival. One reason is that the moon is *yin* and believed to have female characteristics. Women pay their respects to its goddess with food, candles, and incense. The Chinese believe the sun to be *yang* or male; therefore men feel closer to the sun than to the moon. This day is also considered the Kitchen God's birthday. A saying advises men not to worship the Moon Goddess, women not to sacrifice to the Kitchen God, and men and women to honor one or the other on this day.

Birthday offerings set before the Kitchen God traditionally include apples, grapes, melons, peaches, and pomegranates, all fruits with special meanings. Apples and grapes symbolize prosperity; the seeds of melons and pomegranates are wishes for the many children most Chinese families would like to have; and the peaches are wishes for longevity. These three wishes are Chinese people's most common desires.

Young people and children also adore this festival. Some gather in parks, where they sing and eat meals and snacks under the full moon. This is a good time for matchmaking. The man in the moon, called *Yueh Lao*, ties couples together with invisible red threads. It is customary for men and women to write poetry, particularly love poems.

Round cakes looking like a full moon are still made on every anniversary of this moon holiday. They remind people of the rebellion. They are filled with sugar paste, fruit and/or nut stuffings, seeds such as the lotus, beans made into a paste, or any other heavy filling. Moon cakes are usually made with gray or white flour because those with yellow flour might be thought to belong to the sun. The larger round cakes often have different fillings.

Traditional moon cakes have designs on top that represent what is inside. Some are stamped in red with a word that indicates their contents. Most are hand-shaped, their exterior a thin dough lining the wooden form each one is made in. This dough is filled; the overhanging dough is sealed; and the cake is knocked out of the mold onto trays, glazed, stamped, and then baked. Most moon cakes are about three inches in diameter and half that thick, though they can be of any size and any design. Some are made in the shape of *Shou*, the God of Prosperity, who carries a scepter in his hand; *Fu*, the God of Happiness, who carries an incense burner and wears a green robe with storks embroidered on it; or *Lu*, the God of Longevity, whose white beard is near the peach in his hand. Some are in the shape of birds, animals, and even houses; others are stylized; and some have beautiful scenes or lovely people. Whatever the design, first it must be carved in wood, making a mold to put dough and filling in.

Moon cake fillings often are regional. In the north, they can be white sugar paste, brown sugar paste, or both. The Chinese in the south prefer their moon cakes filled with nuts, fruits, spices, seeds, even quail and duck eggs. Some temples stack 13 moon cakes to recognize and celebrate the years that have an intercalary month.

Restaurants and bakeries nowadays make moon cakes all year long, some shaped like fish, crabs, lions, and dragons. People say moon cakes are now used for promoting harmony among men. Earlier they were to promote harmony between man and the moon. Whatever their purpose, moon cakes are given as gifts on this day, as are paper lanterns, small statues of animals, and toys. There is something to delight children and adults alike.

Moon cakes are not the only foods used as gifts now. So are melons, pomelos, yams, peanuts, water caltrops, and tea. Moon cakes, fruits, and nuts symbolize fullness of family life, vigor, numerous progeny, and longevity. Many are put on altars along with cosmetics, particularly face powder, to invoke blessings on their female devotees. They symbolize wishes to have handsome, healthy, intelligent children.

These wishes for children may be rooted in a moon dream about a Han Dynasty queen who saw the moon entering her womb at this harvest festival. Later she gave birth to a son who, when he grew up, learned of her dreams. She told him the sun and moon come from the essence of *yang* and *yin* as emblems of rank and nobility. Thus, he knew that her dreams meant that her sons and grandsons would flourish.

Dragon Boat Festival

This Upright Sun Festival, as it is also called, is celebrated on the fifth day of the fifth month, and in Chinese is called the *Tuan Wu* holiday. In another time, noblemen gave gifts to one another. Some gave cakes made with apricots, cherries, mulberries, peaches, or water chestnuts; others gave rose cakes; and still others gave cakes whose tops illustrated the five poisonous animals: the centipede, lizard, scorpion, snake, and toad. The likeness of one or the other was a spiritual wish that these creatures could be avoided.

The Dragon Boat Festival is a summer festival that features boat races to honor those who tried to save a beloved scholar-statesman-poet named Qu Yuan. He served in the time of the Warring States (403–221 B.C.E.). The boats used are narrow. Each one has a carved dragon on the bow and one large drum set in the stern. A drummer keeps the two dozen or more oarsmen in one boat rowing together, and the drum's noise is said to frighten away anyone who would harm Qu Yuan. Those watching these races drink protective wines and eat special dumplings.

A story is told that Qu Yuan jumped into a river circa 295 B.C.E., very distressed to learn that he had earned the king's displeasure and was to be exiled. Another tale calls him a statesman who was a victim of palace politics. Whichever is accurate, he did throw himself into a nearby river on the fifth day of the fifth month. Local people used their boats to try to save him. They were unsuccessful. So they made and threw packages of *zongzi* to divert any predatory sea creature from eating him. These *zongzi* pitched into the river were made of cooked sticky rice mixed with meat and stuffed into pieces of bamboo to keep them together.

After this, his mourning became an annual festival. Tradition has it that the rice was originally put into bamboo tubes, closed with lily leaves, and tied with colored silk thread to assure that the scaly dragon would not steal them. These days, the dumplings are triangular and wrapped in bamboo leaves. Leaf strips or strings hold them together.

These tribute foods generally have one of three fillings. The first is made of meat, mostly pork, mixed with rice and chestnuts. A second kind is rice and beans with a bit of sapan wood preserved in an alkaline solution such as lye; it is to act as an evil-dispelling agent. The third type is rice powder mixed with pomegranate juice and honey. The last two kinds are said to have medicinal properties that increase as they age. They are recommended for dysentery. Like moon cakes of the previous festival, these dumplings are popular year-round and now can be purchased in many Asian markets ready for cooking. Some folks freeze theirs on the holiday and cook them after it.

Protective wine was part of the festival. Some of it was dried and painted on foreheads, noses, even ears of children. It was to ward off poisonous creatures. Some was used wet for writing the character *wang* or *guowang*, which means king. It was also painted on foreheads for the same purpose. Leaves of calamus and mugwort, two ancient plants, were dipped in wine and put on the gates of homes, also to ward off evil. The calamus looks like swords, and mugwort leaves resemble tigers, both clearly evil items. All the wine-related activities were protectors against one calamity or another.

Double Ninth Festival

This Hill Climbing Festival, known also as the Double Ninth, is celebrated on the ninth day of the ninth month. It is a day go to the countryside, preferably up a hill, and bring along foods and beverages such as roast meat, wine, and cakes. On this festival, people make time to hike, eat, read poetry to one another, and do things to stay healthy. Visiting a temple set on a hill or mountain is an appropriate thing to do. Many do that on this day eating roast pig or roast goat. Northerners would be more apt to have the roast goat or maybe some roast lamb, while southerners would prefer the roast pig.

This holiday began in the late Han Dynasty, but for a different reason. A well-known martial arts gentleman who was a Daoist magician told a friend to leave home and take his family to the hills, saying that if he didn't, something dreadful would happen. It did—that is, all his animals suffered a violent death. This man had advised his friend to take chrysanthemum wine when he left home because this flower looks like the sun and is said to have life-giving properties.

With that in mind, people now take that wine, pickled crabs, and special fruits such as persimmons, quince, and red hawthorns. Some call this Vegetarian Cult Day and eat a dry black vegetable dish made from hair seaweed, also called hair vegetable, at their hillside picnic. The Chinese call it *fatsai* and eat this vegetable because its name sounds like words meaning to grow prosperous. As this is not a usual vacation day, only a few people get to celebrate it in the traditional manner. Some just celebrate by eating the special foods after work.

Not everyone eats only vegetables on this particular holiday. Meat abstinence began in China thousands of years ago when the legendary emperor Huang Di said that one secret of long life was fasting, and another avoiding meat. Many think that admonition enough to not eat meat, at least on this particular holiday. Others, particularly Buddhists, deem eating meat always a sin.

A story is told about a pious vegetarian son who was ill. His mother made him a meat soup to help him recover. They ate it together. He got well. She denied eating the soup's meat and said that if she had, she deserved a trip to hell. An instant after saying this, she was about to be taken away. Her son offered to change places and take her punishment. At that second, Buddha himself came to his rescue. That act may be why some people eat no meat that day or ever.

Winter Solstice

This holiday is also called Eighth of the Twelfth Month Gruel Day. It is the time to celebrate the winter solstice and honor the five spirits of the house: the Gods of the Door, Main Gate, Kitchen Stove, Center of the House, and Alley. The twelfth month is called the *La* month. A special gruel is made to eat on the eighth day of this month. The day before, millet, two kinds of rice, water chestnuts, regular chestnuts, small red beans, and dates have their seed coats removed. They are then soaked and readied. Almonds, melon seeds, peanuts, hazelnuts, and pine seeds are measured and readied too. On the eighth day these are mixed together, with white and red sugar and raisins added, then cooked. When done, it is called *laba*, and it is offered to the ancestors, taken to the temple and offered to Buddha, and then offered to friends and relatives. The family eats *laba* with pickled cabbage, and it is said that the quality of the cabbage determines the future prosperity of the household.

Other Festivals

In ancient times there were a plethora of reasons and occasions to pay filial duty to one's ancestors, times to celebrate various gods, and times to make merry for other reasons. In Beijing alone, there were many dozen celebration and festival days. One month had only 5, another 6, another 7, two had 8, and the rest had 10 or more. The first lunar month had 21, the last had 23. All were opportunities and reasons to feast or eat special foods, but most have been forgotten. Rare is one still celebrated, other than by temple folk.

Many of these days showed respect for filial piety; others celebrated people of different ages, though most were for the young and the elderly. Some were to honor seasonal things such as skating and the cutting of ice, and others showed respect for animals, plants, and places. For example, the tenth month included a celebration for kites, shuttlecocks, and other toys. One celebration was for Manchu cakes, another for birds of the season; one was a day honoring the troops; one was for the sale of calendars;

and one for the lighting of fires. Fifteen of these 145 Beijing festivals specifically mention food. Some of the foods were elm-seed cakes, pomegranates and oleander, sweet melons, ice seeds, sour prune drink, water chestnuts, chicken-head seeds, dates and grapes, nine-jointed lotus roots, lotus petals, watermelons, flower cakes, fruits and foods of the season, chestnuts, sweet potatoes, various candies, bamboo shoots, silver fish, boiled gruel, and New Year's pudding.

The kinds of dishes served, restaurants where they might be eaten, and the number and kinds of dishes at any festival were indications of the wealth and intentions of the host. People showed appreciation of the finest edibles to eat or offer to "the deities at the back of the house." These deities were homeless roaming spirits with no family or friends to venerate them. To honor them people put foods at their rear doors as their offerings. Not all holidays were for offerings; some were outright times of enjoyment, no reasons given.

Major festivals, such as those listed above, and even minor ones were excuses to enjoy a family feast or a banquet, be it the first of the month, the equinox, a wedding, an anniversary, a special birthday, or to honor gods and goddesses. Differences of opinion exist on how any festival should be practiced. These depend upon where one lives, ethnic and regional heritage, and the way ancestors may have practiced that particular festival. For example, if one eats roast pig at a wedding or gives a roast pig to one's parents-in-law as a funeral gift, that can be a local, regional, or cultural food behavior. No matter the food gift, its quality demonstrates regard for those who eat it. To the Chinese, foods are an ostentatious display of wealth and show that the giver really does care about the receiver.

FAMILY CELEBRATIONS

Family events honor important occasions in the life-cycle. Most important is the birth of a son because it assures continuance of the family tree. Birth of a girl, now that the government encourages and sometimes allows only one child, is taking on increased importance. So are all birthdays, even though special ones were the only times to celebrate. They and weddings and funerals have major dining components that honor family.

Births

The birth of a child, particularly a son, is still an important event. One month after it, eggs are colored red and given to family and friends, sometimes to all in the village. They announce and celebrate this auspicious event (*manyue*). The parents of the mother of the newborn are sent nine red eggs. They and others are given cakes of glutinous rice filled with mung bean paste or ground peanuts, and gifts of rice. The baby's gender can be announced by the shape of the cake. Tortoise-shaped and round cakes announce a male child, and peach-shaped cakes a baby girl.

At the one-month festivity, many foods are given; some colored yellow to wish gold and other riches for the tiny tyke. This event is the first time mother and baby are allowed to leave the bedroom. It is also the first time the mother washes her hair after giving birth. Hard-cooked red eggs are sent and others eaten this day to symbolize mother and baby's life and energy. Bright and attention-getting, the eggs also symbolize courage. In ancient times, some families were sent more than one egg. Even numbers meant a girl. Odd ones, which are considered luckier numbers, said it was a boy.

Birthdays

Traditionally, Chinese celebrate a child's coming into the world when the child is one month old, and they celebrate again when the child reaches the age of two. To them that is 12 months after birth. That calculation is because they considered the baby one year old if it lives to the end of the first month. At the first anniversary of birth, they celebrate the child's second birthday, and so on. Years ago, many children died soon after birth, so waiting a month was prudent, as was the giving of eggs symbolizing life and energy for the baby. After the first or second birthday, it was not common to celebrate a birthday each year because calling attention to it might invite evil spirits. Now parents say ignoring it might do likewise. The solution is to have the immediate family gather and eat long noodles, wishing for long life. Other dishes can accompany the noodles, but the long-life noodle dish must be the last dish at that meal. The kind of noodles vary; they can be made of rice, wheat, even bean flour, and can be yellow or white. Most likely they will be bathed in the birthday person's favorite sauce.

Once a year, a birthday for everyone is celebrated communally. It is on the seventh day of the New Year. Two cooked eggs are served to each person, along with noodles and sugar. The noodles, sugar, and eggs wish for a long, sweet life and the courage to live it fully. Other birthday foods might include a roast pig, sweetened steamed bread, dumplings, and other filled foods such as egg rolls. The Chinese use of noodles and eggs at birthdays is an ancient custom; it has been recorded frequently since the Han Dynasty (206 B.C.E. to 220 C.E.).

Weddings

Marriage celebrations begin when a couple is engaged. Four-colored Chinese biscuits, sometimes named *call cakes*, are given with other foods to announce an upcoming marriage. They can be given months ahead because many preparations are needed. Some families still receive a bride price from the groom or his family in return for dowry received. Current government regulations frown on that, but it is still practiced in some places in China. One or more animals and other foods, including pre-wedding cakes, dried fruits, even a cock, a hen, a goose, and/or a gander, can be sent to the bride's family. Well-to-do families send beautifully decorated pre-wedding cakes with wheat-flour dolls adorning them long before the event. And for the event, the groom's family sends for the bride. A red carriage is sent to bring the bride to the groom's house, as was traditionally done. Some send this before and others send for the bride on the wedding day.

These pre-wedding cakes, sometimes just called wedding cakes, are an inch or two thick, filled with fruits and nuts, and quite heavy. Before the event, the groom's family also sends noodles and items in groups of five, such as sweet bean paste biscuits, roasted nuts, peanut cakes, and glutinous rice cakes. They send them in fives because five is one of China's many lucky numbers. Some cakes are made with grains put together with caramelized sugar; they look like Rice Krispies. They also send lots of candies, sweetened fruits, nuts, and seeds. People from different parts of the country may not make round cakes; some make them five-sided, others hexagonal or octagonal, and others can roll them so they look like rolls of money.

On the wedding day itself, a lantern wishing double happiness is found hanging in the room set aside for the newlyweds. After the bride arrives at her new home, she makes tea for her new in-laws. Then she goes to that room to wait for her husband. Her new home has traditionally been a room in the groom's parent's home. The bride's job is to cook for and serve not only her new husband but also his parents. When friends come to honor bride and groom on the wedding day or the next day, the newly married couple awaits these friends in the bridal chamber and are served fruit and tea by them. The bride and groom are subject to much teasing the night they are married, before they can consummate their marriage.

Funerals

The Chinese believe that when and how one dies is determined at birth. They think that death is one of the most important events in life because it allows reverence for ancestors. An old Chinese book called *Greater Record of Mourning Rites* details appropriate behaviors at the time of death and calls death a return journey to where the person came from and their ancestors.

The Chinese do not bury their parents until an auspicious place is found to inter them and set up their ancestral tablets. Funeral rites used to last for 49 days before the body was buried. When the actual burial comes, sons and nowadays daughters must cry profusely. All members of the immediate family mourn for three additional years.

One of the few food behaviors mentioned in this mourning rites volume has to do with putting dried fish near the coffin at the funeral, along with bundles of wood, uncooked rice, salt, and oil. These essentials are for the afterlife. They are to keep the deceased's spirits from being hungry and speak to the fact that the family will no longer be cooking for the person.

Being buried well is very important to the Chinese. While still alive a person selects coffin or burial urn and burial clothing. The hallway near the front door is a typical place to keep the coffin until needed; it is also where the coffin used to stay until the burial occurred. This practice, observed since Han Dynasty times, allowed everyone to see how fine a coffin has been selected.

Ceremonial food offerings discovered in Neolithic tombs include Chinese celery, cassia, and *fagara*. The last two items are spices better known as Chinese cinnamon and Sichuan pepper. Along with them, a person's prize possessions were taken in a processional to the burial location and put in the tomb. Recently excavated tombs show replicas of items thought needed in the afterlife, such as boats, farm animals, houses, magicians, musicians, and stoves.

As they aged or when illness predicted imminent death, people began their funerary preparations. The rich selected coffins and items at considerable cost. The less affluent might pay for a fine urn by scrimping and saving. They did so to not embarrass themselves or their families. All spent the most they could afford. One person who died sometime during the Han Dynasty and was found in 1968 was buried in a jade body suit. That is the richest funeral attire found to date.

After the funeral and the burial, it is customary to hold a funeral banquet. Spouse, eldest son, and/or all the children invite everyone to celebrate the deceased's return to heaven. It is not uncommon for family and friends to give money to the family of the deceased to help defray the costs of this elaborate feast. Providing a paltry meal would not be a propitious way to send off a relative.

RECIPES FOR SPECIAL OCCASIONS

The Chinese have foods associated with many of their special occasions. Probably the most frequently eaten food item is the New Year cake. For birthdays everyone enjoys long noodles. For the Dragon Boat Festival, most popular are the bamboo leaf wrapped dumplings. At Winter Solstice people enjoy glutinous rice dumplings in broth. At the mid-autumn Moon Festival, they eat moon cakes.

New Year Cake Patties

- 10 Chinese black mushrooms, soaked in warm water for 20 minutes
- 1/2 cup raw shrimp, diced into one-eighth-inch pieces
- 1 tablespoon corn or peanut oil
- 1/4 cup Yunnan or Smithfield ham, diced into one-eighth-inch pieces
- 10 water chestnuts, minced
- 1 teaspoon sugar
- 1/2 teaspoon salt
- 2 cups glutinous rice flour
- 2 cups corn or peanut oil
- 1 scallion, minced

1. Remove stems from the mushrooms, and dice them into one-eighth-inch pieces, then mix with the shrimp.
2. Heat the oil, and fry the mushroom and shrimp mixture for 1 minute. Add ham and water chestnuts and fry a minute longer. Remove pan from heat and allow to cool, then add the sugar and salt.
3. Put glutinous rice flour in a bowl, and mix with two-thirds of a cup of very hot, but not boiling, water until totally wet. Allow to cool, then make into 20 balls of dough. Flatten each on a small sheet of wax paper or plastic wrap with your hand. Make them as thin as possible.
4. Put one tablespoon mushroom mixture on one side of each rice patty and a small amount of the minced scallion. Fold the other half over it, and press the edges together gently.

5. Heat oil. Remove five patties from the paper and fry them until golden brown, then drain them on paper towels. Repeat until all are fried and drained. Serve hot, warm, or at room temperature.

Long-Life Noodles with Brown Bean Sauce

- 1 pound fresh long noodles
- 8 Chinese black mushrooms, soaked for 20 minutes in warm water
- 2 tablespoons brown bean sauce, mashed thoroughly
- 1 clove garlic, minced
- 2 slices fresh ginger, minced
- 1/4 teaspoon chili sauce with garlic
- 1/2 pound boneless chuck or flank steak, thinly sliced, then slivered
- 2 tablespoons hoisin sauce
- 1/2 teaspoon sugar
- 2 tablespoons dark soy sauce
- 1 tablespoon water chestnut, yam, or arrowroot flour
- 3 tablespoons corn or peanut oil

1. Boil long noodles for up to 5 minutes, testing each minute or so. Remove and drain when cooked through but not too soft. Reserve 1/2 cup of the noodle water.
2. Drain the mushrooms, then squeeze the water from them and set them aside. Remove mushroom stems, and thinly slice them.
3. Mix bean sauce, garlic, ginger, and chili sauce, and allow to set for 10 minutes.
4. Mix steak, hoisin sauce, sugar, soy sauce, and flour, and allow to marinate for 10 minutes.
5. Heat wok or fry pan, add oil, and when hot add the bean sauce mixture and stir for half a minute before adding the mushrooms. Let them fry for 1 minute, then add the meat mixture and stir-fry for 2 minutes or just until the meat is no longer pink. Add the noodle water and cook this for 3 minutes, then pour sauce over the hot noodles and bring this to the table. Toss, then eat: The birthday person is served the first portion.

Dragon Boat Festival Dumplings

- 1/2 cup shelled peanuts, paper skins removed, soaked for 12 hours in cold water
- 8 Chinese black mushrooms, soaked for 20 minutes in warm water

- 2 tablespoons dried shrimp, soaked in warm water for half an hour, then minced
- 1/2 pound boneless pork, diced into one-quarter-inch cubes
- 2 tablespoons corn or peanut oil
- 2 cups raw glutinous rice
- 1 tablespoon thin soy sauce
- 1 teaspoon dark soy sauce
- 1/2 teaspoon mixed ground black and white pepper
- 1/4 teaspoon coarse salt
- 1/2 cup chicken or beef broth
- 24 bamboo leaves, soaked in warm water until soft, about an hour
- straw or white twine

1. Rinse, drain, then coarsely mince the peanuts and set aside.
2. Squeeze water from the mushrooms and set aside. Remove their stems, and mince them coarsely, then mix with the peanuts and the shrimp.
3. Heat oil and fry the pork for 2 minutes, add the mushroom mixture and stir-fry for 1 minute, then remove from the pan, leaving remaining oil in the pan; set aside to cool.
4. Fry the rice in the remaining oil for one minute. Then add the soy sauces, peppers and salt, broth, and 1/2 cup of the reserved mushroom water. Stir, then cover and simmer on very low heat until the rice is cooked. If needed, add another quarter cup of remaining mushroom water, just enough so that it is absorbed by the rice. Allow the rice to cool until it can be handled.
5. Put two bamboo leaves slightly overlapping, inside up, and fold down the top quarter of them, making a cuplike shape. Put 4 tablespoons of rice onto this cup. Put another leaf crosswise where the rice ends. Top the rice with two tablespoons of the meat mixture, cover with four more tablespoons of rice, and fold leaves over each other so that you get a solid triangle, and seal the contents. Tie with straw or twine and repeat until all leaves and mixtures are used up.
6. Steam these dumplings over rapidly boiling water for 90 minutes and serve. Or refrigerate and resteam them for 40 additional minutes, then serve. They last three days in the refrigerator. If they are frozen, they need to be resteamed for an hour.

Winter Solstice Soup

- 1/4 pound black sesame seeds
- 1/2 cup rice, soaked for two hours, then drained

- 1/4 cup sugar
- 1 cup glutinous rice flour
- 1 teaspoon corn oil
- 1/4 pound ground pork
- 1/4 teaspoon sesame oil
- 1/4 teaspoon ground black pepper
- 1 tablespoon minced shallots
- 1 teaspoon cornstarch

1. Bake sesame seeds in a low oven until fragrant, then grind in a blender with the soaked rice and 1/2 cup water. Add 6 cups cold water and the sugar, and simmer this soup for half an hour.
2. Mix glutinous rice flour with 1/2 cup boiling water and allow to cool. Then wet hands and knead the dough for 5 minutes. Allow to rest for 10 minutes, and knead again for another minute or two. Make gumball-sized balls and set aside, covered, until ready to use.
3. Heat corn oil, fry the pork, sesame oil, pepper, and shallots for 1 minute, then add cornstarch and set aside to cool.
4. Make indentation in each ball, and fill with a teaspoon of the pork filling. Squeeze the rice dough around this to seal it inside, and reroll so that each one is again round. Let these rest for one hour, covered, in the refrigerator.
5. Boil in two quarts of water for several minutes until they float, then remove them, putting them into the sesame seed soup. Simmer, then serve.

Sweetened Moon Cakes

- 1/2 cup minced Yunnan or Smithfield ham
- 1/2 cup shredded coconut
- 1 1/2 cups sugar
- 1/8 cup white sesame seeds, toasted
- 1/8 cup hulled sunflower or watermelon seeds, toasted
- 1 cup corn or peanut oil
- 1 uncooked pie crust, rolled out and ready for two dozen four-inch pies
- moon-cake mold or 24 disposable four-inch aluminum pie plates

1. Mix ham, coconut, sugar, and both kinds of seeds.
2. Heat wok or fry pan, add oil and heat that before adding the ham mixture. Fry ham mixture for 1 minute, then cool.

3. Press pie crust dough into a wooden moon cake mold, covering bottom and sides, then fill with two tablespoons cooled filling, put piece of dough on top, seal by crimping by hand and tucking the crimps into the top mold edging. Knock this out of the mold upside down onto a cookie sheet, and repeat until done. Or put bottom crust into a small pie pan, fill as indicated, and put top crust over it, seal, crimping with a fork.

4. Bake in a 400 degree oven for 20 minutes until crust is golden brown, remove, cool, then serve.

8

Diet and Health

The Chinese believe that appropriate food selection is important for maintaining good health. For thousands of years they have investigated and developed elaborate traditions about food consumption and medicinal cooking, including the use of herbs. To them, cooking and eating are healing arts. They believe that food is medicine and medicine is food. Therefore, eating good foods ensures and prolongs life, and the right amount of each food group and which combinations should be consumed together are important considerations.

They believe that grains are the foundation of the diet. Meats, fruits, and vegetables should supplement grains, not take their place or exceed their consumption. They think beverages, particularly soup, should be consumed with foods at main meals. Some of this information was discussed in earlier chapters. All of it relates to the way they think about food, nutrition, and health. Their beliefs were developed and written about thousands of years ago.

ANCIENT CONSIDERATIONS

At least since 3000 B.C.E., the Chinese explained all phenomena of nature as symbolic forces in fixed patterns. They believe that these forces interact and work with or against other forces. Though the exact date of publication is not sure, one of the earliest written volumes about Chinese diet, nutrition, and health is the *Yellow Emperor's Classic of Medicine*, or

Huangdi Nei Jing. To the Chinese, it is an essential text of health and healing.[1]

Some think the Yellow Emperor isreal; others say he is mythical. All agree that no one person could do all he is credited with. One such credit is he is the father of medicine, diet, and health. Another is that he is also said to be Shennong (in earlier times often spelled Shen Nung), the King of Farming, who tested foods for their health effects. Historians, archeologists, and others who study the past believe he probably did exist. However, they believe that he alone did not write this tome credited to him. Maybe the true authors, who will forever remain nameless, got together and wrote the *Huangdi Nei Jing* and attributed it to him.

The *Yellow Emperor's Classic of Medicine* comprises 18 volumes with 162 chapters. It is a two-part set of observations that some people simply call *Nei Jing* for short. In English it is known by several names, a few of which are the *Yellow Emperor's Classic,* the *Classic of Internal Medicine,* and the *Yellow Emperor's Medicinal Classic.*

Some editions claim to be and probably are the original. They read like a dialogue between the Yellow Emperor and Qi Bo, his chief counsel and imperial physician. In them, the first half deals with anatomy, physiology, and pathology. These are called *Su Wen,* or *Plain* or *Ordinary Questions.* The second half, called *Zhen Jing* or *Ling Shu,* has chapters that discuss acupuncture, *qi,* and more. These parts probably reached their present form by the end of the Warring States period in 221 B.C.E. A third part is called *Tai Su* or *Great Purity.* That section, scholars believe, was added in the seventh century C.E.

In the first part of this classic, the emperor questions his doctor about origins of disease. He writes about everything as under the influence of four seasons and interactions of *yin* and *yang.* He wonders whether people understand the extent of these influences. The physician goes beyond telling his sovereign that his are excellent questions. He describes the five natural influences of dryness, wind, cold, heat, and humidity and indicates that each has an effect on the internal solid organs and each imparts a particular flavor—pungent, sour, salty, bitter, or sweet (see Table 8.1). Also discussed are plants including herbs, animals, and minerals. They are from land and sea, and are components of diet and health, and are also discussed.

Besides this medicinal text, there are several thousand traditional medicinal texts, many extant but spoken about in later books. A few are famous, including another attributed to Shennong. It was done shortly after the *Nie Jing* and is called the *Shen Nung Ben Cao Jing,* or *Shennong's Classic Materia Medica—Materia Medica* for short. This book may be the earli-

Table 8.1
Five Tastes and Their Actions

Taste	Believed Action
Sweet	Clears toxins
	Harmonizes drug actions
Sour	Contracts
	Alleviates sweating related to deficiencies
Salty	Softens and eliminates
	Lubricates large intestine
	Combats swelling in lymph system
Bitter	Activates blood
	Sends Qi (energy) downward
	Assists urinary function
Pungent	Disperses foods

est systematic pharmacology volume to have survived. It contains instructions on how to process as it prescribes 365 different drugs. They are divided according to their toxicity and referred to as superior, common, and inferior.

In the Zhou Dynasty (1045 to 221 B.C.E.) another book had a large impact on Chinese food and medicine. It was the *Zhou Li* or *Rituals of Zhou*. It prescribed foods and medicine and indicated that dietitians attached to the court are among the highest class of medical personnel. It reports a large number of specialized cooks and details the importance of nutritional medicine and culinary arts in and outside of the imperial household. Its contents are considered important; they are characteristic of Chinese civilization's medical and food thoughts from earliest times to today.

Other well-known works, most written later, discuss drugs, tell how to evaluate the pulse and conduct clinical examinations, examine symptoms and treatments for various diseases, and so on. Better-known ones have been revised many times. They change their names, so it is difficult to tell where and when the first one was written. The *Materia Medica* had a major revision in 1578 by Chen Lixi. It was translated as *The Chinese Pharmacopoeia* or *Compendium of Materia Medica*. Later it became a four-volume tome with many of the original 365 medicinals and the described therapeutic properties of 1,892 different kinds of medicines. It includes more than 1,100 prescriptions, all detailed; has more than 1,100 illustrations; and is still used. Many editions have various additions and omissions, and tell how some medicines should be consumed and that a few should only be taken when absolutely needed and in very small quantities.

Diet, nutrition, food, and herbs remain part of traditional Chinese medicine, known by its initials TCM. It is the oldest practicing medical system in the world, and many of its beliefs are unique to the Chinese culture. Its approach of "you are what you eat" truly speaks to China's ancient food and health traditions.

Recently, archeologists have unearthed traces of medicinal plants and medical artifacts from Shang Dynasty tombs from 1600 to 1045 B.C.E. They confirm the early medicinal practices and believe that some even date from Neolithic periods. The archeologists discovered early forms of treatment with acupuncture needles and believe that their purpose was to send messages to the brain and other vital organs. They found indications of herb-burning on acupuncture needles, a practice now called moxibustion. And they unearthed medicinal liquors. The oracle bones, silk rolls with writing on them, and other findings confirm a strong body-centered approach to China's ancient health traditions.

ILLNESS IS DISHARMONY

Then and now, the Chinese believe that food relates to health and that illness is a disharmony within the body. They believe that maintaining harmony and balance insures health and longevity. When this balance goes awry, they see a need to restore it to make a person's body work more efficiently. This, they say, helps the body heal itself. The Chinese still use traditional and herbal medicinal efforts to restore the body's harmony and balance.

More important, the Chinese pay attention to the body long before illness sets in. They use food as preventive medicine and as restorative medicine. To them, food is healing cuisine. The correct foods aid life and health and assure longevity. The science of diet therapy is a respected component of their medical and pharmacological practices.

Confucius (551–479 B.C.E.), a great sage, used and expanded this thinking 25 centuries after the *Yellow Emperor* in a volume attributed to him called the *Book of Songs*. He wrote about foods, rules and ethics, and what and how to eat. He explored the principles of balance and gave examples of specific foods with health implications. He expanded upon the interplay of positive and negative, dominant and recessive, better known as the opposing forces of *yin* and *yang*. He considered their duality important for order and harmony in the universe and in the human being. He explained they were not rigidly fixed but rather relationships reflecting dynamic interactions, interpretations of everything on earth and in the heavens. He saw the *Yellow Emperor* as reflection of diet therapy and medical knowledge before the twenty-first century B.C.E. It was pre-Qin Dynasty, and its concepts, he mused, underlie most aspects of Chinese existence, including medicine and health.

Confucius postulated that *yin* and *yang* work with the five elements or five phases of wood, fire, earth, metal, and water. He believed that they and the five virtues of benevolence, justice, propriety, sincerity, and wisdom were cosmic forces exerting additional effects on things and more importantly on the eternal cycle of life. Confucius and others saw the five elements as most important because they were the basis of science and cosmology. They were part of everything, including nutrition, health, and medicine.

Why five? The Chinese like to divide things into groups, many having five items. The number five is thought to be lucky because it is uneven and male. Westerners see four points on a compass—north, south, east, and west—but the Chinese see five directions including east, south, center, west, and north. They envision many other groups of five, including five colors of: black, green, red, white, and yellow; and five sacrificial animals to place on their alters—the ox, goat, pig, dog, and fowl. They have five general animal classes with feathers, with shells, with scales, with hair, and naked. They discuss five body fluids of tears, sweat, saliva, mucus, and urine, and speak of the five emotions of anger, joy/fright, worry, sadness/grief, and fear. Inside a person's body, they believe, are five solid organs of: liver, heart, spleen, lung, and kidney; five hollow organs of: gallbladder, small intestine, stomach, large intestine, and bladder; and five bodily tissues of: tendons, blood vessels, muscles, skin, and bone. They also think of five pures that include moon, water, pine tree, bamboo, and plum tree; and even five classics of their literature: the *Book of Documents* or *Shujing*, the *Book of Songs* or *Shijing*, the *Book of Changes* or *Yijing*, the *Book of Rites* or *Liji*, and *Book of Ceremonies* or *Yili*.[2]

There are additional groups of five with special importance for food, diet, nutrition, and health. One is the five aromas of rancid, scorched (or

Yin/yang.

burned), fragrant, rotten, and putrid. Westerners do not limit themselves to five and have at least two others: sweet and floral. Many believe there are even more. The Chinese also have five categories of healing herbs: grass, tree, worm, stone, and cereal. The Chinese word *herb* includes plants, animals, and minerals. Other items in fives are cereal categories (wheat, glutinous millet, millet, rice, and beans) and meat groups (chicken, mutton, beef, horse, and pork). And there are others.

Not everything is divided into fives. Major causes of disease in Western medicine include germs, mostly bacteria and viruses. In China's ancient medicinal thinking, there are four major causes: external, internal, food, and fatigue. The external causes are sixfold: wind, cold, summer heat, dampness, dryness, and fire. There are seven internal causes: anger, joy, worry, thought, sadness, fear, and shock. There are other groups important to the Chinese, but the most important revolves around and relates to the five elements. Understanding them is the basis of their medicinal thinking.

THE FIVE ELEMENTS

The five elements are important tenets of feeding and healing. They network and influence each other and are associated with many things, including parts of the body. Each element travels through the body using a particular meridian or pathway as it interacts with the others. Think of a five-pointed star with the element fire as the top point. Next envision lines around the points going from one to the next. This helps understand which element interacts with others. These are unidirectional, going from one exterior point to the next all the way around the star. Other interactions go across the star. Now think of drawing a five-pointed star without lifting the pencil off the paper. These other interactions are following those lines. There is another item of importance because in one of these lines an element generates or creates the other and in the other it subjugates or controls the next. Generating is going around the outside; controlling or subjugating is going across as when drawing the star.

The generating directions are fire to earth to metal to water to wood. The controlling directions are fire to metal to wood to earth to water and back to fire. When generating, think wood burns and generates or creates fire; fire produces ashes that decompose and generate earth; earth creates or generates metal taken from earth; when heated the metal becomes molten; and water helps things grow, generating or creating more wood. Alternately, when thinking controlling, think wood breaks up the earth as it grows; earth controls or subjugates water, keeping it in one place;

water subjugates or controls fire, putting it out; fire controls metal by melting it; and metal subjugates wood by cutting it.

Each of these elements is associated with body parts and body pathways.
Therefore, together these interrelationships determine not only direction
but also actions of food and herbs when consumed. For example, salty
herbs relate to the element water and include items such as seaweed. They
are cooling foods that act on the kidneys and the bladder. The Chinese
consider sweet foods and herbs tonifying and nutritious. They believe that
pungent ones mobilize and disperse blood and impact lungs and large intestine. Bitter ones are helpful with coughs and cooling, and they direct
things downward to the heart and small intestine. Sour or astringent foods
are used for sweating; they act on the liver and gallbladder.

Easier understanding can come when looking at the elements alphabetically, starting with earth. The Chinese say that earth is associated with late
summer, the sweet taste, the emotion of worry, and the body parts of stomach, spleen, mouth, and muscle. Fire is associated with summer, bitter taste,
joyous emotions, and heart, tongue, blood vessels, and small intestine.
Metal's season is fall, its taste pungent, its emotion grief, and the associated
body parts of lungs, nose, skin, and the large intestine. Water's season is winter, its taste is salty, emotion is fear; and its related body parts are bladder,
bones, ears, hair, and the kidneys. The fifth element is wood. Its season is
spring, taste is sour; and body parts are liver, gallbladder, tendons, and eyes.

Table 8.2 shows interactions of foods, organs, and elements. Begin by
looking at an element, then read down to see those things related to it.

Table 8.2
Chinese Fives: Foods, Organs, and Elements

Elements	Fire	Wood	Earth	Metal	Water
Yin Organs	Heart	Liver	Spleen	Lungs	Kidney
Yang Organs	Small intestine	Gallbladder	Stomach	Large intestine	Bladder
Colors	Red	Green	Yellow	White	Black
Aromas	Scorched	Rancid	Fragrant	Goatlike	Putrid
Animals	Horse	Chicken	Cow	Dog	Pig
Fruits	Apricot	Plum	Date	Pear	Chestnut
Grains	Sweet rice	Wheat	Millet	Rice	Legume
Tastes	Bitter	Sour	Sweet	Pungent	Salty
Herbs	Tangerine peel	Magnolia	Orange peel	Ginseng	Licorice
Other foods	Ginger	Sugar	Vinegar	Lemon	Salt

Then think of the star and other elements and items in that element's column, picturing directions around the circle, that is, the lines outside the star and those made across it when drawing it. This helps explain food's relationship to the body and vice versa. It also explains why food is medicine and medicine is food.

Examples of foods and medical conditions expand the five element theory. One example is salt's being associated with water and the kidneys. The Chinese believe that a salt deficiency leads to hardening of body tissues, while too much salt increases dampness. This is not simple or clearcut, and more specific knowledge is needed because not all salts function as one. Rock salt, thought to be salty, has different properties. It is considered a stimulant with the ability to soften enlarged lymph nodes and hard swellings. Garlic impacts *qi* or a person's vital energy. It increases the circulation of *qi*; its taste is pungent; it is associated with skin and lungs; and it increases sweating. Lemon is believed to be sour. It is associated with the liver; and it is believed helpful when someone has diarrhea.

The relationships are complex, as are most things medical. A medical person trained in TCM needs to determine and explain a correcting balance, therefore. This cannot be done just by looking at the element's star and the above table. People in China, and Chinese people living in countries where most people are not Chinese, view nutrition, health, and vitality using the above conceptualization. They may not be able to verbalize their behavior because many TCM prescriptions were initially learned under the tutelage of a TCM doctor or knowledgeable family member. They may use traditional foods and dishes to reflect this complicated balance, particularly when a condition such as pregnancy warrants.[3] When the condition is serious, even if they know these relationships, they will seek professional TCM diagnosis. They do not and one should not prescribe food cures for serious conditions without medical help.

The Chinese know that pungent and sweet are heating, and that other tastes are more cooling. They know that heating and cooling are not actual temperatures, but rather philosophic impacts foods and dishes can have. They know which body parts are stimulated by pungent tastes. They have familiarity with the idea that sour tastes cause contractions, bitter ones send vital energy or *qi* downward, and sweet ones tonify the body. They also know that all food is nutritious when eaten in proper balance, and that eating foods in proper balance means adequate amounts of grain foods with just a few other foods to accompany them. Because they view disease and related organs as weak and unable to resist, they compare them to excess use of alcohol. They see need of control to monitor their bodies. Chinese medical practitioners, TCM doctors, help them understand the five elements and help them put into practice ideas gleaned from the above table.

TCM doctors are trained to diagnose disease by interviewing patients, observing them, listening to them, feeling their pulse, and looking at the color and surface of the tongue. Interactions between many of the fives already mentioned are important parts of diagnosis. TCM doctors do not separate food and medicine because both maintain balance and assure a healthy life. They consider other traditional ways such as the Dao, and they prescribe *qigong* exercises and traditional medicinal foods. They worry about evil winds and think about the body's upward and downward movement of food and medicine. *Qi* is the spirit or invisible nature that surrounds and permeates everything. They prescribe ways to live in harmony with *qi*, a word that literally means breath or vital energy.

TCM practitioners use these and many other things to determine a person's general well-being and whether the person has a condition. They use the word *condition*, while Westerners think of the word *disease*. They visualize the location of the condition's imbalance; consider *yin* and *yang*, the five elements, and other fives; and recommend foods to bring the body back into harmony or balance. If the condition is thought to need additional intervention, they can recommend a herbal prescription as additional treatment, probably one from Shennong's *Ben Cao*.

ROLES OF FOOD AND HEALTH

People in the United States and other Western cultures discuss, some say obsess about, new healthy diets, fat-free foods, and the like. In China, medicinal conceptualizations have not changed for millennia. There, the role of cuisine, medicine, herbs, and health are as ancient as China itself. They are based on theories, already mentioned, about the body's *qi*, and the traditional Chinese medicine (TCM) components of acupuncture, herbology, reflexology, and feng shui.

While most items TCM practitioners prescribe are appropriate and healthy, they and their predecessors have concern for toxicity. Therefore, they give specific amounts of each ingredient in each prescription. They speak of concern about misuse of food and herbal items and know that some should be used in small amounts. This serious concern for toxicity and overuse began in early dynasties. Then, anyone who served toxic food faced a flogging of 90 strokes. For foods deliberately sold knowing they were poisonous, the punishment was banishment for a year. If the consumer died, the offender faced hanging. Chinese emperors deemed health and diet important, and they took strong steps such as these to keep themselves and their subjects healthy. They considered their dietary doctors near the top when classifying their medical staff and had nutritionists watch their food and serve it.

BALANCING DISHES AND DIET

It is hard to think of a Chinese dish that is not in some way based upon an ancient sage who designed or wrote about it. Most Chinese people know their history and the important people who influenced it. They know, from thousands of years of traditional practice, how to balance their diet. They discuss the body's energy or *qi*, but they do not think that food gives energy in the Western sense, but instead in the philosophical sense.

Chinese people know that *yang* means bright, dry, hot, and male and that *yin* means dark, moist, cold, and female. Each of these properties does not appear 100 percent in each food item, but all foods and health conditions, even organs and aromas, have some *yin* and some *yang* qualities. There is a predominance of one or the other in larger amounts in each food. They serve some *yin* or cold foods and some *yang* or hot foods at every meal. Foods can also be warm or cool, and a few are considered neutral. What is interesting is that Chinese people may not be able to tell which food is which, but they do put a meal together with foods of all of these qualities, and they know what foods not to serve when a person has a particular condition.[4]

FOODS THAT ARE *YIN* AND *YANG*

Yin or cold food-related items include eating, white foods, bland foods, and boiled foods. Examples of some foods that have mostly *yin* qualities are bean sprouts, cabbage, carrots, celery, congee, daylily, gingko, greens, and honey. *Yang* or hot food-related items include drinking, red foods, fried and broiled foods, and spicy foods. Some examples of foods having *yang* qualities are bamboo, beef, black pepper, chicken, cinnamon, eggs, eggplant, fatty meats, garlic, dried ginger, and more. Neutral, warm, and cool foods are few in number, but nonetheless important in the *yin/yang* dichotomy (Table 8.3). Neutral foods can include Chinese cabbage, figs, licorice, noodles, peanuts, red dates, shiitake mushrooms, and soft rice. Cool foods include asparagus, bean curd, bean sprouts, citrus peel, eggplant, and tangerines.

Some foods appear in more than one category, for several reasons. One is that China is a large country, and not everyone everywhere agrees with

Table 8.3
Yin (Cold), Yang (Hot), and Neutral Foods

Yin (Cold) Foods	Yang (Hot) Foods	Neutral Foods
Agar agar	Brown sugar	Carrots
Banana	Chicken egg	Cauliflower
Bean sprouts	Chicken fat	Cherries
Bitter melon	Garlic	Dates
Clams	Ginger	Frog
Crab	Green pepper	Hot boiled water
Cucumber	Goose meat	Pigeon meat
Dried Chinese black	Oyster sauce	Pine nuts
mushrooms	Pomegranate	Pork blood
Green tea	Pork liver	Red or black tea
Hawthorn	Sesame paste	Rice gruel
Shrimp	Sticky rice	Soy sauce
Silk squash	Taro	Tea eggs
Snake meat	Walnuts	Wheat flour
Soy bean milk	Wintermelon	

the items on every list. Other foods are both cooling and cold depending upon how they are prepared or what they are served with. There are regional variations and variations within groups, including some between Hand and various minority populations. There are variations about foods thought sweet, bitter, and in-between. Yet another consideration is that some food categorizations are seasonal, such as dog meat, snake meat, guava, and the like, which are thought better for men, and are recommended only in winter. There are a plethora of other reasons and situations.

Related beliefs, referred to by some as folk medicine, are practiced in India, the Near East, and many places in Europe and Central and South America. These practices are related but not the same. Heating and cooling foods and conditions remain in use in China not only because people believe they work, but also because they fit well with the yin/yang, five elements, qi, feng shui, and other systems that impact balance, order, and harmony.

OTHER DIETARY CONSIDERATIONS

Not all diet therapy is based upon yin and yang. Another concept is called bu or pu. All animals are bu to some degree, especially if they are steamed or simmered slowly and herbs added to the pot. Bu foods are easy to digest, rich in protein, and often have many minerals. This category of foods is strengthening and supplementing; it can put the body back into harmony.

Another consideration is foods that look like what they are supposed to strengthen. For example, because they look like a brain, walnuts are thought to increase intelligence. Jujubes, particularly the red ones, are considered to be good for the blood. Ginseng fits into this type of consideration and is the highest class and perhaps the most expensive of medicines. Some believe it looks like a person. It is said to help people, particularly as a *yang* energy tonic because it is thought to replace lost *qi* or vital energy. The Italian explorer Marco Polo thought ginseng a wonderful tonic.

There are other rare and exotic items, also costly, that are thought to serve the same or similar purposes. They include sea cucumber, bird's nest, deer antler, shark fin, white fungus, abalone, and other hard to find and expensive items. The Chinese consider them nourishing foods— that is, nourishing in its philosophic sense. All of them can provide the power of suggestion, and Chinese people take them because they believe they work.

Chinese traditional beliefs keep people healthy, diversify food production, and use foods that are available. They are not based upon Western science but rather upon generations of empirical observations, such as when Shennong tried out foods and herbs on himself and recorded his findings. If they were good enough for him, many Chinese people reason, they should work on them.

The Chinese system of TCM uses easily obtainable food items to gently strengthen the body and soothe it. For the most part, it uses small, sometimes minute amounts of more powerful and dangerous remedies that the people believe will work. Western researchers are beginning to look at and understand the therapeutic value and power of certain foods. The West is beginning to look at and understand how these foods and herbs heal.

The use of traditional items and thoughts about them are so ingrained that combining them at meals is part of Chinese thinking, even when people do not think about or focus on them. Most Chinese people balance foods and conditions without even knowing they are practicing harmony and balance. They may not be aware of which food or herb is classified which way, which condition is *yin* or *yang*. They may not know its relation to one of the elements. But they probably do know and practice balance and harmony because their parents and grandparents did.

Some Chinese speak about the philosophical taste or flavor; others cannot. Many do not realize that the foods they are serving and eating have five philosophical tastes and five philosophical temperatures. They may not know that *yin* foods are bitter, cool, and salty and that foods considered hot, sweet, and pungent are believed to be *yang*. They may not be able to say which is which, but when they make a dish they balance the ingredients so that they harmonize. Some are copying their mothers' and grandmothers' way of preparing foods; others have just learned to like those taste combinations.

People may know that a person who has a *yin* condition should be served *yang* foods and one with a *yang* condition needs to eat *yin* foods to return to health. They may not be able to verbalize that *yin* health conditions include shivering, cancer, and women's issues including menstruation, pregnancy, lactation, and the time after childbirth. They may not know that *yang* health conditions that need treatment with *yin* foods include constipation, hangovers, hypertension, and most infections including a sore throat, a toothache, an upset stomach, and venereal disease.[5] But know or not, in practice—that is, when eating—they do balance the right food with the right condition.

SPECIFIC FOODS USED AS MEDICINALS

Foods discussed below indicate how the Chinese and their TCM practitioners perceive their medicinal qualities. Written about are which parts should be used, their nature, bodily organs for which they have an affinity, and on which meridian they travel through the body. There are more than a thousand specific foods and herbs or parts of them in the Chinese pharmacopoeia. Each has a different use, nature, and affinity. People spend years learning about them before they diagnose and use them. Each has different dosages for different conditions. Because there are so many, it would require volumes to discuss even a quarter of them.

No matter the item, it is important to note that no food or drug should be used for acute conditions without consultation with one or more medical persons. This discussion does not replace appropriate medical diagnosis and treatment. Rather, it is given to show how the Chinese and their TCM practitioners view food as medicine. The items are simply illustrations of their conceptual perspective; they are illustrations of foods as medicine and medicines as food.

It is particularly important to be sure that any medicinal food is the botanically correct one. There are many foods that are of the same genus but a different species. In addition, there are many foods and medicines named colloquially or misnamed. One such example is silk squash; some refer to it as Chinese okra, but in no way is this food okra. Another incorrect identification is referring to the insides of apricots as almond pits.

Incorrect names distort an item's intended use. Inaccuracies are to be avoided, particularly in medicinal uses, because there can be serious health consequences.

For any illness or condition, only a physician should judge a medical condition and only a qualified TCM practitioner or licensed physician should prescribe a specific part of plant, animal, or mineral to treat it. For example, the Chinese tout turtle, but they use only the inner or outer shell for a particular medical purpose. While they use the praying mantis, only its egg casing is used for a specific medical condition. They do recommend pumpkin to cure some conditions, but limit that specifically to the seeds of the pumpkin. Furthermore, TCM practitioners specifically state that their prescriptions are effective only if used against the ailment for which they recommend them. They say that prescriptions must be used in proper dosage, taken at the suggested times, and mixed only with the recommended compatible ingredients.

Some foods as medicines are intended as tonics, and others are used in a more curative fashion. Still others are used to prevent a medical condition. It is important to know that some TCM recommendations can be toxic when taken incorrectly.

Foods, when recommended as medicines, are most often made into decoctions. That is, they are to be boiled or simmered, and many for a long time. Most are bitter and taste unpleasant. The Chinese believe they do more good that way. In addition, all of them need to be prepared the day they are consumed and prepared exactly as prescribed.

Numbers have meaning to the Chinese. The number 8 is among the meaningful numbers, as is the number 2; and the list that follows has 2 times 8, or 16, foods to illustrate their medicinal roles. These 16 illustrate some understandings of how TCM practitioners view them. Each short explanation is but part of the entire picture. Each is given with its Chinese name and the botanical family to which it belongs. Each mentions its Chinese nature, such as sweet, pungent, bitter, and the meridians believed it impacts.

Boxthorn

Boxthorn, in English, is known as Chinese wolfberry or Chinese matrimony vine. It is a *Lycium* member of the *Solanaceae* botanical family. While English names are often used interchangeably, not so those in Chinese because they are indicative of a different member component of this herbal. TCM practitioners say the fruit of *Lycium Chinense*, called *gouqizi*, is sweet and neutral, a liver and kidney tonic, a remedy for those with mild diabetes, and something to improve vision. The root of *Lycium barbarum*, most specifically the exterior layer or skin of the root, is believed sweet and cold, called *digupi*, and used to reduce blood in the urine, as an antitussive to reduce coughing, a help for asthmatics, and treatment for general weakness and fever to reduce *yin* deficiencies.

Chicken

Chicken, or *Gallus gallus domesticus*, is a remedy in many cultures when made into chicken soup. The Chinese consider chicken sweet and neutral and use this bird, called *xiaoji*, to make a fine *tang* or soup. TCM practitioners also recommend using the gizzard as a digestive. Chicken has an affinity for the small intestine, spleen, and stomach. When fresh, it is believed to move excess food out of the stomach. The gizzard, when fried and mixed with charcoal, makes a paste that can reduce painful abscesses in the mouth.

Chinese Olives

Chinese olives or *ganlan* have many TCM uses. This member of the *Burseraceae* family, known botanically as *Canarium album*, has pits with very thin ends that remove food stuck between the teeth. The fruits are used medicinally, considered sweet and sour, and known to be neutral. Some TCM practitioners recommend Chinese olives for some seafood toxicities and other allergic reactions. They say they have an affinity for lung and stomach conditions.

Chinese Quince

Chinese quince, *mugua*, is called *Chaenomeles lagenaria* by botanists. The fruit of this member of the *Rosaceae* family is considered sour and warm. It has an affinity for the liver and spleen. TCM doctors recommend it for those with arthritis, people who have weak backs, and for stomach cramps due to vomiting. They also prescribe quince for those with rheumatism and others suffering from swelling in the lower limbs or cramps in the calves.

Chrysanthemum

Chrysanthemum flowers used in dishes and tea are known as *juhua* in Chinese. In TCM, the flowers are believed sweet, bitter, and cool. A member of the *Compositae* family specifically known as *Chrysanthemum morifolia*, they have affinity for liver and lungs. They are used to improve vision and lower blood pressure, and as a sedative. Chrysanthemum is also used to reduce fever from wind-heat and headaches from problems with the liver.

Cinnamon

Cinnamon, that is, bark of the cinnamon tree, is an item in the *Lauracea* family, specifically *Cinnamomum cassia*. The Chinese call it *guizhi* and believe it pungent, sweet, and warm. They say it has affinity for bladder, heart, and lungs and should be used when a person has wind-cold chills and fever. They suggest it for fevers without sweats, menstrual disorders, and nausea, and recommend it with other food and herbal items.

Ginseng

Ginseng is an important food item in TCM. This all-important Chinese medicinal is called *renshen*, is a member of the *Araliaceae* family, and botanically is called *Panax ginseng*. Ginseng is considered sweet and neutral, a plant with affinity for lungs and spleen. Chinese believe that it has a positive impact on and increases a person's *qi*. It is recommend for the elderly and for those with a weak pulse, heart palpitations, and diabetes. Even though considered great, ginseng and many other food items are not prescribed without warnings. TCM doctors say one should not drink tea or eat turnips when consuming this remedy.

Honey

Honey, known as *fengmi* to the Chinese, is called *Apis mellifera* by botanists. This excretion from bees is in the *Apidae* family. Categorized as sweet and considered neutral in the hot/cold dichotomy, it has an affinity for large intestine, lungs, and spleen. It is used as a laxative, an emollient to relieve dry throat and cough, and a nutrient for all except those suffering from diarrhea.

Job's Tears

Job's tears are believed sweet and only slightly cold. Called *yiyiren* in Chinese, they are members of the *Gramineae* family, botanically known as

Coix lacryma jobi. They have affinity for lungs, spleen, and stomach. A liquor is made of their seeds and is believed to relieve pains from rheumatism. Unfermented seeds are used as a digestive, to reduce swelling, and to treat ulcers in both stomach and lungs.

Lotus

Lotus plants have many parts, all eaten and all used in TCM. The stem is used to rid a person of constipation; seeds get rid of insomnia; and leaves reduce pressure on the brain. As a member of the *Nymphaeaceae* family, specifically *Nelumbo nucifera,* this plant is called *heye* in Chinese. It is said to have affinity for liver, spleen, and stomach. TCM practitioners use it for ailments associated with summer heat and to increase urine in those who have difficulty urinating and to treat those with dark urine.

Mandarin Orange

Mandarin orange rind is believed to be pungent, bitter, and warm. Known as *chenpii* in Chinese, it is a member of the *Rutaceae* family, and is called *Citrus retulata* by botanists. It has an affinity for lungs and spleen, with the fibrous part just under the skin used as an expectorant. TCM practitioners recommend the seeds as an analgesic and the skin of the fruit to relieve nausea, vomiting, and general stomach aches. The entire fruit can relieve coughing and act as a general energy regulator.

Peaches

Peaches are used most in TCM for their pits, extracting the inner seed found inside them. Considered bitter, sweet, and neutral, they have an affinity for heart, large intestine, and liver. They are given to women after birth and to anyone with blood clots. The Chinese use peaches to relieve pain from appendicitis, and recommend them for lowering blood pressure. TCM doctors point out that high dosage of these seeds can be toxic.

Puffballs

Puffballs, used in TCM, are called *mabo* by the Chinese. This fungus is a member of the *Lycoperdaceae* family and botanically known as *Lycoperdon perlatum.* It is believed pungent and considered neutral. When made into a poultice, it is used as a coagulant. Other uses are to reduce coughing and assist breathing in very hot weather, and it is also used as an anti-dote for several poisonous substances.

Scallions

Scallions, members of the *Liliaceae* family, are botanically known as *Alium fistulosum*. Some literature calls them spring onions; the Chinese call them *congbai*. Medicinally, only the roots and the lower white part of the stalk are used. They are believed pungent and warm, but not sweet. They have an affinity for lungs and stomach, and can be used externally as a mild antiseptic when made into a poultice. Internally TCM practitioners use them for colds and chills and believe them effective reducers of wind-chills when mixed with fresh ginger and sugar. As antiseptic agents, they mix them with honey.

Silk Squash

Silk squash, a gourd in the *Curbitaecae* family, is botanically a *Luffa cylindrica*. When dried, this luffa sponge, called *sigua*, is prized by bathers. Sweet and neutral, mature fruits are considered cooling. They have an affinity for liver, lungs, and stomach. TCM practitioners use them to relieve pains in the chest cavity and to reduce painful tumors of the breast.

Soybeans

Soybeans, the black ones, are sweet, and slightly bitter. The Chinese do not use them raw, but rather fermented. Known in Chinese as *douchi*, this member of the *Leguminosae* family has the same name as regular soybeans, *Glycine max*. Soybeans have affinity for lung and stomach, and in TCM are used to alleviate headaches from wind-heat and for treating colds and fevers. They are sometimes used as a sedative.

RECIPES FOR HEALTH

The recipes below are neither medicines nor cures in the Western sense but are provided to give a feel for Chinese traditional practices. They can be consumed by healthy persons but should not be taken to cure an illness. Medicinally, they should be consumed only after consultation with a trained Chinese medical person. TCM doctors, before they prescribe, check pulse, tongue, meridian flows, and blockages, among other things, and then recommend prescriptions based upon discerned need, and they determine quantity and frequency. Many of the recipes below are soups or other liquid decoctions, and many are bitter. Before the actual recipe, a few symptoms a TCM medical practitioner might use it for are discussed.

Pork Soup with Lotus Seed and Lily Bulb

TCM practitioners believe that pork soup with lotus seed and lily bulb calms the mind, alleviates headaches and insomnia, and is good for the spleen and the kidneys.

- 8 cups chicken or mixed meat broth
- 1/4 pound dried lotus seeds, soaked for two hours in hot water, then drained
- 3 tablespoons dried lily bulb leaves, soaked for two hours in hot water, then drained
- 1/2 pound lean pork loin, sliced thin, then cut into one-inch squares
- 1 teaspoon thin soy sauce
- 5 drops hot oil (or Tabasco)
- 1 tablespoon cornstarch mixed with 1 tablespoon cold water
- 1 scallion, cut into one-quarter-inch pieces

1. Bring broth to the boil, reduce heat, add lotus seeds and lily bulb pieces, and simmer for two hours or until they are soft.
2. Mix pork with soy sauce, hot oil, and cornstarch, and let rest for 10 minutes.
3. Add pork mixture to broth mixture and simmer for half an hour. Add the scallions and then serve.

Chicken Soup with Mushrooms and Chestnuts

TCM practitioners recommend chicken soup with mushrooms and chestnuts for eliminating fatigue, nourishing vitality, strengthening the body, and helping with blood circulation.

- 1/4 pound dried chestnuts, soaked in hot water for one hour, drained and dark skin removed
- 8 Chinese black mushrooms, soaked in hot water for 20 minutes, drained, with water reserved
- 15 bamboo mushrooms (also known as bamboo fungus), soaked for 5 minutes in warm water, then drained, and each one cut into five pieces
- 1/2 chicken, cut in half
- 2 tablespoons Chinese rice wine
- 1/4 teaspoon salt

- 1/2 teaspoon corn oil
- 2 slices fresh ginger, sliced
- 2 cloves garlic
- 8 cups chicken broth
- 2 scallions, one tied in a knot, the other cut into one-inch pieces

1. Simmer chestnuts in water until soft, 40 minutes to an hour, remove them and set aside.
2. Remove stems from black mushroom and discard, then slice thin, add bamboo mushrooms, and set aside.
3. Put chicken into in boiling water. Take it out after 1 minute, cool, and chop into two-inch pieces, then mix with rice wine and salt and let rest 10 minutes. Discard this water.
4. Heat corn oil in the bottom of a four-quart pot. Stir-fry ginger and garlic in it until fragrant, about half a minute, then add the chicken pieces, broth, chestnuts, and the scallion tied in a knot. Simmer for 40 minutes, remove the scallion knot, add the scallion pieces, then serve.

Bitter Melon and Date Congee

TCM practitioners advise that bitter melon and date congee relieves rheumatism, is good for the eyes, reduces swelling, and helps detoxify the body.

- 1 bitter melon, seeds and white interior tissue around the seeds removed
- 1/2 pound spareribs, cut into individual ribs, then chopped into one-inch pieces
- 2 tablespoons water chestnut flour
- 1 tablespoon thin soy sauce
- 1 teaspoon cornstarch
- 5 dried lily bulb petals
- 8 red dates
- 2 tablespoons glutinous rice
- 1 cup long-grain rice
- 5 Chinese celery stalks, rinsed and diced
- 1 dash each of ground Sichuan pepper, white pepper, and salt

1. Cut bitter melon into one-inch cubes. Put them into boiling water and simmer for 3 minutes, discard the water, and set aside in a bowl.
2. Mix spareribs with thin soy sauce and water chestnut flour and set aside for 15 minutes.

3. Simmer lily bulb petals for half an hour, add dates and cook another 5 minutes, then drain, and pit the dates. Add both of these to the bitter melon.

4. Put glutinous rice in 8 cups of boiling water, boil for 5 minutes, then reduce heat to simmer and cook for half an hour. Next add the long-grain rice and cook for another half hour. Then add the spareribs, lily bulb petals, and red dates, and cook another half hour.

5. Add celery, ground peppers, and salt, and simmer 10 minutes more, then serve.

Beef and Lotus Root Stew

TCM practitioners say that beef and lotus root stew relieves heat, reduces swelling, and strengthens the body.

- 1 pound sirloin of flank steak, cut into thin slices one-inch square
- 3 tablespoons cornstarch
- 3 sections lotus root, peeled and sliced thin
- 3 scallions, 2 cut into thin slivers, and 1 cut into one-inch pieces
- 3 sprigs coriander, minced
- 3 slices fresh ginger, peeled, each cut into three pieces
- 3 cloves garlic, minced
- 3 whole star anise
- 3 tablespoons Chinese rice wine
- 3 tablespoons dark soy sauce
- 1 tablespoon black rice vinegar
- 1/2 teaspoon salt
- 1 scallion, green part only, coarsely chopped or cut into slices

1. Mix beef with cornstarch. Set aside for 15 minutes.

2. Put meat, lotus root pieces, scallions, coriander, ginger, garlic, star anise, Chinese rice wine, soy sauce, vinegar, and salt into a heavy pot with one cup of water, and simmer for half an hour. Check to see if meat is tender, and if not cook another 15 minutes and check again, cooking until the meat is tender.

3. Add chopped scallions, then serve.

Duck and Abalone

TCM medical doctors say that duck and abalone prevents miscarriages, strengthens women after childbirth, cures backaches, strengthen tendons and bones, and tones liver, kidneys, and *qi*.

- 1/2 fresh duck, rinsed and dried with paper towels
- 1 can abalone, drained and sliced
- 1 tablespoon eucommia bark or *Cortex eucommiae* (Chinese call it *da zhong*), optional
- 30 pieces wolfberry, also called *fructus lyci*, or the fruit of *Lycium Chinense* (called *gouqici*)
- 1 knob ginger, peeled and sliced
- 3 tablespoons rice wine
- 1 teaspoon coarse salt

1. Put duck into boiling water for two minutes, remove and drain, then cut into two-inch pieces.
2. Put duck, abalone, eucommia bark, wolfberry, ginger, rice wine, and salt into a heavy pot with two cups of boiling water. Reduce heat and simmer two hours or until duck is soft, then serve.

NOTES

1. Maoshing Ni, trans., *The Yellow Emperor's Classic of Medicine* (Boston: Shambala, 1995).

2. Woolfram Eberhard, *A Dictionary of Chinese Symbols* (London: Routledge, 1986).

3. E. K. Ludman, J. M. Newman, and L. L. Lynn, "Blood-Building Foods in Contemporary Chinese Populations," *Journal of the American Dietetic Association* 89: 1122–24 (1989).

4. Ibid.

5. Ibid.

Glossary

bokcai Commonly spelled bok choi or bok choy.

bu (*or* pu) foods Strengthening foods, from a philosophic perspective.

cai Vegetable and meat foods, used to flavor staple grain foods; also can mean just vegetables.

cha Tea made from leaves of *Camellia chinensis*, dried and processed; from least to most cha is white, yellow, green, oolong, or black, and when infused with hot water is one of China's most popular beverages.

chifan Common greeting; literally means to eat rice, but also used to mean a meal or to eat.

congee Cantonese word for rice cooked with a lot of water and consumed as a gruel; *pinyin* word is *juk*.

conpoy Dried scallop.

cumquat A citrus fruit also transliterated as *kumquat*; has sweet skin and sour/acidic pulp.

dadao Soybeans, can be yellow, black, or brown; domesticated in the north about 3000 B.C.E.

daikon Japanese word commonly used for a specific large, white-skinned radish.

dianxin Northern Chinese *pinyin* name for dim sum.

dijiang   Plum sauce; often served with Peking duck, hence also called duck sauce.

dim sum   Translates to "dot the heart"; a morning or afternoon snack meal with many small dishes; also known in the south as *yumcha*.

donggua   Winter melon, huge and often white and flourlike on its dark green skin; sometimes used as container for steaming foods, then eaten with the foods.

doufu   Chinese word for tofu, a coagulated product made from soy milk; coagulated with calcium sulphate, nigeri, or another coagulating agent.

doujiou   Chinese long beans, also called yard-long beans; an 18-inch or longer starchy legume, can be light or dark green and string-bean-like.

doumiao   End leaves and tendrils of the pea plant, a very popular vegetable.

fan   Staple food of China, most often rice in south and wheat and other grains in the north.

feng shui   Also known as geomancy, the flow of good wind and water; a divination used for kitchen placement, burial, and other sites.

fu   An ancient pot used to steam foods, as were others called *xien* and *zeng*.

fuyu   Fermented bean curd, can be white, red, or green depending on what it was fermented with.

gailan   Chinese broccoli, not the same as headed broccoli, a member of the same *Brassica* family.

gambei   Means "bottoms up" and said when consuming alcoholic beverages in one gulp.

ganlankeng   Inside of olive pit/stone that is dried and rolled and used in cooking; Western countries substitute pine nuts.

gaoliang   Also known as *kaoling* or sorghum, a staple grain food, and when fermented a famous liquor called *maotai*.

guo   *Pinyin* word for a wok.

Han   Major population group in China, 93 percent of the country's people.

Hanyu pinyin   Chinese ideographs written in phonetics; government approved and most popular way to transliterate Chinese so that others can say the words.

hoisin   Slightly piquant, sweet, fermented bean sauce.

hsien   Salty; one of the five basic Chinese tastes.

hsin   Pungent; one of five basic Chinese tastes.

huangcai   Lily bulb, also known as lily petals; used as a vegetable.

hunton   A ravioli-type dumpling, commonly spelled *wonton.*

jaozi   Dumpling filled with minced meat and other foods; popular, especially on New Year's Eve and New Year's Day.

jiang   Savory, ancient term for one of China's five basic tastes, now called *xian;* another more common meaning is sauce.

jiangyou   Ancient name for sauce, but not soy sauce because *you* means oil and soy sauce has no oil.

jiu   Wine or any alcoholic beverage, no matter its strength or proof.

ju   Peel of a tangerine, slightly bitter citrus flavor used dry and in many dishes.

jujubes   Chinese dates, a different fruit from those in the West; red, black, or brown jujubes are popular.

kan   Sweet; one of the five basic Chinese tastes.

kao   Another Chinese word for wok.

kaoling   Chinese word for alcoholic beverage made from sorghum.

keng   Stew, an early culinary technique.

kimchee   Korean pickled vegetables, probably originated in China.

ku   Bitter; one of the five basic Chinese tastes.

kuaizi   Chopsticks, literally running boys or quick boys; the most common eating implements in China today, often made of bamboo.

laba   Gruel eaten on eighth day of the twelfth month of the lunar calendar in preparation for Chinese New Year.

lamien   Hand-pulled Chinese noodles.

lianhou   Lotus root; rhizome of a water-lily plant eaten as vegetable or sugared and as a candy; can also be stuffed.

liianzi   Lotus seeds, from the rhizome of a water-lily plant; eaten fresh, dried, and reconstituted, sugared as a candy, dried, and as flour.

lingjiao   Water chestnut, a starchy bulb used as a vegetable or made into flour; not the winged starchy vegetable popular in Tang Dynasty times.

lizhi   Lichee fruit, domesticated in China, eaten fresh and dried; used to make a liquor; its leaves are used to make tea.

mala   Hot and spicy, a term most often used about foods from the Sichuan province.

maotai   Distilled alcoholic beverage made from sorghum, often 200 proof.

mapo doufu   Most popular dish in Sichuan province, hot and spicy doufu.

mei   Small fruit related to apricot, often mistakenly called a plum.

mein   Noodles of any variety.

moer   Fungus called cloud or wood ear, can be black, white, even pale pastel colors; black ones frequently consumed with tiger lily buds, white ones popular in sweet dishes.

popia   Wrapped vegetable or meat roll popularly taken to gravesites or ancestral tablets at Qing Ming festival; also eaten throughout the year, particularly in southeastern China.

qi   Energy, breath, air, and other things; in and around everything, vital in mind-body functioning, and needed to maintain a person's balance.

qiguo   A Yunnan or ceramic pot with funnel-shaped center that allows steam to slowly enter; used in a steamer.

sacha   Fermented sauce usually made of brill or krill; also known as Chinese barbecue sauce.

shaobing   Baked wheat flour leavened bun usually topped with sesame seeds, can have a filling.

shaomai   Steamed thin-skinned wheat-flour dumpling often filled with pork and shrimp.

shi   Persimmon, often dried and cooked or eaten as candy, many found in Han tombs.

shih   To feed, eat, or drink; or excellent grain.

shiitake   Common Japanese word used for Chinese black forest mushrooms; cultivated on logs or grow at the base of oak trees; preferred dried as flavor is more intense.

shiliu   Pomegranate; its many seed represents a wish for having many sons.

shu   Millet, one of China's first grains, still used in the north, also made into an alcoholic beverage.

sigua   Long, often ribbed, squash that needs peeling.

suan   Sour; one of the five basic Chinese tastes.

su foods   Vegetarian cuisine.

tao   Peach, a revered Chinese fruit held in hand of God of Longevity; kernel inside the pit used in some dishes and in traditional Chinese medicine.

tonghaocai   Chinese vegetable known as garland chrysanthemum.

wengcai   Water spinach, known as hollow stem vegetable.

wuxing   Five elements of: water, wood, fire, metal, and earth; philosophic energy permeating everything including foods, themselves attributed to one of these cosmic forces needing balance.

xiangyou   Sesame oil made from toasted sesame seeds; brownish in color and very aromatic, used after dishes are cooked for its taste and aroma.

yaotiao   Cruller-type long, thin fried dough eaten at breakfast in many northern regions.

yin and yang   Opposite forces, fundamental to understanding astrology and divination; *yin* is dark, female, even numbers, cold, and passive; *yang* is light, male, odd numbers, hot, and active; health conditions are one or the other and treated with food of the opposite polarity.

yum cha   Southern term for dim sum; literally means to drink (or take) tea.

zheng   Steaming, one of the earliest Chinese cooking techniques.

zhimajiang   Sesame sauce made of mashed white or black sesame seeds; used to flavor dishes and stuff dumplings.

zhurou   Pork, the main meat of China.

zongzi   Rice-filled dumplings usually wrapped in dried bamboo leaves; popular at Dragon Boat Festival.

Resource Guide

COOKBOOKS

There are literally thousands of Chinese cookbooks available. Here is a diverse list.

Blofield, John. *The Chinese Art of Tea*. Boston: Shambala, 1985.

Chan, Millie. *Kosher Chinese Cookbook*. New York: Harmony Books, 1990.

Chang, Wonona W., Irving B. Chang, Helene W. Kutscher, and Austin W. Kutscher. *An Encyclopedia of Chinese Cooking*. New York: Crown Books, 1970.

Chao, Buwei Yang. *How to Cook and Eat in Chinese*. London: Faber Books, 1972.

Chen, Joyce. *Joyce Chen Cookbook*. Philadelphia: Lippincott, 1962.

Dunlop, Fuchsia. *Sichuan Cookery*. London: Michael Joseph, 2001.

Fu, Pei Mei. *Pei Mei's Chinese Cookbook*, Vol. 1. Taipei, Taiwan: T & S Industrial, 1969.

Hom, Ken. *Illustrated Chinese Cookery*. London: BBC Books, 1993.

Hsiung, Deh-Ta, and Wendy Lee. *Simple Chinese Recipes*. North Vancouver, Canada: Whitecap Books, 1997.

Huang, Su Huei. *Chinese Cuisine*. Taipei, Taiwan: Wei-Chuan Foods Corp., 1972.

Hush, Paul, and Joanne Hush. *Chinese Cooking the Healthful Way*. Rocklin, Calif.: Prima Publishers, 1996.

Hutton, Wendy. *The Food of China*. Boston: Periplus Editions HK, 1999.

Keyes, John D. *Food for the Emperor: Recipes of Imperial China with a Dictionary of Chinese Cuisine*. San Francisco: Ward Ritchie Press, 1963.

Kuo, Irene. *The Key to Chinese Cooking*. New York: Random House, 1977.

Kwong, Kylie. *Kylie Kwong Recipes and Stories*. Camberwell, Victoria, Australia: Penguin, 2003.

Lapidus, Dorothy Farris. *The Scrutable Feast: A Guide to Eating Authentically in Chinese Restaurants*. New York: Dodd, Mead, 1977.

Leung, Mai. *The Classic Chinese Cookbook*. New York: Harper's Magazine Press, 1976.

Lin, Hsiang Ju, and Tsuifeng Lin. *Chinese Gastronomy*. New York: Pyramid Publications, 1972.

Liu, Christine Y. C. *Nutrition and Diet with Chinese Cooking*, 5th ed. Ann Arbor, Mich.: Author, 1983.

Liu, William T., and Mary L. Liu. *The Essence of Chinese Cuisine*. Nashville, Tenn.: Aurora, 1970.

Lo, Kenneth, ed. *The Complete Encyclopedia of Chinese Cooking*. New York: Crown Publishers, 1970.

Mark, Willy. *Chinese Cookery Masterclass*. Secaucus, N.J.: Chartwell Books, 1984.

McLaren, H. W. G., ed. *Towngas Cookery Book*, 11th ed. Hong Kong: Hong Kong and China Gas, 1972.

Miller, Gloria Bley. *The Thousand Recipe Chinese Cookbook*. New York: Atheneum, 1966.

Sakamoto, Nobuko. *The People's Republic of China Cookbook*. New York: Random House, 1977.

Tropp, Barbara. *The Modern Art of Chinese Cooking*. New York: Morrow, 1982.

Wong, Ella-Mei. *Yum Cha Dims Sims and Other Chinese Delights*. London: Angus and Robertson, 1981.

Wu, Sylvia. *Madame Wu's Art of Chinese Cooking*. Los Angeles: Charles Publishing, 1973.

Yan, Martin. *Martin Yan's Feast*. San Francisco: Bay Books, 1998.

Zhang, Enlai. *Chinese Cuisine–Recipes and Their Stories*. Beijing: Foreign Language Press, 2001.

Zhuo, Zhao, and George Ellis. *The Healing Cuisine of China*. Rochester, Vt.: Healing Arts Press, 1998.

VIDEOS

Asian Health Secrets with Letha Hadady. New York: Wellspring Media, 1999.

Basic Chinese Cuisine. Indianapolis: Kartes Video Communications, n.d.

Chinese Cooking with Rosa Ross. Great Neck, N.Y.: Best Films and Video, n.d.

The Chinese Kitchen with Jeff Smith. Chicago: WTTW/Chicago, 1992.

Chinese Video Cookbook with Roger Hong. San Francisco: Panda Foods International, 1985.

A Guide to Chinese Cooking with Ken Hom. New York: Videoclassics, 1985.
Quick and Easy Chinese Cooking with Rocky Aoki of Benihana. Great Neck, N.Y.:
    Best and Video Corp., 1987.
Stir-fry with Helen Chen. Billerica, Mass.: Joyce Chen, Inc., 1995.

CDS

Annie Chun's. San Rafael, Calif.: Annie Chun's Inc., 2002.
The Best of Hong Kong, Food for Friends. Hong Kong: The Culinary Chronicle,
    n.d.
Culinary Excursions through China. SunMedia Inc., 1995.
Easy Cooking Chinese with Madeline Greey. Buffalo, N.Y.: ARC Media Inc., 1995.
Matsu: Taiwan's Guardian Goddess. Hong Kong: Sinorama Magazine, n.d.
Music and Recipes of the Orient. New York: SPD Entertainment, 1999.
Seek Sip Savour Asian Cuisine. Singapore: SunRice, 2000.
Taiwan Food Showcase 2001. Taipei, Taiwan: Visual Trade Mart, 2001.
Visual Chinese Cookbook. Baldwin, Calif.: Video Turos Institute, 1995.
Wonders of Hong Kong. Hong Kong: Hong Kong Tourist Association, n.d.
World Cuisine: Chinese, by Madeleine Greey. San Leandro, Calif.: Oasis Blue Pro-
    ductions, 1996.

WEB SITES

Asian Books and Asian Pantry

www.orientalpantry.com

Asian Cooking

www.orientalfood.com
www.goodcooking.com/asia
www.asiafood.org/

Botanical and/or Common Food Names

http://198.93.235.8/cfdocs/examples/treessd/botanic/cfm/BotanicSearch.cfm
http://198.93.235.8/cfdocs/examples/treessd/botanic/cfm/CommonList.cfm

Chinese Cooking

www.chinavists.com/culture/cuisine/recipes/html
www.techart.nia.edu.tw/-suchu/www-cook

www.pasture.ecn.purdue.edu/-agenhtml.agemc.china
http://techart.nia.edu.tw/~suchu/www-cook/
www.chinavista.com/culture/cuisine/recipes.html
www.china-yz.com/food/list.htm
www.chinats.com/shanghai/index42.htm
www.taipei.org/teco/cicc/currents/53/Html/food2.htm

Chinese Food History

www.flavorandfortune.com
www.tsinoy.com/Roots/Cuisine.cfm
www.sinorama.com.tw

Chinese in America

www.chineseroots.com

Culinary History, Maps, and Cooking Links

www.gti.net/mocolib1/kid/food1.html
http://cookingmedia.com
www.foodchannel.com/maps/2_maps.cfm
www.pazsaz.com/ffodliunk.html

Ethnic Recipes

www.godzilla.eeecs.berkeley.edu/recipes/ethnic

Food Ingredient Links

www.gti.net/mocolib1/kid/food/html

Global Gastronomy

www.cs.yale.edu/homes/hupfer/global/gastronomer
http://WorldCulinaryInstitute.com/main2.shtml

Links

www.cookingconnect.com
www.whatweeat.com
www.gourmetsleuth.com/index.asp

Mini Asian Food Directory

www.sintercom.org/makan

Nutrition (with Chinese foods included)

www.nutri-facts.com/main.asp
www.nal.usda.gov/fnic/foodcomp/Data/

Selected Bibliography

Anderson, E. N. *The Food of China*. New Haven, Conn.: Yale University Press, 1988.

Bensky, Dan, and Andrew Gamble, trans. *Materia Medica*, rev. ed. Seattle: Eastland Press, 1993.

Buell, Paul D., and Eugene N. Anderson. *A Soup for the Quan: Introduction, Translation, Commentary, and Chinese Text [of the Essentials of Dietetics, in Chinese the* Yinshao Chengyao, *abbreviated at YSCY]*. London: Kegan Paul, 2000.

Chai, Chu, and Winberg Chai. *Confucianism*. Woodbury, N.Y.: Barron's Educational Series, 1973.

Chang, K. C. *Food in Chinese Culture*. New Haven, Conn.: Yale University Press, 1977.

Compendium of Materia Medica. See Bensky and Gamble, above.

Debaine-Francfort, Corinne. *The Search for Ancient China*. New York: Harry N. Abrams, 1998.

Eberhard, Woolfram. *A Dictionary of Chinese Symbols*. London: Routledge, 1986.

Fieldhouse, Paul. *Food and Nutrition: Customs and Culture*. London: Chapman and Hall, 1995.

Gittings, John. *A Chinese View of China*. New York: Pantheon Books, 1973.

Goody, Jack. *Cooking, Cuisine, and Class: A Study of Comparative Sociology*. Cambridge, England: Cambridge University Press, 1986.

Huang, H. T. *Joseph Needham Science and Civilization in China*, VI:5. Cambridge, England: Cambridge University Press, 2000.

Keightley, David N., ed. *The Origins of Chinese Civilization*. Berkeley: University of California Press, 1983.

Keyes, John D. *Food for the Emperor*. San Francisco: Ward Ritchie Press, 1963.

Koo, Linda-chih. "The Use of Food to Treat and Prevent Disease in Chinese Culture." *Social Science and Medicine* 18:757–766.

Koo, Linda Chih-ling. *Nourishment of Life: Health in a Chinese Society*. Hong Kong: The Commercial Press, 1982.

Latourette, Kenneth Scott. *The Chinese, Their History and Culture*, 4th ed. New York: Macmillan, 1964.

Lin Hung. *Lin Hung's Basic Provisions for Rustic Living*. In Chinese; written in Song Dynasty (960–1279), no date given.

Lu Yu. *The Classic of Tea*. Trans. F. R. Carpenter. Boston: Little, Brown, 1974.

Madame Wu's Recipe Book. In Chinese; written in Song Dynasty (960–1279), no date given.

Mennel, Stephan, Ann Murcott, and Anneke H. van Otterloo. *The Sociology of Food: Eating, Diet, and Culture*. London: Sage Publications, 1992.

Mintz, Sidney W. *Tasting Food, Tasting Freedom: Excursions into Eating, Culture, and the Past*. Boston: Beacon Press, 1996.

Ni, Maoshing. *The Yellow Emperor's Classic of Medicine* [new translation of the *Neijing Suwen* with commentary]. Boston: Shambala, 1995.

Nizan the Painter. *Cloud Forest Collection of Rules for Eating and Drinking*. Dated circa 1360.

Passmore, Jacki. *The Encyclopedia of Asian Food and Cooking*. New York: Hearst Books, 1991.

Qi, Xing. *Folk Customs at Traditional Chinese Festivities*. Beijing: Foreign Languages Press, 1988.

Roberts, J. A. G. *China to Chinatown: Chinese Food in the West*. London: Reackton Books, 2002.

Rozin, Elizabeth. *Ethnic Cuisine: The Flavor Principle*. Lexington, Mass.: Stephen Greene Press, 1983.

Simoons, Frederick J. *Food in China: A Cultural and Historical Inquiry*. Boca Raton, Fla.: CRC Press, 1991.

Waley, Arthur, trans. and ed. *The Analects of Confucius*. New York: Vintage Books, 1938.

Watson, James L., ed. *Golden Arches East: McDonald's in East Asia*. Stanford, Calif.: Stanford University Press, 1997.

Wilkenson, Endymion. *Chinese History, A Manual*. Cambridge, Mass.: Harvard University Asian Center, 1998. [This comprehensive English-language volume lists major Chinese-language publications. It deals with basic knowledge, has sections on agriculture, food and the environment and medicine, and describes the different branches of historical writings. It provides literary sources and other primary sources for each historical period, Qin to Qing, and uses only *pinyin* transliterations.]

Wittwer, Sylvan, Yu Youtai, Han Sun, and Lianzheng Wang. *Feeding a Billion, Frontiers of Chinese Agriculture*. East Lansing: Michigan State University Press, 1987.

Wu, David Y. H., and Sidney C. H. Cheung, eds. *The Globalization of Chinese Food*. Honolulu: University of Hawaii Press, 2002.

Wu, David Y. H., and Chee-beng Tan, eds. *Changing Chinese Foodways in Asia*. Hong Kong: Chinese University Press, 2001.

Zee, A. *Swallowing Clouds*. New York: Simon and Schuster, 1990.

Zhou Cuncai. *The Yellow Emperor's Medicine Classic: Treatise and Health and Long Life* [a comic book-type translation]. Singapore: Asiapac Books Pte. 2000.

Index

abalone, 94, 192, 201
abalone sauce, 42
alcoholic beverages (includes beer, wine, and liquor), 5, 14, 16, 19–20, 22, 32, 35, 37, 40, 44, 51, 59, 64, 70, 89, 95, 98, 106, 113, 116, 117, 146, 147, 157, 164, 168, 169, 184, 189, 197
alfalfa, for horses, 12
almonds, 57, 170
amaranth, 54
Analects. See Confucius and Confucianism
ancient natural phenomena, 181–84
ancient recipes, 25–28
Anhui Province, and its foods, 91, 93, 99
animal foods. See meat and poultry; seafood
animal months as a yearly cycle, 161
anise, 33, 46
Annuls of Linzi County, 17
Anyang, 11
apples, 16, 160, 166

apricot, and other seeds, 47–48, 193. See also nuts and seeds
apricots, 16, 168
arable land, 4
arrowroot, 57
asafetida, 19

baked foods, 9, 15, 18, 38, 59, 79–80, 159, 160, 162–63, 166, 167, 168, 169, 172, 173
baking, 38, 72, 82, 93, 95
balancing dishes and diets, 190
bamboo records or strips, 17
bamboo shoots, roots, leaves, and stalks, 51, 160
bamboo tools, 12
Banpo Village, 2
banquets, 100, 116, 117, 123, 130, 132–37, 138, 147, 174–75. See also guest behaviors and responsibilities at meals
barbecuing, 46, 72
barley and tsampa, 2, 9, 12, 39–40, 97, 116

Basic Provisions Rustic Living, 41
basil leaf, 45, 50, 100
bean curd. See *doufu*
beans and peas, 19, 50, 51–52, 97,
    116, 170
bean sauces and pastes, 42, 43, 44.
    See also sauces and pastes; soy
    beans and soy sauces
bean sprouts and other shoots,
    52–53
bear, 59, 99
beef, 2, 97, 98
beer. *See* alcoholic beverages
Beijing, 8, 91, 94–95, 114, 116
betel leaf, 17
beverages and their use, 5, 9, 14, 17,
    33, 63–64, 105–6, 111–12, 116,
    117, 129–30, 138, 139, 142, 146,
    147, 181. *See also* alcoholic bever-
    ages; *specific types of beverages*
bird's nests, 21, 30, 60, 94, 133, 138,
    157
births and birthdays, 132, 154,
    171–73
bitter melon, 32–33
bitter taste, 32–34, 53, 183, 194
black bean pastes, mashes and sauces,
    16, 42–43. *See also* sauces and
    pastes
blanching, 70
boiling, 5, 20, 59, 69, 70–71, 77, 82,
    190, 194
bokcai (bok choy), other cabbages,
    and leafy greens, 53, 90
Book of Ceremonies, 185
Book of Changes, 185
Book of Etiquette, 109–10
Book of Rites, 185
Book of Songs, 184, 185
bowls, plates, saucers, and glasses, 19,
    79, 107, 108, 117, 146. *See also*
    ladles and spoons
boxthorn, 194–95

braising, 5, 15, 18, 46, 49, 50, 59, 70,
    90, 95
brassica vegetables. *See bokcai,* other
    cabbages and leafy greens; broc-
    coli, and related flowering and
    non-flowering relatives
breads. *See* baked foods
breakfast, 108, 119, 159
broccoli, and related flowering and
    non-flowering relatives, 54
bronze vessels, 14
buckwheat, 40
Buddha's hand. *See* citrus fruits
Buddhism, 5, 8
buffalo. *See* water buffalo
butter. *See* dairy foods

cai foods. *See* vegetables and meats
calendars, 154, 155, 156
calligraphy, 7
camel, 59
candy. *See* sugar, other sweeteners,
    and sweets
cardamon, 46, 50
carp (goldfish), 20, 94
carrots, 55
cashews, 50
cassia, 32, 33, 45, 67, 71, 174, 196
CD resources, 211
celebrations and special occasions,
    131–32. *See also* holidays and
    special occasions; other or lesser
    holidays; *specific occasions*
celery, 174
Celestial Sovereigns, 10
cereals. *See specific types*
Chang-An. *See* Xian
changes in food consumption, 12,
    144–45
characters. *See* calligraphy
charcoal braziers, 75
cheese. *See* dairy products
cherries, 168

chestnuts, 16, 50, 95, 168, 170, 171
chicken, 2, 16, 20, 60, 72, 94, 98, 99, 160, 195
chili, long, and other peppers, 17, 44, 50, 51, 53
chili bean sauces, 44. See also sauces and pastes
chili peppers, and chili bean sauces, 41, 50, 51–54, 89, 96. See also sauces and pastes
China's borders and land mass, 3, 4
Chinese celery, 54
Chinese celery cabbage. See vegetables
Chinese chives, 54
Chinese fives, 187; five aromas, 185; five body fluids, 185; five cereals, 5; five classical grains, 60; five colors, 185; five directions, 185; five elements, 16, 186–89, 191; five emotions, 185; five flavors, five and six tastes, and five seasonings, 5, 31–34, 182, 183, 186, 192; five foods as medicinals, 193–98; five general and sacrificial animals, 185; five healing herbs, 186; five major causes of disease, 186; five natural influences, 182; five nourishing animals, 5; five poisonous animals, 168; five solid organs, 185; Tables of these and other fives, 183, 187; five virtues, 185; five vegetables to sustain, 5
Chinese food abroad, 142–45
Chinese food beliefs, rituals, and sayings, 5, 93, 109, 116, 117, 131, 132, 146–47, 157, 159, 160, 162, 166, 169, 174, 194. See also Chinese fives
Chinese language. See Putonghua
Chinese olives, 195
Chinese Pharmacopoeia, 183

Chinese population, 4, 5
Chinese sayings. See Chinese food beliefs, rituals, and sayings
chopsticks, 5, 18, 78, 80, 105, 107, 108, 110, 111, 146
chrysanthemum and its leaves, 54, 195–96
chrysanthemum pots, 19, 20, 22, 80–82
cinnamon, 45–46, 196. See also cassia
cilantro. See coriander
citrus fruits (including Buddha's hand, mandarins, lemons, oranges, etc.), 61–62, 95, 164, 167, 188, 197
clams, 20, 59, 95
Classic of History, 10
Classic of Poetry, 10
Classic of Tea, 14
clay-pots and clay-pot cooking, 72, 82. See also Yunnan pots
cleavers, 77, 79
Cloud Forest Collection of Rules for Drinking and Eating, 20
clover, 12
cloves, 33, 45, 46, 50
coffee and coffee substitutes, 106, 123
cold beverages and soda, 63, 106, 117, 162
cold food, 74, 147, 163–64, 192
Cold Food Festival, 74, 163–65
conch, 95
Confucius and Confucianism, 5, 8, 16, 17, 48, 64, 100, 133, 155, 184
congee. See soups and congee
conversation at meals, 138–39, 140–41
cookbook resource, 209–10
cooking, 69–83. See also specific cooking techniques
cooking and eating equipment, 9, 18, 20, 72–74, 75–82, 107. See also specific types of equipment

cooking techniques and their use, 15,
    59, 69–82, 91, 92–93, 114–16.
    See also specific types of cooking
cooling, 74
coriander (cilantro), 12, 15, 22, 48,
    50, 55
corn, 21, 40, 94. *See also* maize
crabs, 94, 98, 99, 164, 169
crock-pot cookery, 97
cucumber, 5, 15
cumin, 50
cumquats, 15, 62
curing, 93, 96, 97
curry, 50
cutting boards, 78

daikon, 55–56
dairy foods (including cheese), 9, 15,
    97
Dao and Daoism, 5
dates, 50, 157, 169, 171
Dawenkou culture, 2
decoction, 194
deep frying, 72. *See also* frying and
    deep-frying
dialects, 7
dian xin. See dim sum
diet and health, 181–99
dietetics, 17, 183
dim sum, 18, 93–96, 119–24,
    141–42, 164
ding, 12, 14
dog, 2, 60
donkey and mule, 16, 19
Double Ninth Festival, 154, 169–70
doufu, 17, 30–32, 34, 52, 100, 160
Dragon Boat Festival, 153, 155,
    167–68
dragon eye fruit, 157
dried foods, 3, 5, 50, 59
drinking and eating games and be-
    haviors, 112, 113, 130, 145–46

duck, 16, 19, 60, 72, 94, 95, 97, 98,
    114, 164
duck sauce. *See* plum sauce
dumplings, 4, 15, 18, 19, 94, 96, 116,
    124, 158–59, 168, 172. *See also*
    snack foods

early food and food changes, 10–12,
    13–14, 15–23, 90–91
early regional differences, 88–91
earthenware and pottery jars, 80
eastern cuisine (including Shanghai),
    88, 90, 117, 120, 135–36
eating games. *See* drinking and eating
    games and behaviors
eating out, 129–48. *See also* restau-
    rants
eating tools. *See* cooking and eating
    equipment
eel, 98
eggplant, 15, 51
egg rolls. *See* dim sum; snacks and
    snack foods
eggs, 16, 60–61, 98, 116, 172
Emperor Wudi (King Wudi), 3, 12
Essentials of Dietetics (YSCY), 20
*Essential Techniques for the Peasantry
    (QMYS)*, 15, 16, 41
ethnic customs. *See* minority popula-
    tions
European settlers, 22
extant materials, 16

fagara, 174. *See also* peppers
family meals, 105–24
fan or grain food use, 19, 105. *See also*
    staple and grain foods
fennel, 33, 46
fenugreek, 50
fermented foods (including black
    beans and pastes), 35. *See also*
    sauces and pastes; soy sauces

fire-pot and hot-pot cookery, 71, 93, 97
fish, and imitation fish, 16, 20, 34, 41, 95, 98, 99, 159, 164, 174
fish maw, 59
fish sauces, 34, 97
flour, 4, 15, 42, 73, 95, 98, 166. *See also* noodles
food for elders, 115–16
Food Menus by Revered Zhu Ping, 18
fricasseeing, 73
fruits, 3, 15, 21, 31, 34, 35, 61–62, 173, 181. *See also specific types*
frying and deep-frying, 15, 18, 38, 69, 71, 72–74, 95, 99
fu, 12
Fujian Province, and its foods, 37, 38, 42, 44, 56, 91, 93, 95, 98
funeral foods and behaviors, 110, 154, 171, 174–75
fungi. *See* mushrooms

gambei. *See* drinking and eating games and behaviors
Gansu Province, and its foods, 91, 95
garland chrysanthemum, 54
garlic, 50, 73, 89, 95, 116, 188
garnishing, 93
General Annuls of Shandong, 18
geoduck, 59
ginger, 17, 31, 44, 46, 47–49, 50, 56, 73, 89, 94
ginger graters, 77
ginseng, 157, 192, 196
gluten, 20
goat, 2, 16, 19, 59, 97, 169
Goddess of Mercy, 163
Gods of Prosperity, Happiness, and Longevity, 167
goldfish. *See* carp
goose, 20, 94
grain foods. *See* staple and grain foods

grain payments, 13
Grand Canal and other canals, 12
grapes, 12, 15, 166, 171
Greater Record of Mourning Rites, 174
grilling, 82, 95
grills, 75
gruel. *See* soups and congee
Guangdong Province, and its foods, 2, 18, 91, 93, 106, 114
Guangzhou, 2, 93, 106, 114
Guangzi Province, and its foods, 2, 91, 93
guava, 21
guest behaviors and responsibilities at meals, 138–41
guilds, 19
guo. *See* wok and wok tools

Hainan cuisine, 91, 98, 100
Hainanese cuisine, 100
hair seaweed, 160, 169
Hakka cuisine, 93, 99, 100
Han Dynasty, and its foods, 2, 3, 4, 6, 10, 15, 17, 30, 32, 52, 70, 90, 116, 161, 169
Han people, 6, 156
Hanyo pinyan. *See Putonghua*
hawthorn, 169
hazel nuts, 16, 170
hemp, 11, 116
Hemudu, 11
Henan Province, and its foods, 91, 95
herbal cures, 17
hoisin sauce, 43
holidays and special occasions, 75, 131–32, 153–75. *See also* other or lesser holidays; *specific occasions*
Hom, Ken, 144
honey, 196. *See also* sugar, other sweeteners, and sweets
Hong Kong, 91, 93
honored guests, 107

horse and horsemeat, 12, 16, 19, 60
hot and cold foods. *See yin* and *yang*
    foods and philosophy
hot-pot and fire-pot cookery, 71, 93,
    95, 97
hot rock use, 82
hu, 12
Hua (or Huizia) people, 6
Huangdi. *See* Yellow Emperor
Hubei Province, and its foods, 91, 95
Human Sovereigns, 10
Hunan Province, and its foods, 12,
    53, 91, 93

ideographs. *See* calligraphy
illness, 184–86
Imperial Dynasties. *See* dynasties
imported foods, 2
ingredients, 29–64. *See also individual*
    foods
intercalary months, 154
invitations and responses, 113–14
Islam, and peoples of Muslim faith, 5,
    6, 8, 9, 100
I Yin, 31

Japanese food influences, 23, 24
jelling, 74
jelly fish, 20
Jia Sixie, 16
Jiangsu Province, and its foods, 12,
    91, 93, 99
Jiangxi Province, and its foods, 91
jicama, 55
Jin Dynasty, and its foods, 19
Job's tears, 40, 197
juk. *See* beverages; soups and
    congee

kaoling. *See* sorghum
Keyes, John, 31
King Liuan, 52

King Wudi, 3
Kitchen God, 155, 157–59, 166
knives, 107, 159. *See also* cleavers
kowtow, 112, 164
Kublai Khan, 19
kumquats. *See* cumquats

ladles and spoons, 5, 79, 80, 102, 107,
    117, 146
lamb and mutton, 2, 9, 16, 18, 19, 20,
    59, 95, 96, 97, 98, 169
language. *See Putonghua*
Lantern Festival, 153, 155, 160–63
lazy Susan, 107
leafy greens, 50. *See also bokcai*, other
    cabbages, and leafy greens
Legendary Period, 10
lesser known cuisines, 99–100
li, 12
Liaoning Province, and its foods, 91
licorice root, 46, 50
lily bulb, 57
Lin Yutang, 31
liquor. *See* alcoholic
    beverages; Maotai
Little New Year, 158–59
lizhi (litchee), 62
lollipop pedlars, 21
longans, 62
long beans, 52. *See also* beans and
    peas
loquats, 62
lotus root, stems, and seeds, 20,
    55–56, 171, 197
Lunar New Year, 153–55, 156–59
Lu Yu, 14, 64

Macao, 93
mace, 46
Madame Wu's Recipe Book, 18, 41
main dishes, 106
main meals, 105, 108–9, 118–19

maize, 40. *See also* corn
mallow, 5. *See also* vegetables
maltose, 50. *See also* sugar, other
  sweeteners, and sweets
Manchu cuisine and its people, 22,
  100. *See also* Qing Dynasty, and
  its foods
mandarin oranges. *See* citrus fruits
manners. *See* table manners
Maotai, 147. *See also* alcoholic beverages
Mao Zedong, 23–24
Marco Polo, 192
marinating, 73
mastic, 19
Materia Medica, 183
meals, meal preparation, and meal
  times, 22, 74–75, 105–24, 131,
  133
meat and poultry, and their uses, 15,
  19, 20, 59–60, 131, 141, 173,
  181. *See also specific types*
meat pastes, 34
medicinal cuisine, 100
medicinal texts, 181–84
mein. *See* noodles
melon seeds, 3, 170
menus. *See* suggested menus
Middle Kingdom, 1, 6
millet, 1, 4, 12, 19, 35, 39
Ming Dynasty, and its foods, 5, 20,
  24, 89, 159, 161, 165
minority cuisines, 88, 90. *See also*
  minority populations, languages
  and behaviors
minority populations, languages and
  behaviors, 6, 8, 9, 97, 114
modern Chinese food, 23
modern taste equivalents, 32
Mongolia, 2
Mongolian grills and hot-pots, 20, 22,
  80–82

Mongol Rulers, 20, 165. *See also* Yuan
  Dynasty
monosodium glutamate (MSG), 23,
  33, 48
moon cakes, 165, 167. *See also* baked
  goods
Moon Festival, 153, 155, 165–67
mother sauce, 59
mulberries and other berries, 168
mung beans, 52. *See also* bean sprouts
  and other shoots
murals and reliefs, 15
mushrooms, 16, 20, 31, 33, 42, 48,
  56, 57, 192, 197–98
Muslim. *See* Islam
mustard, 48–49
mutton. *See* lamb and mutton

Nanjing style, 60, 114
Neolithic period and settlements, 1,
  4, 36, 62, 174, 184
neutral foods. *See* yin and yang foods
  and philosophy
Ningxia Province, and its foods,
  95
Nizan, the painter/author, 20, 21
noodles, 4, 15, 20, 38, 40, 95, 97, 98,
  108, 131, 160, 172, 173. *See also*
  staple and grain foods
northern cuisine, 88, 90, 94–96, 117,
  134, 167
nourishing foods, philosophically,
  192
nutmeg, 46, 50
nuts and seeds, 3, 16, 21, 50, 51,
  57–58, 117, 139, 166, 171. *See
  also specific types*

oats, 40
offerings, 5
olive kernels, 47–48, 95
onions, 5, 90

oracle bones, 11, 39, 184. *See also*
    bamboo strips
origins of Chinese people, 5
other or lesser holidays, 154, 155. *See
    also* holidays and special occa-
    sions; *specific occasions*
ovens, 79–80
oysters, 59, 94, 99
oyster sauce, 43, 94. *See also* sauces
    and pastes

Paleolithic times and settlements, 1,
    4, 11
pan cooking, 72–73. *See also* wok
    and wok tools; wok cooking
pau, 18. *See also* wok and wok tools;
    wok cooking
peaches, 22, 62, 160, 166, 168, 197
peanuts, 21, 40, 50, 57, 94, 95, 97,
    167, 170, 172
Pearl River, 3, 4
pears, 16, 160
peas. *See* beans and peas
Peking. *See* Beijing
Peking Man, 11, 12
Pengtoushan, 12
penttiao, 16, 87
People's Republic of China (PRC),
    2, 3
peppers (black, white, and Sichuan),
    15, 17, 33, 45, 46, 50, 94, 95, 96,
    97, 174
perilla, 55
Period of Mythical Sages, 10
persimmons, 16, 62, 169
pheasant, 19
pickling, 69, 96, 99. *See also* salt, salty
    taste, and pickled foods
pictorial language. *See* calligraphy
pine nuts, 50, 95
pinyin. *See Putonghua*
plate grabbers, 77–78
platters and trays, 79

plums, 16, 31
plum sauce, 44–45
poaching, 59
pocket soup, 119–20. *See also* soups
    and congee
poetry anthologies (i.e, *Shijeng* and
    Chuci), 17. *See also* Yuan Mei
pomegranates, 12, 15, 160, 166, 168,
    171
popia, 164
population, 4, 6
pork and pork products, 2, 16, 19, 20,
    60, 94, 95, 97–98, 164, 168, 169.
    See also meat and poultry
potatoes, 2, 40
pots and pans, 18, 19, 72–74, 75. *See
    also specific cooking equipment*
poultry. *See* meat and poultry
preventive medicine, 184. *See also*
    diet and health
Prince Liu An, 30
puff balls, 197–98. *See also* mushrooms
pumpkin, 21, 194
pungent, 32–33, 183, 188, 192
Putonghua, its written language, 6, 7.
    See also calligraphy

Qi and *Qigong*, 188–89, 190, 192
Qimin Yaoshu (QMYS), 16. *See also
    Essential Techniques for the Peas-
    antry*
Qin Dynasty, and its foods, 2, 6, 15
Qingdao, 63, 95
Qing Dynasty, and its foods, 2, 15,
    20, 22, 23
Qinghai Province, and its foods, 91
Qing Ming Festival, 153, 155,
    163–64
quince, 169, 195
Qu Yuan, 168

rabbit, 19
radishes, 90

raw food consumption, 19
recipes: ancient, 25–28; Beef and Lotus Root Stew, 201; Beef and Water Chestnut Packets, 148–49; Bitter Melon and Date Congee, 200–201; Boiled and Baked Peanuts with Red Bean Curd, 84; Braised Shanghai-Style Soybean Sprouts, 84; Cantonese Soya Chicken, 67; Chicken Soup with Mushrooms and Chestnuts, 199–200; by cooking technique, 82–85; Corn Kernels and Red Nuts, 126; Dragon Boat Festival Dumplings, 176–77; Duck and Abalone, 201–2; for formal and informal occasions, 148–51; Golden Tofu, 126–27; Greens with Fu Yu, 66; Hainan Fried Rice, 103; Hakka-Style Stuffed Salt-Baked Chicken, 100–101; Hangzhou's West Lake Sliced Fish and Watershield in Soup, 101–2; for health, 198–202; Lotus Root Chips, 84–85; using major ingredients, 65–68; Meatball and Cellophane Noodle Soup, 124–25; Ming Dynasty Stir-Fried Chinese Cabbage, 27–28; New Year Cake Patties, 175–76; Noodles with Brown Bean Sauce, 176; Northern Song Dynasty Tungpo Pork, 27; Pork Soup with Lotus Seed and Lily Bulb, 199; Red-Cooked Duck and Daikon, 150–51; by region, 100–104; Sacha Beef Lo Mein, 125–26; Sichuan Mapo Doufu (Tofu), 102; Southern Song Dynasty Shrimp Appetizer, 25; for special occasions, 175–79; Steamed Dumplings, commonly called *shumai*, 148; Steamed Pork with Seasoned Rice Flour, 83; Steamed Sea Bass in Black Bean Sauce, 151; Steamed Shrimp with Garlic Sauce, 150; Stir-Fried Beef and Chinese Broccoli, 66–67; Stir-Fried Shrimp with Chinese Vegetables, 83; Stuffed Pork Omelets with Oyster Sauce, 125; Sweet and Sour Spareribs, 65; Sweet Potato Balls, 149–50; Sweetened Moon Cakes, 178–79; Tang Dynasty Empress Chicken, 26–27; Two-Way Hot Cabbage, 127; for typical meals, 124–28; Velvet Shrimp Beijing-Style, 102–103; Winter Solstice Soup, 177–78; Yangzhou Fried Rice, Vegetarian Style, 67–68; Yuan Dynasty Carp Soup, 25–26
red cooking, 70
red envelopes, 156, 159
regional and provincial foods, 87–100, 123–24
religious influences and beliefs, 5, 9. *See also* Islam, and minority populations
restaurants, 23, 38, 74–75, 89, 129–32, 137–38
rice, 1, 2, 4, 5, 9, 19, 20, 35–37, 97, 108, 162, 168, 170, 172, 174. *See also* staple and grain foods
rice bowls, 80
rice cookers, 78
rice wines. *See* alcoholic beverages
Rites of Zhou (also *Rituals of Zhou*), 17, 32, 183
roasting, 5, 9, 15, 46, 72, 99
rock and other sugars. *See* sugar, other sweeteners, and sweets
rock salt, 72. *See also* salt, salty taste, and pickled foods
rolling pins, 79
root vegetables (including *daikon* and *jicama*), 55–56
rye, 40

sacha sauce, 43

salt, salty taste, and pickled foods, 3, 5, 32–34, 41–43, 51, 60, 72, 73, 96, 99, 114, 174, 183, 188, 192

Sandai, 10, 14

sashimi, 19

sauces and pastes, 30, 33, 35, 40–45, 48, 50, 59, 89, 96. *See also specific types*

savory, 32–33

scallions and leeks, 53, 73, 95, 116, 197

scallops and imitation scallops, 20, 116

scallop sauce, 42

sea cucumber, 59, 60, 133, 192

seafood, 19, 20, 58–59, 97, 98. *See also specific types*

sea horse, 60

seasonings. *See* spices and seasonings

seating arrangements at meals, 112–13

seaweed, 32, 48

seeds. *See* nuts and seeds

sesame oil and sesame paste, 12, 45, 50, 89, 97. *See also* sesame seeds

sesame seeds, 12, 15, 18, 50, 99. *See also* sesame oil and sesame paste

seven necessities, 18

Shaanxi Province, and its foods, 91, 95

shallots, 73

Shandong Province, and its foods, 93, 94–95

Shang Dynasty, and its foods, 5, 10, 14, 16, 31, 36, 184

Shanghai, 1, 42, 49, 91

Shanxi Province, and its foods, 95

shao mai, 96. *See also* dim sum; snacks and snack foods

shark's fins, 21, 30, 94, 98, 133, 138, 192

Shennong, the Yellow Emperor, 10, 182–83, 189, 192

Shennong's Classic Materia Medica, 182–83

shih, or food for the people, 13

shrimp and prawns, 59, 98, 99

shrimp sauce, 42, 43–44. *See also* sauces and pastes

Sichuan pepper. *See* peppers

Sichuan Province, and its foods, 12, 14, 42, 50, 53, 91, 93, 96–98

Silk Road and related routes, 5, 21, 38, 62, 88

silk squash and other squashes and gourds, 56–57, 193, 197

simmering, 59, 77, 82, 194

smoking, 72, 97

snacks and snack foods, 3, 18, 24, 35, 50, 75, 93, 106, 116, 129, 131, 141–42, 164, 166. *See also* dim sum

snake, 94

soda. *See* cold beverages and soda

Song Dynasty, and its foods, 5, 12, 18, 19, 30, 41, 59, 90, 95, 100, 130, 133–34, 142

sorghum, 12, 39–40, 95, 97

soups and congee, 12, 50, 63, 94, 98, 99, 105, 106, 107, 108, 110, 119–20, 124, 147, 157, 181

sour and sour foods, 32–34, 96, 183, 188. *See also* vinegar and other sour tastes

southern and southwestern cuisine, 88, 90, 93–94, 117, 133, 135–36, 142

soy beans and soy sauces, 16, 19–21, 30–31, 32, 34, 40–42, 43, 52, 59, 70, 73, 89, 95, 97, 99, 197. *See also doufu*; soy milk

soy milk, 52, 99

spices and seasonings, 40, 45–50. *See also specific types*

spoons. *See* ladles and spoons
spinach, 15
Spring Festival. *See* Lunar New Year
staple and grain foods (*fan*), 4, 13,
    35–40, 105, 115, 116, 181. *See
    also specific types*
star anise, 45–46
steamers and steamer baskets, 18, 19,
    69, 71–72, 75–76
steaming, 5, 9, 15, 18, 35, 69, 71–72,
    87, 90
stem lettuce, 54
stewing, 95, 99–100, 116
stir-frying, 5, 59, 70, 73, 90, 93, 95
stoves, 75, 174
street venders and street food, 15, 74,
    116, 117, 129, 141
sugar, other sweeteners, and sweets, 9,
    17, 24, 32–34, 42, 43, 44, 48–50,
    62, 73, 97, 98, 116, 157, 159, 160,
    162, 166, 168, 171, 172, 188, 192,
    196
suggested menus, 118–19, 120–23,
    133–36
Suiyuan Shidan (Yuan Mei), 21–22
surimi, 21
sushi and sashimi, 18–19
sweet potato, 21, 53, 56, 97, 98, 171
sweet potato leaves. *See* bean sprouts
    and other shoots
symbols. *See* Chinese food beliefs, ritu-
    als and sayings, and Chinese fives

table and stool use, 19
table manners, 109–11, 138–41
Taiwan food. *See* Fujian Province
tamarind, 46
Tang Dynasty, and its foods, 14, 15,
    17, 18, 115, 142, 161
tangerine peel, 46, 50
taro, 5, 55
TCM. *See* Traditional Chinese Medi-
    cine

tea and tea shops, 2, 14, 19, 21, 22,
    56, 63–64, 78–79, 80, 97, 98,
    106, 112, 117, 123, 129, 142, 147,
    157, 160, 164, 167, 173
tea cups, kettles, and teapots, 19,
    78–79, 80, 107
tea sauce. *See* sauces and pastes
Terrestrial Sovereigns, 10
Three Gods, 167
Tianjin, 91
Tibet. *See* Xizang
tomato, 21, 33, 94
tomb reliefs. *See* murals
Traditional Chinese Medicine, 184,
    188–90, 192, 194
tsampa. *See* barley and tsampa
turkey, 21
turmeric, 46
turnip, 55
turtle, 162, 194

umami, 32

Vegetarian Cult Day, 169. *See also*
    Double Ninth Festival
vegetable and meat use (*cai*), 1, 3, 5,
    10, 20, 105, 108
vegetables, 33, 34, 50–58, 106, 181.
    See also specific types
vegetarian or *su* cuisine, 200
velveting, 95, 97
venison, 19
vinegar and other sour tastes, 15, 16,
    18, 31, 37, 43, 44, 73, 95, 96, 97,
    98, 117

Wade-Giles writing system, 7
walnuts, 15, 50, 57, 192
water, 64, 84, 106, 116, 117
water buffalo, 4
water caltrop, 167
water chestnuts and other bulbs, 57,
    170

watercress, 54
weddings, 154, 171, 173
Wei Dynasty, and its foods (including Jin, Southern and Northern, and Three Kingdoms periods), 16
western cuisine (including Hunan, Sichuan, and others), 96–98, 136
western foods, 23–24
wheat, 2, 19, 35, 37–39, 41, 97, 116. See also staple and grain foods
whetstones, 79
white-cooking, 70–71
wild cats and other wild meats, 19
wine, 63–64. See also alcoholic beverages
wine houses, 113, 129, 130
wine vessels, 107
Winter Solstice, 170
wok and wok tools, 17, 72–74, 75–78
wok cooking, 72–74

Xia Dynasty, 10, 14
Xian, 2, 7, 114, 115
xien, 12
Xinjiang cooking, 91
xizang, 91

Yale writing system, 7

Yan, Martin, 144
yang. See *yin* and *yang* foods and philosophy
Yangzhou Culture, 1, 4
Yangzi River, 3, 4, 36
Yellow Emperor, 10
Yellow Emperor's Classic of Medicine, 181–82, 184, 185
Yellow River, 1, 3, 4
yin and *yang* foods and philosophy, 13, 167, 182, 184, 185, 187, 190–91, 192, 193
Yinshao Chengyao (YSCY), 19
Yuan Dynasty, and its foods, 2, 20, 24, 89, 95, 115
Yuan Mei, 21
Yue cuisine, 3, 93
yum cha. See dim sum
Yunnan pots, 82
Yunnan Province, and its foods, 2, 91, 92, 98

zeng, 12
Zhejiang Province, and its foods, 12, 93, 91, 99
Zhongguo. See Middle Kingdom
Zhou Dynasty, and its foods, 10, 12, 14, 41, 59, 91, 115, 163, 183
Zhoukoudian, 11
Zhouli and *Chili*, 32. See also *Rites of Zhou*

About the Author

JACQUELINE M. NEWMAN is a retired Professor in the Family, Nutrition, and Exercise Department of Queens College, Flushing, New York, and the editor of *Flavor and Fortune*, a quarterly about the science and art of Chinese food.

**Recent Titles in
Food Culture around the World**

Food Culture in Japan
Michael Ashkenazi and Jeanne Jacob

Food Culture in India
Colleen Taylor Sen